THE
METAMORPHOSES

Ovid's Roman Games

Edgar M. Glenn

UNIVERSITY
PRESS OF
AMERICA

LANHAM • NEW YORK • LONDON

Copyright © 1986 by

University Press of America,® Inc.

4720 Boston Way
Lanham, MD 20706

3 Henrietta Street
London WC2E 8LU England

Printed in the United States of America

Library of Congress Cataloging in Publication Data

Glenn, Edgar M.
   The metamorphoses : Ovid's Roman games.

   Includes index.
   1. Ovid, 43 B.C.-17 or 18 A.D.   Metamorphoses.
2. Metamorphosis in literature.   3. Mythology in
literature.   I. Title.
PA6519.M9G54   1986   873'.01   86-15828
ISBN 0-8191-5582-9 (alk. paper)
ISBN 0-8191-5583-7 (pbk. : alk. paper)

All University Press of America books are produced on acid-free
paper which exceeds the minimum standards set by the National
Historical Publications and Records Commission.

To Milly with love

THE *METAMORPHOSES:* OVID'S ROMAN GAMES

Table of Contents

PREFACE

Greek and Latin have been ushered out of the curricula of most American secondary schools with the unfortunate result that the young no longer have the opportunity to come into direct contact with the remoter linguistic and literary traditions of their culture. It is gratifying, therefore, that there has been such a brisk business recently in the translating of the works of classical antiquity, for at least the young and readers in general have fresh renditions in contemporary English. Since the translators are also scholars, some of the results of research have doubtless been incorporated in these translations, which have also benefited from contemporary frankness and lack of inhibition. Just as important, however, scholars have been aiding the general reader by producing helpful interpretations of some of the major works. The result is that these works have been even further removed from the academic anatomy theater and brought into the arena of everyday understanding and experience, for the interpretations bridge the gap between the reader and the works of literature. This book is intended to provide such a bridge.

Readers of Ovid's *Metamorphoses* especially need such a bridge, for the poem as a whole and sometimes in particular parts is puzzling and difficult to come to grips with. With regard to sequence, it seems rather whimsical, and it is full of clutter. One never knows what will come next or why, and sometimes it is not at all clear why something has been included or what its significance is. The result is that the poem sometimes has been regarded as a mere handbook of myths or as simply a bunch of tales of uneven interest. It might also appear as a bewildering array of Pitti Palace walls and ceilings. Further confusion has been produced by moralizing the narratives or analyzing the structure of the poem. This last approach, however, is one that could be most helpful, and though Professor Brooks Otis systematically examined the architectonics of the poem for scholars, I did not find that his study provided me with the sort of illumination I sought. Therefore, I turned to the leads of the New Critics of the 1930's and the general guidance of some of Professor Fränkel's insights in order to determine what is going on in the poem and why.

My basic approach, then, was to regard the poem as an artistic whole, a coherent entity into which each part fits meaningfully. Hence, I had to go to the poem itself and see what is there, asking myself, What is going on in the *Metamorphoses* passage by passage and book by book? Then, how do these parts relate to one another? What unifies each book, if anything does? Is there an overall plan to the poem, and is it carried through consistently? (In the process of answering these questions, I found that I was producing a thematic survey of each book and that overall the poem had a consistent attitude.) Having scrutinized the poem thus, I asked, what conclusions about it may I legitimately reach. Long ago I became convinced, thanks to Professor Fränkel, that Ovid knew

vii

what he as doing as artist and that it was not valid for me to say that here he was dull or that there his genius flagged or that somewhere else he did not make sense. Instead, I have assumed that lack of understanding or appreciation was mine and that it was my obligation to determine what was happening in the poem. Once I took this stance, I found myself involved in an exhilarating scrutiny of a viruoso and his finest performance.

My major purpose in answering the above questions was that of making the poem accessible to the reader, but as I worked, I found that it does, indeed, contain a good deal of non-Christian moralizing and that it is an elaborate and high-spirited kind of game. I am not alone in holding these opinions. For example, Professor Maurice Cunningham notes in his "Otis on the *Metamorphoses*" (*Classical Philology*, 1966) that the poem adheres to the traditional ancient view that poetry is and should be instructive and that in the poem Ovid uses myths as moral patterns, that is, uses them to present attitudes and behavior that led or might lead to certain results. Cunningham regards the poem as "a generously inclusive repository of this accumulated wisdom and experience." And Peter Levi, fellow of St. Catherine's College, Oxford, agreed with me in conversation that the *Metamorphoses* is essentially a game.

In short, Ovid has created a poem that provides those truly classical results, profit and pleasure. There is much to be learned from the *Metamorphoses* about art, human nature, and human values. Alison Elliott stressed Ovid's "perceptive insight into human psychology, normal and abnormal" (*The Classical Journal*, 1973). Dr. Freud would undoubtedly concur. Elliott, Freud, Cunningham, and Hermann Fränkel all indicate the ways in which every person can come in contact with the *Metamorphoses* and derive pleasure and profit from it. And their views imply that we can and should take Ovid out of the anatomy theatre and get on with the game.

One needs some initiation into the sport, of course, but once he has it, he can participate in it on his own. Whether the reader remains an initiate or engages in the game more deeply, he will learn what a fox Ovid is and should come to admire him immensely.

Ovid is good at engaging the reader in what is going on in the poem and at the same time frustrating him. One expects brilliant narrative and clearly relevant sequences of events, as in the *Iliad*, the *Odyssey*, or the *Aeneid*, and is given them, at times, but the reader is also given inconsequentialities, or clutter; stories that apparently lack meaning; and unpredictable sequences. My own experience with the *Metamorphoses* has made me feel that I was involved in an imaginary fox hunt in which red jacket and Ruddy Brush watched admiringly from the hedge while one chased the other over meadow and stone wall. We know that Ovid exuberantly admired his poem, for he stated so at its end. But that spectator and participant should be the same seems too clever to be true. Yet it is true: one does stand off with the poet and admire Ovid as one pursues him through his work and becomes familiar with his craft and art. Indeed, he is so crafty that, because of his unexpected transitions, he has been called the sleight-of-hand man. Because of his ingenious variations and taking off in unexpected directions, he might also be called the artful dodger.

But beneath Ovid's artistry and his changing forms, moods, and tones, as well as his glitter, novelty, and lightness, there is more than gamesmanship or divertissement. This assertion does not mean that the *Metamorphoses* has a chocolate coating that lures adolescents into biting into and assimilating the spider myth of Arachne and other bitter proteins. Nor does it represent the position of Thomas Walsingham, who explained in his *De Archana Deorum* that Actaeon's fate was that of any country gentleman overly fond of hunting, namely, that his hounds ruin him by devouring his substance. Such moralizing aside, Ovid does deal with human values; he does make his readers feel certain ways about particular human situations; he does, like any great writer, have significant things to say about his subjects; and since he does these things, he moralizes. Ovid was, for all his baroque qualities and apparent trifling, a perceptive and intelligent human being addressing his contemporaries who, like us, enjoyed art and novelty, but who were not necessarily as shallow, insipid, insensitive, or stupid as one sometimes likes to think the members of the world of fashion and power are. On the other hand, bright and right are not necessarily consequent upon one another, nor are morality and talent, power and responsibility. The cosmos and its cities and beings are not as simple as we should like them to be, nor as consistent, nor as monolithic. Therefore, we should not stereotype Ovid as all good or all wicked, as all artist and nothing else, or as all glitter and no substance.

For the moment, suffice it to say that my position is that in the *Metamorphoses*, Ovid has written a work that entertains, that is mostly not very serious in surface and approach, yet one that gives psychological insights and instruction as it goes, that pays its respects—and its disrespects—to the mighty and, finally, with comic hyperseriousness (because only partially true, but definitely exaggerated) and with ambiguity, praises the poet's self. Thus this novel and shocking light masterpiece ends with a stunning bit of heroico-comico effrontery. In the poem, Ovid demonstrates that he can do anything. And in addition, it is, as mentioned above, a fox hunt.

My pursuit, however, does not include source hunting. Although it is important to know Ovid's sources, because then one can compare Ovid's renditions with them and better determine his meaning, artistry, and originality, such an undertaking would mean reproducing a vast amount of material and is beyond the scope of this book. Fortunately for the lover of literature, it is not of crucial importance to know where the bits and pieces came from or what they are like in the sources. The truly important process is that of determining what is going on in Ovid's versions of the tales. Such analysis allows the perception of motifs and the

ix

determination of themes book by book, the meaning of each book, and, cumulatively, the meaning of the poem as a whole. In an informal way, each chapter gives such an analysis of a book of the *Metamorphoses*, the title of the chapter presenting the dominant theme of the book. If each book of the poem is a meaningful unit, then perhaps the books combine to form a meaningful whole, but we can ascertain this only in a final overview.

I should note that I have not everywhere called attention to the morals implicit in Ovid's myths nor to each transition, but I have done enough to demonstrate that both exist and to indicate their nature. Doing more in these areas seemed tedious. After all, I wished to start readers on their way, not stifle them. I should add, however, that the best way to use this work is to read it in conjunction with the *Metamorphoses*, preferably chapter after book.

I hope that my readers and I shall agree as to what is going on in the poem, but if we do not, perhaps I shall irritate them sufficiently so that they will be spurred on to entirely different interpretations. This book should be something of a seminal work, not a dead end. For one thing, I cannot claim to answer all the questions about the narratives, but I trust that I have opened a rich vein that needs working and that I have aroused some enthusiasm for a very great poem and have generated some interest in the game.

Before proceeding, I wish to acknowledge general indebtedness to many scholars for information, insight, and stimulation. I cannot name all of them, but readers might like to know some of the authors and works that I turned to most often and from which I have occasionally quoted. These are Hermann Fränkel, *Ovid: A Poet Between Two Worlds* (University of California Press, 1945); L. P. Wilkinson, *Ovid Recalled* (Cambridge University Press, 1955); Brooks Otis, *Ovid as an Epic Poet*, second edition (Cambridge University Press, 1970); G. Karl Galinsky, *Ovid's Metamorphoses: An Introduction to the Basic Aspects* (University of California Press, 1975); William S. Anderson, *Ovid's Metamorphoses Books 6-10* (University of Oklahoma Press, 1972) and his edition of the entire *Metamorphoses* (B. G. Teubner, 1982). To this list I should add the following that I made use of, namely, the editions of various books of the *Metamorphoses* with notes and introductions by A. G. Lee, G. M. H. Murphy, Charles Simmons, A. H. Allcroft and B. J. Hayes, and W. Michael Wilson. Translators Golding, Riley, Miller, Gregory, Humphries, and Innes have also been helpful. I regret that the informality of my approach required omitting notation of each particular debt to author and source in the customary formal academic fashion. This lack does not mean that I wished to purloin the perceptions and arguments of others or to deny them their due—I trust that the admission of general indebtedness is adequate and proper—but that I was striving for a text that read more smoothly than academic form and punctiliousness allow.

For the Latin text of the *Metamorphoses* and for the translations in my work I have relied upon the easily available Loeb Classical Library editions of 1916 and 1921. On occasion I have done my own translations, but the fact is not difficult to ascertain. I wish to thank the Harvard University Press for graciously granting me permission to quote from the Loeb editions of the *Metamorphoses*, translated by Frank Justus Miller, and from the Loeb edition of *The Roman Antiquities of Dionysius of Halicarnassus*, translated by Earnest Cary (1937). Wherever the meaning of an ancient Greek proper noun is given in quotes within parentheses, I have used, almost exclusively, the index to Robert Graves' two-volume *The Greek Myths* (Penguin Books, 1955).

Anyone wishing to learn details about Ovid's life should consult the biographical sketches in the works of Fränkel and Wilkinson, named above, or the more recent one in Peter Green's "Introduction" to his translations entitled *Ovid: The Erotic Poems* (Penguin Books, 1982). The careful study *The Mystery of Ovid's Exile*, by John C. Thibault (University of California Press, 1964), is available for those who wish a survey of theories about something that cannot be proved.

I should add that Cicero, who died in the year Ovid was born, was aware of the logical fallacy of contradictory premises. The significance of this apparently irrelevant remark will become clear later.

The citizens of Sulmona deserve our gratitude for preserving a long-standing appreciation of Ovid and his worth that has resulted in a valuable collection of printed editions of his works. I have benefited from their efforts and from their hospitality, for which I express my thanks. I am especially indebted to Professore Mario Marcone for his enthusiastic support of my scholarly efforts and for his many kindnesses, to Mr. and Mrs. W. E. C. Haussler for theirs, and to my colleague Victor Lams, who read the manuscript and gave it his imprimatur.

Edgar M. Glenn
California State University, Chico
May 1986

INTRODUCTION

The Roman had a good many games, or *ludi*. These included, according to the Roman way of naming things, such diverse activities as horse racing, gladiatorial combats, centennial celebrations, priestly dances, physical exercise, gaming with dice and other devices, playing with toys, school instruction, legal and political apprenticeship, quasi-military drill for boys and youths (e.g., the Trojan Games), and theatrical shows, that is, plays, dancing, mime, and pantomime. Ovid developed a new one, an intellectual literary game, that of matching wits with the reader and in the process teasing him, frustrating him, puzzling him, and often outwitting him. For modern readers, this is Ovid's major Roman game, what I have referred to earlier as a game in which the hunter pursues a fox.

I used this metaphor because one never knows what Ovid is going to do next or why or how he is going to get to the next tale or what he will do with it when he gets there. Each of Ovid's transitions from one story to another is effected by means that one can anticipate no more than one can a magician's devices. These transitions are one dimension of the game sketched in the opening lines of the *Metamorphoses:* the setting up of an impossible task, namely, that of dealing with change of shapes in one continuous poem moving from the beginning of the world to Ovid's own time. They provide the continuity. But as for the task, one believes that it can be accomplished as much as one believes that a magician can produce a coin out of thin air. One immediately puts oneself in opposition to the poet: the thing cannot be done. But Ovid dupes the reader further, for the subject of the poem is itself so vague that it gives the audience little upon which to base any expectations. Homer's stating that the *Iliad* is about the wrath of Achilles and the sorrows that it brought the Greeks is much more helpful in guiding the reader as to what to expect.

In addition to this sort of playing with the reader, it is not always clear what Ovid is getting at in some passages. Why should Pelops, when mourning for his sister, display his ivory shoulder? Why bother with the story of Ceyx and Alcyone at all? It seems relatively pointless. Why tell the story of Syrinx so soon after the similar one of Daphne? Why does Medea's story fade away after a strong beginning? What is the point of including the episode about Procris' dog and its metamorphosis? Why is Europa introduced and then written off, so that anticlimax results? And why the youth in the doorway? All of these puzzlers are also parts of Ovid's playing with the reader. Then there are other game devices, such as the rapid change of mood or tone, exemplified by the horror created when Phaëthon scorches the earth and the sudden shift to sympathy for the lad when Jove blasts him from the sky. And Ovid uses other ploys.

But this is only one of Ovid's Roman games. Another is that of outdoing the Greeks. Most of the material that Ovid used came to him through Greek authors and derived from Greek myth and legend. Of course, he did not slavishly imitate the Greeks when he retold their tales, but redid them for his own purposes. However, merely by composing his own versions, he unavoidably set himself in competition with the Greeks as a storyteller, and his artistic challenge is that of surpassing them. To decide whether Ovid wins in this competition, one would have to compare his tales with their Greek counterparts in Hyginus or Apollodorus or elsewhere, a project outside our purview. We cannot here demonstrate that the Roman is a better storyteller than the Greeks. But we can ask another question relative to this competitive game without going outside Ovid's poem. And that question is, how does Ovid present the Greeks in contrast to the Romans? The answer will emerge in the following chapters.

Ovid's third game is one that he played with Augustus. This one is complicated and requires extended consideration. And it is unusual because it was one-sided for a long time, as far as we know. Put simply, it amounts to this: in his poetry Ovid blandly opposed, both directly and indirectly, Augustus' program of moral reform, specifically in the areas of marriage and sexual behavior. Ovid's direct opposition took the form, not of attacking the institution of marriage or of ridiculing chastity as a value, but of encouraging men to have extramarital affairs and women, ostensibly not the respectable or aristocratic ones, to be fascinating, alluring, and engaging in bed as well as out. He presented love as an exciting pastime, free of expense, hazard, and routine and thus unlike political endeavor, war, and marriage. The *Amores* and the *Art of Love* are the chief early documents of this opposition.

Indirectly, Ovid later undercut Augustus' moral program whenever he presented arguments for aberrant sexual behavior, such as the ones he gave Byblis in the *Metamorphoses*, or showed love triumphant over restraint, law, and reason, so that it produces criminal behavior, as it does with Myrrha and Medea in the same poem. Ovid also undermined the program when he used unedifying myths, such as those of the rape of vestal virgin Rhea Silvia by Mars, Faunus' attempt to spend the night with Omphale but finding himself in bed with Hercules, or Priapus' trying to make love to Lotis—all tales found in the *Fasti*. Whenever Ovid made illicit love exciting or engrossing or gave it divine status, as he often did in the *Metamorphoses*, and whenever he showed the individual ardently striving to be free of custom, law, authority, or restraint and sympathized with that figure, as he did with Byblis and Phaëthon, he crossed Augustus. Part of Ovid's game with Augustus, then, was that of ignoring the Princeps' official views and of sapping them by presenting opposite or incompatible ones. Other devices emerge in the chapters that follow.

Apparently, either by his own reading or by means of reciters, staff, or talebearers, the busy Imperator kept himself informed about the writings, published or in progress, of various authors, especially those who were the best and those who were most in favor with the upper classes. Because of the patronage system and because of Augustus' constant use of propaganda, it would have been advantageous for Augustus to know which authors were enhancing his image and supporting his official views and which were not. Augustus definitely knew that Ovid had not supported the imperial position on sexual morality because one of the reasons for exiling Ovid was his poem on the art of love. Augustus clearly resented Ovid's opposition.

This punishment is better understood if one reviews Augustus' career. As a boy, he received training in literature and philosophy and, presumably, rhetoric. Later he wrote some poetry and began a tragedy about Ajax. But these were minor matters. From his youth he had been groomed for high political position by his great-uncle Julius Caesar, who adopted Augustus and made him his heir when Augustus was eighteen. He was still eighteen when Caesar's assassination forced him into active political participation in order to capitalize upon his inheritance. The situation was perilous, and handling it required ability and acumen. From 44 B.C., when Caesar was murdered, until the death of Marcus Antonius in 30 B.C., Augustus was constantly exercising his talents to improve his position as one of the rulers of Rome, with the result that he finally emerged as her sole ruler and master of the peoples subject to her.

At that point, he could not stop. He continued his strenuous administrative and political activities, or what was called "life in the sun." To buttress his position and to bring Roman citizens back to greatness, he advocated an austere devotional and moral program. He refurbished decaying temples, built new ones, revitalized the rituals, and gave new life to the declining official Graeco-Roman religion of the familiar myth deities. He was responsible for so much building of various sorts, much of it religious, that he is said to have found Rome brick and left it marble. Augustus also tried to re-establish the traditional Roman virtues, conspicuously those having to do with the res publica, the family, and marital fidelity. For he wanted more and better Romans to man the empire. These activities were a fraction of his duties and responsibilities. And of this fraction, poets, though useful, were only a part, dwarfed when compared with Agrippa or Maecenas and, of course, Augustus himself.

What Augustus stood for officially, however, was not to the liking of everyone, certainly not Ovid, who gave up the taxing life of civil service and was not temperamentally suited to the military, but rather to "life in the shade." There were many other men and many women who represented what may be called the New Establishment. They were interested in themselves first, not the state and not in having families that would produce soldiers and administrators or the wives of magistrates and senators. The New Woman, whose emancipation had begun a hundred years before Augustus' austerity program, had money and freedom. She could be a very willful dame, like Mark Antony's independent and bellicose wife Fulvia. Or she could lust after pleasure as well as political power, like Clodia Pulchra, against whom Cicero defended Caelius. The New Woman had her male counterparts, who also thought more of self-glorification and power, like Catiline, or of luxury, like Lucullus, than of administrative problems, the long run, and the common good. And then there were the out-and-out playboys that Clodia was accused of consorting with. The examples come from a generation or so before Augustus, it is true, but they show that the New Establishment was well entrenched by the time that Augustus tried to revive a bygone era.

Poets like Virgil tried to change the tone of and to improve Roman morals and dedication to the *res publica*, but Augustus did not receive unanimous backing from all poets. Poetry was polarized like the society. At one extreme was Virgil, whose work consistently supported and elaborated the official views. He was not alone in writing heroic epic, which *per se* glorified valor and military life and might well add to the prestige of Rome and Augustus, for among Ovid's friends in middle life were Cornelius Severus, who produced an epic on the war between Octavius and Sextus Pompeius; Macer, who wrote one on the Trojan War; and Tuticanus, Rabirius, Montanus, Sabinus, Largus, Camerinus and Varius—all authors of epics. In the middle were poets like Horace, who wrote about amorousness and the convivial life of the country gentleman, but who also praised Augustus and Maecenas and Roman valor, deplored the times, and wrote the Secular Hymn for one of Augustus' great public celebrations. At the other extreme were the elegists like Propertius when he preferred to sing of love, not war, and Tibullus, who wrote of love's trials and triumphs. To this group belonged Ovid, who early wrote of his loves and of the love of ladies of note, almost all legendary, whom he labeled the daughters of Hero, or Heroides. After exhausting the field of amorous and boudoir elegy—Ovid worked it for about twenty years—he suddenly shifted and composed a largely, though perhaps only superficially so, erotic epic counterbalance to Virgil's *Aeneid*, namely, the *Metamorphoses*. Often irreverent to gods and to their earthly counterparts, it could hardly have been looked on with official pleasure by officially pious and proper Augustus, even though it was being balanced at the time by a patriotic religious calendar of the Roman year that Ovid was writing, the *Fasti*.

For in the *Metamorphoses*, Ovid plays the game of indirectly pressuring Augustus to give up the austere principles about sexual behavior that Augustus' legislation implemented and to accept the freer sexual mores of the New Establishment. If Ovid can gain such acceptance, he becomes on this matter his ruler's ruler and wins the game.

To accomplish this end, the *Metamorphoses* piles up stories to demonstrate that sexual activity is a natural phenomenon (something every Roman knew), that it should be regarded tolerantly (here Augustus disagreed), and that it has the sanction of the gods, the Greeks (at least in their myths and legends), and the Italian fertility tradition. The tales, as will be seen, do not give blanket approval to all kinds of sexual behavior. Some types, such as incest and revenge for rejection, are criminal or despicable. Yet, even in such instances, Ovid sometimes sympathizes with the offender, though he condemns the offense. What would be worse to an austere moralist is the fact that, even when labeling some love as criminal or offensive, Ovid engrosses the imagination, makes one

xvi

understand how a person could commit the offense, and opens eyes to amorous possibilities that one might never have thought of.

What is worst, Ovid can always disclaim responsibility for the substance of a twice-told tale sired by some unknown Greek or rude forebear, or he can claim that his version of it is a sport and, hence, not to be taken seriously. In this way he allows himself the luxury and safety of being able to adopt incompatible positions, varying his views to meet those of the audience of the moment: he could take either the moral position or the immoralist's or that of the moral man who likes a dirty joke.

If Ovid were writing with Augustus on part of his mind—and he probably was, for the Princeps was too important and his views too well known—Ovid's game strategy, in part, was to compliment Augustus and to cater to his likes. Although Augustus lived plainly, he had a fondness for Greek art and literature and the myths that both often used. For example, one of Augustus' dwellings, the "house of Livia" on the Palatine, had wall paintings displaying Polyphemus and Galatea and Mercury, Argus, and Io. This taste for artfully done Greek myth the *Metamorphoses* gratifies abundantly. One of the wall paintings, according to Mr. Galinsky, makes use of visual hoodwinking, the game of trompe-l'oeil, in which flat becomes three-dimensional, outside becomes inside, and urban inexplicably elevates into rural. These, in part, are the visual equivalents of Ovid's ingenious and deceptive transitions and his sliding from one mood or tone to another within an episode. The painting indicates an Augustan fondness for this kind of intellectual ingenuity, playfulness, and amusing deception, and again Augustus would find his fondness for these gratified by the *Metamorphoses*.

If, as Ovid asserted late in his career, his *Art of Love* had offended Augustus because it was a technical manual on a touchy topic and was perhaps more erotically exciting than the *Amores*, Ovid ingratiatingly struck a middle ground in the *Metamorphoses*, which is titilating without being a text designed to produce the successful wencher and thus without directly encouraging men to sow their seed abroad rather than in the lap of a productive wife or women to receive it outside marriage. Augustus is said to have liked jokes, and Ovid's poem has many wonderful bits of humor. It is also a brilliant piece of writing, one of the outstanding works of Latin literature, and for this reason alone, it should have pleased the ruler of Rome. But it does more, for it ends with high praise of him.

Yet if Ovid were attempting to lead Augustus by the nose and convert him to Ovid's views or if he were merely attempting to show veiled contempt for the father of his country, the attempt was risky. Either way, the poem was the device of a pert, brazen, talented opponent who used a deadpan manner and false obsequiousness. The danger to Ovid lay in the wariness and cunning of his antagonist in the game. He or his staff might have been too intelligent not to perceive what was going on, namely, that Ovid was trying to outwit him. As for the compliments in either the *Fasti* or the *Metamorphoses*, it is not surprising that Augustus was little moved by them. Not only are they offset by what amounts to covert ridicule or by a conspiratorial attitude of superiority to bygone Roman simplicity and sober morality, but they and the toned down eroticisim came rather late. Augustus was about seventy years old when Ovid offered them, and Ovid, about fifty. For too long Ovid had occupied one pole and glorified the passions or explored the amatory skills and love's entanglements, and for too long Augustus had looked down from the pole of vigorous and tiring administrative work and a program of family purity and uplift, which had failed in his own family. In 2 B.C. his own daughter, Julia, was revealed as an adulteress, a fact that Augustus angrily publicized. And he applied to her the penalty required by his own law, namely, banishment. In 8 A.D., much the same thing happened in connection with his granddaughter Julia.

In the same year Augustus turned his attention to Ovid and sent him off to Tomis on the Black Sea. Ovid was working on the last stages of the *Fasti* and the *Metamorphoses*, but neither poem had enough in it for the emperor to forgive the poet. It may even be that in the poems Augustus saw that Ovid was trying to please the emperor when with the emperor's friends and to stimulate the spleen of those discontented with Augustus when Ovid was in their company. Be that as it may, the Princeps told Ovid, so the poet records, that there were two charges against him. One was an error of some sort, connected with something that Ovid had seen. The other was the *Art of Love*. Some scholars tend to dismiss this second charge as invalid, but they contradict Augustus, who considered the poem a serious offense. He took his moral reforms and the propaganda for them seriously, and they had not received the support that he desired.

The background and details of the first charge were never recorded. The farthest that Ovid himself would go, has already been stated. Theorists are likely to connect the *Art of Love* with someone's actual sexual behavior, sexual behavior with politics, and both sex and politics with Ovid's error. Ovid was either too popular to be severe with or too insignificant in his connection with a crime that may have involved him without his knowledge or that was very minor. Augustus might have simply disliked him intensely and might have been looking for a pretext to vent his spleen. But Augustus did see Ovid as an adversary. And Augustus did act with knowledge of his victim's personality and circumstances and with information about the climatic conditions and cultural environment of Tomis, so that the sentence that he passed, reeks of spite—against Ovid, for it placed, as far as we know, no material hardship on Ovid's family.

And thus this game ended. As far as writing poetry goes, Ovid spent his last eight or so years at Tomis in trying a new game, that of writing his way back to Rome or to a place more civilized and congenial than Tomis. His pleas in the exilic *Tristia* and *Ex Ponto* were ignored. The game with Augustus had long since ended. Ovid lost, and his end is obscure, but not his fame.

Postlude

You and I, gentle reader, may regard the myths of the *Metamorphoses* as incredible, unbelievable tales, as Ovid assured Augustus they were. But in those far off days, they might not have seemed innocuous to his prince. After all, the myth of Aeneas, son of Venus, gave prestige to the Julians, and the myth of the destiny of Rome as proclaimed by Virgil gave supernatural sanction to Rome's role in world affairs. That myths might be counterproductive would not have seemed strange to Augustus and his entourage. Dionysius of Halicarnassus, who published in Rome about 7 B.C., makes the point in his *Roman Antiquities:*

> Let no one imagine . . . that I am not sensible that some
> of the Greek myths are useful to mankind, part of them
> explaining, as they do, the works of Nature by allegories,
> others being designed as a consolation for human misfortunes,
> some freeing the mind of its agitations and terrors and
> clearing away unsound opinions, and others invented for some
> other useful purpose. But, though I am as well acquainted as
> anyone with these matters, nevertheless my attitude toward
> the myths is one of caution, and I am more inclined to accept
> the theology of the Romans, when I consider that the advan-
> tages from the Greek myths are slight and cannot be of profit
> to many, but only to those who have examined the end for
> which they are designed; and this philosophic attitude is
> shared by few. The great multitude, unacquainted with phil-
> osophy, are prone to take these stories about the gods in the
> worse sense and to fall into one of two errors: they either
> despise the gods as buffeted by many misfortunes, or else
> refrain from none of the most shameful and lawless deeds
> when they see them attributed to the gods.

Augustus might have agreed with his contemporary Dionysius and felt, therefore, that, for the most part, the tales in the *Metamorphoses* were likely to have an unwholesome influence upon most of the people.

METAMORPHOSES I: Discord-Concord

Having written about make-up, about finding and keeping a fascinating mistress, about Cupid and the vicissitudes of loving, and about love's heroines, Ovid had a reputation when he stepped before his listeners to give his first reading of Book I of the *Metamorphoses*. They expected to hear once more the erotic poet of sophisticated Rome. But when he announced in his opening lines that he was going to sing of that sweeping, colorless, passionless subject, change of shape, they must have pricked up their ears and smiled. And when he added in the next few lines that he was going to cover his morphological topic from the creation to the present, they may even have groaned with good-humored curiosity. They must have felt that they would no more hear about love, its varieties, its burnings, its games, its adepts, its underprivileged. Instead, a dull subject of impossible scope. What a shift! How unlike Ovid! And how could any poet cover such a subject without dry résumés, stupifying catalogues of begats, and other lists, statistics, and dullnesses? Even worse, Ovid went on and on with his lofty metaphysics for at least eighty more lines. Later Ovid did return to love stories, so that his beginning is a definite put-on. For by means of it, he initially frustrated audience expectations and thus began his extended playing with his audience, his game of fox and hounds. And the game works, even today.

Yet he must have held his audience in this opening passage, too. He must have swept it along with the novelty and interest of what he had to say, partly because he was off on a new tack, partly because it was not clear just what he was doing, and partly because the listeners received pleasure from recognizing Ovid's use of various philosophers. And if we look closely at this beginning, we see that it is very interesting, indeed.

The first four lines announce that Ovid is delivering a serious poem (it is not completely so) in the epic tradition, for they are in the traditional epic meter and adhere to the opening formulae of epic by calling upon a divine being for aid and by making a dignified statement of an important subject. At the same time, this statement is comic because it is flat, and it is flat because it is circular. For saying that the subject is forms changed into new bodies is rather like saying that it is circles' becoming new rings. The thought is grammatically complete, but it is not particularly meaningful because it has not been advanced beyond its initial term. The *Odyssey* and the *Aeneid* announce heroes and their adventures, and the *Iliad* asserts that its subject is the disasters befalling the Greeks because of the anger of Achilles. Hesiod's didactic epic promises revelations, and Lucretius', the truth about Nature. Ovid's promises precious little. That little is also vague, abstract, and bloodless. But the chief annoyance created by the statement of subject is its relative lack of meaning. As a result, the reader has the feeling that either he is the victim of a hoax or his intelligence is being ridiculed, a feeling increased because the subject seems impossible, it is hard to grasp, and the extent of the project makes it laughable.

1

But if anyone thinks that Ovid is not going to do just what he said he would, that person is mistaken. For having defined his subject and its scope, Ovid begins at once with the promised creation, in the course of which Ovid presents the theme of Book I, for the universe consists of a harmony of discords.

The important things to note about this creation are the following. First, it is materialistic and follows a pattern of natural cause and effect, as far as Ovid can make it. The basic materials for phenomena exist from the outset: earth, air, fire, water—the four elements, which are also the seeds of things. Second, it is dynamic. A god who is a better form of nature, does things: he breaks apart and separates. Then the four elements, each of which is a harmony because each part of an element is like another, move to their own levels because of their specific gravities. The original condition of matter in chaos had been dynamic, all the elements pummeling and interpenetrating one another. The dynamism remains after creation; for example, winds blow and rivers flow. Third, order is necessary for any change beyond chaos, and order involves having things in their proper places. But it is not absolute. For dynamism causes change. Fourth, change is further implicit in the created universe because animate beings are the result of the action of warmth on moist earth and may contain air or, if man, something of the divine fire. In other words, things are composed of incompatible, or warring, elements. Fifth, conflict is implicit in and among things because of the incompatibility of their constituent elements. Sixth, since the elements have qualities, or characteristics, and since all things are composed of them, it seems reasonable that some animate beings might have more of one element than another and, therefore, be characterized by it. Thus, Ovid would come close to having the idea of ruling humors. This assertion is borne out to a degree by some of the characters in Ovid's myths, for some are fiery youths and maidens, and others, yielding or cold like water. Seventh, the four elements suggest that there are polarities in being and, therefore, possible balances.

This list of ideas and their logical extensions is sufficient to show that Ovid's account of the creation is philosophical enough. It presents basic assumptions and develops their consequences, and it is consistent. In short, Ovid begins his poem in a very rational and, for his time, up-to-date way—not a myth way—and lays the foundation for what is to come. What is to come in due time, of course, is myth, but the beginning of the poem suggests that it will be rationalized myth, for the most part, and so it will appear sophisticated and intellectual, though, being myth, very human. Ovid's myths also promise to be humorous, because the indication is that they, like the beginning of the *Metamorphoses*, will playfully undercut expectations. However, they also may be serious, because they will deal with change, and change is not always humorous.

If one wishes evidence of Ovid's wit and humor, aside from his toying with audience expectation, one may consider Ovid's creator god. Ovid is puzzled as to who this god may be—indeed, he may be

Nature—never gives him a name, but simply refers to him as "whoever of the gods it was." Ovid thus whimsically acknowledges the theoretical need for such a deity and brushes him off. He is one of Ovid's expedient gods; indeed, he is expendable, for after the creation, Ovid never refers to him again. As Sterne remarked, "Vive la bagatelle." Surely it is a form of wit to belittle one's audience and write off the creator god almost simultaneously. However, if one wishes a more obvious example of Ovid's wit, there is his remark, involving a pun and a bit of internal rhyme, about chaos: earth was unstandable/unstable ("*instabilis*"); sea, unswimmable ("*innabilis*"). And the word play is witty in another fashion, for it exemplifies one kind of discordant strain that runs through the *Metamorphoses*, that of concurrently playing off the serious against the non-serious.

Discord, of course, is inherent in the created universe. Not all of it is fit for human beings; Ovid notes that the frigid zones are too cold and the central one, too torrid. Yet if black bird is real, so is oriole. For some of the creation is arresting and lovely: the earth hangs magically balanced in air, and the sea-goddess embraces the shores with her arms. Unfortunately, waters rush about and winds create waves; even worse, brother winds contend with one another and almost tear the world apart. Such is nature: conflict is built into it.

This creation ends with myth. Amphitrite, Phoebe, and Titan, whom Ovid noted as lacking in chaos, come into being at the end of creation, as do the wind-gods and Prometheus. It is clear, then, that most gods come into being when the things they govern, do, that these first gods are nature deities, and that they are much like man in some respects. Then man is made—with a touch of the divine in him. From this point until near the end of Book XV, Ovid keeps his reader in the realm of myth, legend, or a combination of both. So it is no surprise at the end of the poem to find Caesars lifted to the heavens: they not only have a touch of Venus, but have the original bit of divinity within them.

Once man has been created, Ovid gives him the appropriate myth-history, beginning with the Four Ages. The Golden Age of human perfection, innocence, and rectitude is a primitive age of golden lacks: the absence of laws, masters, travel, hard work, punishment, war, etc.; and men are content with a culture of gathering from nature's green in her mild, refreshing *Floréal*. There is only one season. The picture is pre-agricultural, pre-idyllic, ideal. It disappears with a god whose dismissal to Hades can be regarded only as sinister. Curiously, Ovid does not lament its going, and he never returns to it. But Ovid's attitude is not as odd as it seems. The Golden Age is woefully limited as to diet: acorns, milk, grain, honey, strawberries, blackberries, cornel-cherries, and arbute fruit. Furthermore, in a Golden Age of harmony all the conflicts, duplicity, sacrifices, meannesses, and savage passions abounding in myth would not exist. Not only would Ovid's subject be eliminated, but so would the need for his rhetoric, legal astuteness, and psychological insight. Augustus would have no meaning, purpose or function. One could not, then, compliment him. Neither poet nor emperor would have occupation.

With the Silver Age the human decline begins, according to a natural law, so says Seneca the Elder, that an inferior state must follow one of perfection. Ovid here avoids describing the moral condition of mankind, merely placing it between primal placid goodness and bronze irritableness and bellicosity. Men, in the Silver Age, therefore, must be unevenly peaceful in their relationships and relatively good. The era is one of house construction, established abodes, basic agriculture, and hard work. Nature is not given high marks for being bountiful, and Jove has modified the calendar so that there are now four seasons. Things are clearly not ideal, but there is instead a desirable real that is attainable and recognizable. Indeed, things are pretty much as they might be, ideally, under the Augustan program for native Italians: a stable society of hard-working farmers living productive lives in peace and following the essential moral principles most of the time. Oddly enough, the Golden Age by contrast is shown to have its defects.

The Age of Brass is not vicious, but men are extremely irritable and severe and inclined to use weapons. This epoch is merely a way to get from Age Two to Age Four. Yet the focus here on the importance of emotional bent indicates that an age is determined by its mood or is its mood. Ovid implies as much when he puns about the Iron Age, saying that it is of baser "vein," for he thus indicates that each age has its mettle indicated by a metal.

The Iron Age is characterized by deceit, greed, and a lack of restraint so gross that the closest relationships are violated without hesitation. Human discord, which has been growing through the Ages, now becomes vile and impious, worse than the disharmony of the winds. Piety is vanquished; Justice flees from the earth; the Giants assault Olympus, but are slain with thunderbolts; and the nadir of depravity is reached when the bloody offspring of the Giants join the unhumankind of the Iron Age. Therefore, Jove does two traditionally epic things: he conceives a prodigious wrath, and he calls a council. Thus far Ovid has moved his poem through the semi-serious didactic type and something like the *Theogony* of Hesiod to something resembling the heroic epic, which is a narrative with plot and characterization, not mere chronology and generalization. What Ovid ends up with, of course, is a composite poem consisting largely of a series of epyllia, "little epics," or dactyllic hexameter renditions of myths. At this point in his narrative, Ovid is almost into the first of these, the Lycaon story.

However, Ovid pauses to compliment Augustus indirectly by comparing Jove's Main Street, the Milky Way, with the Palatine of Rome and to project a sketch of Roman society upon that heavenly concourse. For there are, he says, noble gods and plebeian ones, the former with splendid houses on the best street and with crowded atria. There the great gods have placed their gods, their household ones, that is. This is all very Roman and aristocratic, but also very human and therefore *infra dig.* A bit of air has been released from the lofty gods by making them human, and this diminution lessens the magnitude of the mortals compared to them. Perhaps more important, Ovid is indicating just how he will treat his myth figures, namely, very humanly, contemporaneously, and also archly, for there is something amusing about gods having gods.

There is further delay in getting to Lycaon's metamorphosis because Jove must announce his intention to destroy mankind and justify the action to divine council thus: he must protect the rustic divinities and punish Lycaon for attempting his life. His effort further puts off the tale of Lycaon, for it gives Ovid an opportunity to express his horror at the equally impious murder of Caesar and his approval of loyalty to Augustus, sentiments undeniably laudatory in the author's day, but a damned nuisance to anyone interested in hearing an appalling tale. Finally, Jove is allowed to tell of Lycaon's betrayal of trust, his plot to kill Jove, his attempt to get Jove to dine on human flesh, the destruction of his house, and his metamorphosis into slavering wolf. Jove ends by observing that Lycaon is merely typical of human viciousness and that all deserve to die.

The story of Lycaon is the first of the kind usually thought of as a metamorphosis and is, therefore, an introduction to the type. It represents some of the things that Ovid will be doing later on with variation, with greater detail, at greater length, and with much greater effect. The result, in retrospect, is to make Jove the founder of a genre in which he will be later outclassed, though he is clearly competent here in his thumbnail treatment of a metamorphosis. One of the outstanding qualities of the sketch is its sensationalism. Lycaon commits gruesome crimes, such as cutting the throat of a hostage and serving his still quivering flesh for dinner. After Jove has blasted his house, Lycaon rushes into the fields, and there his change of shape begins with the revolting detail of his trying to speak, but, instead, howling. He foams at the mouth, begins to kill sheep for blood; his clothes become grey hair; his arms, legs; his shining eyes and savage face remain the same. Another dimension of the story is its being something of a mirror for magistrates; that is, it functions morally and ethically. For Jove properly upholds order, law, and piety, in this instance respect for the gods and the rights of a guest and also of a hostage. Lycaon is obviously the opposite of the model king. Also, his nationality is given, a significant fact, for he is the first of the bad Greeks. (One would do well to keep alert for Ovid's appraisal of the Greeks.)

It is important to note, too, that Jove undercuts himself in his own storytelling. At one point he says that he found offenses everywhere; yet he also declares that the common people of Arcadia worshiped him after he gave the proper sign, so that they were not impious; nor does Jove say at this point that the common people were otherwise wicked. Hence, though it is quite right for Jove to punish Lycaon, it is not right for Jove to take Lycaon as typical of all mankind and to punish everyone. Jove's adopting human form in order to spy out or to test man's goodness also seems unsavory because it involves deceit. The result is that one is not sure whether he completely approves of Jove here. One notes further that Ovid does not always label things as black or white, but may present gradations of right and wrong, as he does here with Jove, who is not completely in the right. Indeed, one of Ovid's characters may be right in one way and simultaneously wrong in another: it is right to punish wickedness, but wrong to be indiscriminate or excessive in doing so. Magistrates should take note.

In addition, the myth at hand reveals something about metamorphosis. For a god, such as Jove, a metamorphic change is merely a means to an end and is neither serious nor permanent. Indeed, the implication here, as elsewhere, is that the gods are shape-changers and will naturally appear in various forms or manifestations. But for a human being, metamorphosis evaluates essential nature and may also punish. Transformation into wolf indicates that Lycaon has always been both less than and worse than a man. In his change nature artfully makes the punishment fit the crime. There are two implications here. One is that wrongdoers are punished by the natural course of events. The other is that only in the distancing of art is horror effectively educative; that is, Lycaon can be punished, but he cannot learn from his punishment, whereas the reader can.

In Book I thus far, the Jove-Lycaon episode is part of a sequence that introduces the theme of order at the cosmic level, where warring chaos is turned into creation; carries it to the divine level, where Jove suppresses the Giants; and brings it thence to the human level, where Jove rectifies matters. In the last two levels Jove receives marked attention and respect, as he does in the account of the Silver Age. Order is thus a part of nature and of Jove, a social and administrative being. But the myth also ties Jove close to humanity and makes him seem very Roman at this point. And thus it sets one pattern for future presentations of him and of the other gods.

Structurally, the type of narrative changes with Lycaon's story. Chaos, cosmos, the Four Ages, and the Giants seem sketchy, characterless, and catalog-like. The Lycaon myth gives the reader something he can easily get his teeth into and identify with. Like what has gone before, however, it is best read when read closely and when one tries to determine what the ingenious author is doing.

Now comes the Flood. This catastrophe continues the preceding sensationalism and raises it to the nth degree. Ovid's account of it shows that chaos can come again, in a limited form, because of human depravity: water takes the place of land, and all is topsy-turvily awash. The wash takes the reader back into the generalized kind of narrative used for the creation of the new world and for the Four Ages, but it is full, more detailed and concrete, and more varied. It begins with two somber, sonorous and majestic personifications, those of South Wind and Iris, whose rainbow colors are a sinister illumination in this storm. Then

6

the ingenious operations of these fanciful aerial powers—South Wind has been pouring water from his person and squeezing it out of the clouds while Iris has been lifting water up to refill them—are suddenly contrasted with their real effects for men: the growing grain is flattened and ruined, and the farmers' tearful vows and year's hard work are erased. For two lines, Ovid brings in the harsh reality and indirectly criticizes Jove by sympathizing with the mortals whom the god has seen as so sinful. Then Ovid jumps back to the personified sea and rivers, who do their part to increase the flood. And then, back to the realistic: plains, orchards, houses, and men go under. Holy things and places are overwhelmed. Now the reader is surer that Jove's reformation is excessive. The realism continues with fish in tree tops and sea cows where she-goats pastured. The real is certainly made sensational enough to gratify the tabloid instinct in human nature, but the whole appeals to one's pity, too. Hence, the fairness of Jove is further questioned.

Moreover, Jove's accuracy also comes under question: not all the human inhabitants of earth were killed, as Jove had threatened, for Deucalion and Pyrrha survived. So either all mankind was not guilty and Jove was mistaken, or Jove was ineffective. Both are true. Jove makes faulty decisions and executes them sloppily. Deucalion and Pyrrha not only survive on their own, but they are both innocent and pious. Their piety toward gods and men makes them become the restorers of the human race by following the advice of an earth-goddess who represents various kinds of order and has oracular powers, Themis. They thus fulfill Jove's promise to the assembled gods that he would give them another race of devotees having a marvelous origin. But Ovid gives Jove only this vague promissory role in the matter; and, since Jove takes no active part in the restoration of mankind, one does not feel that he had any hand in it.

Deucalion and Pyrrha function to keep the metamorphoses going by providing the necessary people, who are really stones changed into human beings, but equally important at the moment, Deucalion and his wife lead off the amorous incidents of the *Metamorphoses* by providing a picture of social affection and marital love. Viewing the wasted world and realizing the loss of the rest of their kind, Deucalion voices the couple's sense of solitude and insecurity. He also expresses the general bases for their emotional attachment, an interesting analysis of marriage and doubtless acceptable according to old-fashioned Roman views: he and his wife are of the same race and family; their sexual union was arrived at through marriage; they have had common dangers to face and will have more to strengthen the bond between them; they give each other the consolation and reassurance of companionship. These are rather prosaic, workaday bases for an intimate relationship, but they function, for Deucalion can think of life with Pyrrha, the rest of the world gone; but under the circumstances, he cannot think of it without her. This is not romantic love, yet it may be what made life livable for many Romans, besides making it respectable. Ovid has made his bow to marital fidelity and happiness and, putting Jove in the background, to innocence and piety.

Deucalion and Pyrrha also represent a harmony, the marriage of true minds, which is threatened by discordant natural forces, hostile only because called into action by earlier human discord. Ovid has been keeping to his theme.

Order is restored, of course. But its restoration is slowed down by a baroque description of sea-blue Triton, barnacled about the shoulders and blowing his wreathéd horn in mid-ocean. The sketch is an artistic risk, but it is visually good enough to warrant the gamble. This bit of the Flood story is only one example of Ovid's fine artistic insets that make his poem a virtuoso work. It is like the smiling angel, head cocked, that listens above the pulpit of the Church of St. Mary the Virgin, Oxford, or the angel above the name of Cromwell, her wings lost, that is falling, screaming, through the Chapel Royal, Dublin, into the nether depths.

There is another function that the Pyrrha-Deucalion story performs, and that is to make the reader once again aware of Ovid's subtlety and his sureness of purpose. The story of marital love is a quiet but masterful piece of craftsmanship—all there, yet barely noticeable. The next story is another kind of love story, an unmistakable success, partly because curious and novel, for the love grows out of spite and ends neither happily nor unhappily. This tale, too, is an example of Ovid's mastery, of his ability to handle the complex, to vary his fare, and to keep the reader off balance. The lead into the myth shows Ovid making one of his sleight-of-hand transitions, here a sequence of them. He moves from the subsiding of the Flood to the stony new men and women, to creatures born from the sun-heated slime, to a particular one that terrifies mankind, the Python. Apollo heroically befriends people by killing the monster and self-importantly establishes the Pythian games. Feeling mighty big, he runs into little Cupid, who is playing with his archery set. Apollo is irked by Cupid's using Apollo's weapon and treats him with contempt. Cupid threatens revenge, claiming superiority to Apollo. Thus, neatly varied, the earlier motifs of discord and of divine wrath reappear. However, the epic wrath here is not that of Jove, whose shaking his locks had caused earth, sea, and stars to quake, but the pique of Apollo and the spiteful anger of Cupid—rather comic contrasts with Jove's.

The situation is funny enough, a huff between two incongruously paired flaming archers.   But Ovid changes tone and improves the comedy. Cupid has on- and off-love-arrows, on for Apollo and off for his first love, Daphne. Out of this artillery, Ovid creates a two-pronged situation. One, barely mentioned, is pathetic: Daphne's father wants grandchildren, but gives in to her hubristic request that she remain chaste like Diana, Apollo's sister, ironically enough. The traditional desire for perpetuation of the family is frustrated, but it receives recognition, though here it is not as powerful as Daphne's desire to follow her own impulses.

The other predicament is the ludicrous, though elegant, love situation, which is far from simple. Shot by Cupid, sun-god Apollo burns

8

much brighter because of love for Daphne, who, incongruously enough, has many suitors, though they have not been shot by Cupid. Ovid himself says that Daphne's beauty was the cause of her undoing. Therefore, Daphne does not need Cupid's darts to inspire males with love for her. Her form alone inflames men with desire. In this way, Cupid and his arrows are covertly ridiculed, for the god is unnecessary and is thus merely an expedient figure of speech.

The tale is complicated and enriched in other ways. There is the neat touch of Apollo's looking longingly at Daphne's loose-falling hair and saying, " 'What if it were done up?' " Apollo thus reveals his fastidiousness and his city ways. He is also doing something typical of lovers: remaking the loved one to fit the lover's ideal. His question is ironic, too, because shortly Daphne's hair will be put into a new order, an even more rustic one, the opposite of Apollo's preference. Next, there is something reticently improper, a nice antithesis that people engage in frequently, in Ovid's observing that Apollo praises the exposed portions of his love's anatomy (eyes, lips, hands, and arms), but thinks the covered parts (enumeration unnecessary) even better. Thus comically human are the gods.

It is also funny and also in character that Apollo finds the terrain rough as he pursues Daphne. His protest, however, is that it is far too rough for the lady, to which he adds a complaint that he cannot run as fast as she. The most amusing detail at this point is Apollo's offer to slow down if Daphne will. Clearly he is out of breath, and his ruse is woefully transparent. Incongruously, he still has wind enough to make a long love speech in which he pompously declares his emotions, his lack of rusticity (Daphne, alas, is nothing if not rustic), his real estate, his parentage (most impressive), and his skills (prophecy, music, archery, and healing), none of which is doing him any good. He thus ironically calls attention to his inability to foretell the outcome of this current love and to cure himself of it. Ovid has presented his audience not only with first love, but the prototype of all stories in which the urban magnate's son pursues the country girl.

Then, sore feet or no, Apollo speeds up, and the chase is nip and tuck. The tempo of the narrative speeds up. The tone changes. Apollo has asserted earlier that he is not Daphne's enemy, no beast of prey pursuing a victim; Ovid, nonetheless, now compares the god to a swift hound about to sink his sharp teeth into a flying hare. Ovid sees what Apollo does not: there is an element of cruelty in love; the chaser wants the tender, lovely prey. Love is an animal appetite; it wishes to devour.

At first Daphne's beauty is increased by her exertion, and the reader responds to this loveliness, but as she becomes terrified and exhausted, the reader feels pity for her. When she shows her vanity and prays for the destruction of her beauty, she loses some of that sympathy because of her frigidity. She does not get her wish completely, however, for her transformation into the laurel, or bay tree, does not eliminate all of her loveliness. Yet she remains, when all is said and done, the girl who, when pursued in the rumble seat, turns into a log.

There is a moment of wonder now. What will happen?

Apollo handles the situation perfectly. He really does love Daphne. Instead of cursing her, reproaching her, bruising her bark or stripping it off (a mother does so later to a tree-turning daughter), he honors her by making her his emblem, by giving her the urbane compliment of never parting with her. She will always remain the souvenir of his first love. Thus, in a way, Apollo wins after all—by being the gentleman. Daphne can never be completely his, but she can never escape. Furthermore, although Cupid has clearly defeated Apollo, Apollo has neutralized the sting. His good breeding triumphs over Cupid's pique by turning a loss into a benefit. And though Cupid threatened to humble Apollo and has done so, Apollo, splendid egoist, is unaware that vengeance has been taken or even intended. Surely a threat that passes from the victim's mind and a revenge that the victim ignores, are not completely satisfactory to their perpetrator.

Ovid neatly ends the myth with Apollo's complimenting Daphne by revealing that she will be a functional part of his glory and that of the Romans and Augustus. So Augustus and the Romans are complimented, too, for they are shown to be the concern of the god, and the laurel gains status by their using it for their glory and protection.

Thus the tale of Cupid, Apollo, and Daphne ends on a grand harmonious note. Everyone wins to a degree. But the story is shot through with discord, beginning with the comic confrontation between two archer gods. And if ever there is an arena for discordant harmonies, it is that of love. Moreover, the original warring elements of chaos reappear here. Daphne, daughter of river-god Peneus, is a watery nymph; Apollo, as sun-god, radiates heat; when these two come together, according to Ovid's theories, something animal should be created from the interaction of their discordant harmonies. It is not, because another disharmony, the wrath of Cupid, has intervened. Yet something has been created, namely the laurel tree, emblem of poetry and of triumph.

Again, as earlier, Ovid amply demonstrates that neither harmony nor disharmony is absolute. Yet there is no question that harmony is the better of the two. Courtship, a kind of conflict, has been placed next to marriage and has proved the more exciting, but less fulfilling and less socially meaningful. Cupid's wrath has been presented as powerful, but as less important than Jove's, though more interesting and entertaining.

Preceding commentary indicates that certain themes and contrasts are emerging as episode follows episode in Book I. It implies, too, that some instruction in manners, ethics, and psychology is going on. In manners and ethics, for example, the principles of suavity, or urbane politeness, and respect for others are set forth and upheld. When Apollo violated them in dealing with Cupid, he paid for his rudeness. When he observed them with Daphne, he came out ahead. His experience demonstrates that one cannot trifle with love; that love is a two-way street; that one should not pressure others, for stress may force them into drastic action. Daphne's behavior, on the other hand, indicates that one should be careful what one wishes for; she gets her wish, but it amounts to a diminution of her being.

One of Ovid's psychological insights here is his calling attention to a very real kind of distress experienced by some good-looking girls: their grace and beauty bring them unwanted male attention. Ovid suggests three ethical evaluations of Daphne's frigidity, which, in her case, is a natural reaction beyond her control: it is pitiable; it is wasteful and dehumanizing; it is both, but also understandable and acceptable, because Daphne represents a particular type of woman whose prototype is divine, namely, Diana. Diana stands for and gives status to all women unwilling to be touched by men, all who find womanhood and sexuality repugnant, all who would be free, unmarried, athletic, and independent. It is as natural for Daphne to be this way as it is for her father to wish for grandchildren. Ovid's evaluations are human, but they are not always simple or consistent.

As Ovid emerges thus far in Book I, he seems to belong to an Age of Reason. His use of myth is not religious, but seems related to typology, or classification, of personality, as well as evaluation of it. The gods are seen as persons and as natural forces. For example, Cupid as personified here represents the love drive and its opposite and is a way of presenting the situation in which a male falls in love with a girl who cannot love men. Apollo is both natural phenomena and a variety of young man. Ovid can thus play all sorts of intellectual games with his myths, using them as stories with characters and, hence, for ethical and typological purposes, as examples of a philosophical position, as means of adroit compliment, and as quasi-rational explanation. Since a personified force or natural object or phenomenon is a detachable outer representation of something inner or of an intrinsic quality, it always carries a double nature. It, therefore, encourages and lends itself to creative speculation, to defining notions of being.

And what of Ovid's craftsmanship in the Apollo-Daphne myth? In one hundred and fifteen lines, Ovid has displayed a great deal of learning, ingenuity, art, and perception, freighting the rifts with more ore than here noted. It may be unfair to expect that he can or will do as much every time. But he has demonstrated that one ought to read him carefully and ponder his work. This process includes looking at the connective material between episodes.

Ovid's means of connecting the Apollo-Daphne tale with the next one is clever and novel. Leaving his principals, Ovid rambles on about a minor character in Daphne's life, the river-god Peneus, her father. And, as he rambles, Ovid again varies his fare. First he gives a dignified, vivid, and sonorous description of the actual river Peneus foaming through the Vale of Tempe and misting the tall trees with its spray. Here the river has his rugged, remote, and rustic abode, a cave. At this point Ovid personifies the river as a little Jove giving laws to his water-nymphs, and a purely realistic description is modulated into a scene belonging to human society. To this spot come other rivers to pay their respects, for Peneus has just lost his daughter. Ovid names five rivers, giving each a deft, informed, I-have-traveled-there epithet, and then humorously adds in a lump all the multitude of other river-gods tributary to Neptune, so that there must have been a tremendous mob, but no flooding. In passing, Ovid wryly notes that the situation is ambivalent, because the river-gods do not know whether Peneus should be condoled or congratulated. What Ovid is doing, of course, is providing x number of leads into the next tale, a neat suspense device in his game of catch-the-author, for one cannot tell which lead Ovid will take. He chooses an unexpected one, that of the missing personage, and turns a minus into a plus. One feels that Ovid should be congratulated for his ingenuity and that, when he wrote this passage, he must have done so himself.

The missing Inachus, like Peneus, is a river-god grieving for a daughter who may be lost. Like Daphne's, Io's situation is ambiguous. Like Daphne, watery Io has captivated another god that gives off illumination. Like Apollo (and Ovid in the *Art of Love*), Jove looks for sexual gratification among the lower-class divinities. And like Apollo, he presents his credentials to a girl who runs away. But Jove's escapade is very different from Apollo's, even though both are rural comedies. The whole amorous interlude is over in thirteen lines. And this nymph does not get away.

These are not the only differences between the two tales. Jove seems faster, surer, more experienced than his son Apollo, and more potent. Sexually he is not in need of Cupid; sight is enough, and he is more like the ordinary guy on the prowl. Jove's problems come from other quarters, namely, his jealous wife and his own carelessness. For he makes the mistake of ignoring his own laws of meteorology by producing a covering patch of thick black cloud out of nowhere on a bright, clear day. Not very bright of a sky-god. Thus Ovid launches into another amorous episode, but one with a new kind of comic situation, that of the delinquent husband and the jealous wife. The situation is super-comic because the husband is all-powerful and thus can do no wrong—but he does—and the jealous wife is his everlasting spouse. Unlike a Roman wife, she cannot be divorced. Immortality has drawbacks.

The domestic comedy unrolls with gratifying predictability. Juno, as familiar with Jove's infidelities as was Ovid's Roman audience, misses her husband; spots the telltale concealment, that big Jovial, fertility rain-thunder-and-lightning cloud; suspects the worst; descends; whips off the cover; and exposes her husband with a marvelously beautiful cow, Io metamorphosed. Even Juno has to admire the cow—a perceptive touch on Ovid's part. At the human level, even a wronged wife may admit the beauty of a rival, for cultures standardize feminine beauty for women as well as for men. Indeed, an injured wife might prefer to be replaced by someone more beautiful than herself, rather than someone uglier. Some law of nature or of competitive justice seems to be involved. At the myth level something slightly different is indicated: Io is really a form of bovine, or Junoesque, Juno. Not only does Homer epitomize Hera-Juno as "ox-eyed," but there is reason to believe that Juno in very early antiquity was a goddess of cattle, so that Juno, Io, and Isis are varying embodiments of the same form. Ovid may have been aware of this fact, for in his *Art of Love*, he calls Isis, with whom he identified Io, "the Memphian heifer." In any event, Jove has fallen for essentially the same type of female as his spouse. To continue with the story, Juno knows perfectly well where this cow came from, but both she and Jove play the sophisticated game of pretending that all is perfectly proper and thus save face and avoid a scene. Juno asks for the cow as a gift—she could not ask for Jove's mistress as one. Jove can hardly refuse his wife a cow. So Juno handily eliminates a rival.

Emphasis shifts now to the pastoral scene and to the comic-pathetic portion of the situation, to Io's grief at being a cow. Io does not see herself as beautiful, but as deprived. From a girl's point of view, her new appearance is awful, her diet is bad, and her voice is horrible. Hermann Fränkel says that we feel for Io because we ourselves have gone through similar alterations during life, seeing ourselves suddenly as ugly adolescents or decaying senior citizens, or we have found flaws in our voices or appearance. Or the cow may represent the way a once free attractive girl feels when domesticated to wifehood or motherhood.

Yet for all the pathos here, cows are not serious people. We adults sympathize with Io, but we smile at vocables coming out *moo*, are charmed by her fairy tale literacy when she spells out her story in the dust, chuckle sympathetically at her father's distress when he thinks of having heifers and bullocks for grandchildren, and become rather sober when Inachus observes that, if a god can suffer woes, he must suffer them eternally. More pathetic is watchman Argus' separation of father and child. Once again Ovid has swept the emotional spectrum.

He continues on a more serious note with Jove's pity for Io and his arranging her release from bovine bondage, which involves the complicated and brutal murder of a freak. Mercury accomplishes it by putting all of Argus' hundred eyes to sleep. He does so by means of a very dull telling of an ineffectual love-chase that repeats at a completely rustic level the Daphne-Apollo tale. The story of Pan and Syrinx, like Jove's telling the council of gods his adventures in Arcadia, occurs within a frame, and Ovid here employs a device that he will use much later in the *Metamorphoses* in a more extended and complicated fashion. Here, however, there is humor, as Mr. Fränkel points out, the humor of repeating a story pattern too soon and giving an inferior rendition. This is another artistic gamble on Ovid's part; indeed, Ovid seems to be consciously both using and violating a rule set down by that arch-storyteller Homer-

Odysseus at the end of Book XII of the *Odyssey,* namely, that telling a simple tale over again is wearisome. Once again, however, Ovid proves his ingenuity, this time by making dullness function effectively. For this story would put anyone to sleep. It also shows Ovid as one who does not like those, such as Argus, who participate in punishing lovers and as one who disapproves of mere plot summary as a form of storytelling. The narrative also demonstrates just how good the Daphne-Apollo one is.

The mood throughout the Mercury section is a bit grim, not the drawing-room-comedy atmosphere at all. A harsh guard, Argus, drives Io farther away from her love and kin. An innocent-appearing killer arrives, just a passing goatherd willing to be companionable and entertaining. As soon as this assassin has put Argus to sleep, he sends his severed head to bloody the rocks. Juno in a rage plucks the eyes from the dead head and puts them in the tail of her Indian bird, the peacock, apparently to remind all that jealous wives have many eyes. Juno sends a Fury to drive Io crazy and goad her from Greece to Egypt. Jove promises to be good in order to quench Juno's wrath and, hence, be able to restore Io to her normal shape. Things cease being grim. Jove even makes Io a goddess, albeit an Egyptian and, therefore, an inferior one. Juno can hardly have wished for such an outcome, but Jove is revealed as omnipotent and so is the dominant position of the male; the female is comparatively ineffectual. Playing along with Jove produces substantial benefits.

Ovid closes Book I by preparing for Book II and by leaving the reader in suspense. To do this, he tells of the rivalry between Io's young son, who is now "thought" to have been sired by Jove, and the son of Clymene and that absentee, traveling deity Phoebus Apollo. These scions of prominent personages are proud, haughty poor-little-rich-kids with no adequate resident fathers. The lads bicker about status, and Io's son challenges his friend's descent from the Sun. Phaëthon goes straight home to mother and, childlike, pours out his resentment and his need to be reassured about his paternity. Moved by maternal feeling and perhaps by pride, Clymene foolishly sends her boy off across Ethiopia and India, inaccurately and whimsically described as not far away, to learn the facts from the Sun himself. The situation is all too human, and Phaëthon is all too like his father. Be that as it may, the boy makes this difficult journey effortlessly. Thus a few details fuse fairy tale and psychological realism.

Last, and most important to notice, is that finally, after all the fritter and grandiosity of the creation, the Four Ages of Man, the Giants, Lycaon and reform from the top, the astral Palatine, Triton, and a deal more, Ovid does, he actually does, come around to gratifying initial audience expectation and to writing about love. The fox has doubled back. But even here he has been doubly foxy, for love as Ovid treats it now is a much broader and more mature subject than it is in his earlier works, ranging from sophisticated pursuit and clandestine amour through parental and marital love, so that the fox has gratified expectations and still thrown them off balance.

14

The foregoing analysis is sufficient to show the nature of Ovid's Roman games. They are a subtle and intricate kind of play in which the reader has to be very wide awake to catch Ovid at what he is doing and practically intuitive to anticipate his movements or game plays. The tales that constitute them, moreover, demand—and are worthy of—close attention, involvement, and contemplation, for they are complicated structures unified in their variety, but unexpectedly varied in their movements, both within stories and between them. To this complexity Ovid adds certain ambivalences. Yet he maintains a theme throughout the book. Subsurface or interrupted as the theme may be—or seem to be—this book, like the rest, has one, here that of discordant harmony.

All this artistry would be sterile, however, if Book I did not enrich the human scene with humor, wit, sensibility, vivacity, and joy—if it did not give us a sense of the complex nature of being, its incredible variety and abundance—if it did not make us understand our fellows better and feel for and with them, even when laughing at them or disapproving of them.

METAMORPHOSES II: Advice for Kings and Courtiers

Thus far two gods associated with fire have been moved by love's flames to stoop to creatures of earth, to watery, but very human girls like coy Io. Phaëthon's fires are of a different sort: more pure, less of earth about them, they lead him up to reach exalted origins and a dazzling inheritance. They are the fires of pride and ambition. Phaëthon has an Ovidian identity crisis, for he must prove to himself that he is who he is. His journey of self-assertion is the archetypal journey of all adolescent boys and girls, heroes and heroines, who know they are divinely descended and seek rapport with a divine parent. The tale is gorgeous, funny in spots, and tragic, because when Phaëthon finds his father, he also finds solar power, which has far too many horses for even the average heroic child to handle.

Indeed, everything in the story is on the grand scale, beginning with the gleaming palace of the Sun, which somewhat resembles a temple, and its carved doors. Their baroque ekphrasis, or description of a work of art, depicts the lovely universe that Phoebus Apollo surveys and that Phaëthon will soon be destroying. By emphasizing water, the door reliefs allude to the roles played by moisture and heat in creation through spontaneous generation, a concept Ovid employed for the postdiluvian creation of animals in Book I. The grandeur is sustained in the description of the god and his court, but it is also ironic. Grand and radiant as father Sun and his offspring are, they are not very bright and thus resemble Father Jove. The surprised parent, whose "eyes behold . . . all things," proudly acknowledges his paternity and then, of his own will, swears an irrevocable oath granting Phaëthon whatever he desires as proof of their relationship. What the boy wants is natural enough: he wants to be like his father, that is, to take over his father's job, which means driving the family car. Since Phaëthon is only half grown and half divine, his wanting to be a god is hubristic; since he is a boy, it is pathetic. At this point the modern reader is more likely to blame the parent than the child, especially since the child's father has been away all the time and the boy has only been told about him.

Phoebus, tricked by his pride in his son and implicit trust in his son's common sense, gains some sympathy by groaning heavily and talking long, sensibly, and fast to get Phaëthon to make some other wish. Sol explains the dangers, all of which Phaëthon will find to be true. The father then gives the adamant youth sensible flight instructions, which he cannot follow, one being " 'In the middle is the safest path,' " a clever, yet ironic, use of the doctrine of the golden mean. Then the reader is taken on one of the wildest rides imaginable—pre-Hollywood and television, of course— because it threatens to destroy not only the earth but the heavens themselves, as Jove in Book I had heard, and because it passes close to some awesomely dangerous and active constellations—Serpent, Scorpion, and others. Both dangers result from even the horses' knowing that Phaëthon is a lightweight.

Learning too late that father knows best, Phaëthon is more than willing to be thought the son of a mere mortal, like Ethiopian Merops, his everyday royal father. His ride has taken him only as far as noon when he panics. The daylight skies have become a nightmare. He drops the reins, and the horses rush at will, firing the earth in their course. Finally he himself suffers death by fire, blasted by Jove to save the earth. The account of the ride includes a sonorous and striking survey of mountains set afire, ending with the stunning line, *"aeriaeque Alpes et nubifer Appenninus"* ("the airy Alps and cloud-bearing Apennines"). The long and marvelous description of the results of this close passage of the sun suggests the harm that can be done by giving too much power to the young and inexperienced. Since Phaëthon's earthly father is a king and his divine father dominates and regulates earth, sea, and middle heaven alike, Phaëthon seems like a child who has been given political power too soon. The disaster caused by nepotism suggests that the favoritism almost inevitably engaged in by monarchs is deplorable both for the effects it can have on their offspring and those it may have on the world beneath their sway.

There are other points conveyed by the story, such as caveats against rash promises, being carried away by emotion or overfondness for a child, careless wishing, excessive pride or ambition, thinking that lines of action may be reversible (e.g., that one may grant power and then retract it), thinking that a child will be as competent as his parent, and so on. Hence, there are a good many lessons for a moralizer to derive from the story, but the major one seems to be directed at someone who can delegate power, such as a king or magistrate.

Yet it is clear that, when considering the grand descriptions and the astonishing ride, one is torn between the moralizing and the sensationalism, the latter tending not so much to reinforce the former as to obscure it and to make the reader aware of Ovid's skill as an artist. Such ambivalence takes another form in the epitaph that the Hesperian water-nymphs carve on Phaëthon's tomb: "Here Phaethon lies: in Phoebus' car he fared, / And though he greatly failed, more greatly dared." The reader knows that Phaëthon has done the wrong thing and has had the effect of many atomic bombs, causing untold agony. Yet the reader also sympathizes with him, partly because he represents a certain kind of child: the child with some ability (witness Phaëthon's fantastic journey and his acknowledgment by his father) who is destroyed by trying to imitate or rival an outstanding parent. And the reader may even admire Phaëthon, as Ovid wants him to do, because of the boy's great soul. But from a practical point of view, one must conclude that Phaëthon has caused only grief. As for his being daring, that point, though a possible one, considering the situation, is not one that Ovid has properly stressed and is, therefore, one reason that the epitaph comes as a jolt. Another reason is that Phaëthon is praised for his failure, especially considering the horror and havoc caused by his pride and role-playing.

Ovid makes us pause at that epitaph. It is amazing, we realize, because it is both true and false. It does face up to Phaëthon's ride and to his failure. And he did attempt something great. But the epitaph omits the fact that he caused a natural catastrophe. Hence, it is so incomplete, so much is covered up by those words "greatly failed," that the epitaph is also false. It is woefully slanted.

This quality lays bare the nature of all tender epitaphs. Because men, especially those of high rank, wish to say only good of their dead, they memorialize only their virtues and ignore, even more than the nymphs did, their faults. As a result, official Phaëthons are presented to their contemporaries and to posterity, purified by the condensing fire of lapidary verse and by the desire of relatives to praise and cherish.

Not only does Ovid's epitaph for Phaëthon come as a surprise, but the revelation it presents about epitaphs is also a surprise.

Like the Apollo-Daphne episode in Book I, the one about Phaëthon is filled with numerous artistic effects, as well as value judgments. The doors to Phoebus' palace ought to be splendid to stimulate pride in Phaëthon and to glorify the lordship of the sun over the earth. They also glorify Ovid, a fact that he does not fail to call attention to in his comment that "the workmanship was more beautiful than the material," an indirect way of saying that great art is more valuable than the materials out of which it is made, or that art is more precious than substance. The implication, of course, is that Ovid's *Metamorphoses* is worth more than the myths (substance) out of which it is made or than any content his retellings may have. And so we have an example of Ovid's patting himself on the back—delicately and covertly, of course.

The allegorical figures Day, Month, Year, Century, Hours, Spring, Summer, and the rest of Phoebus' court suggest orderly change and recurrence and tend to stress the importance of the sun as a responsible regulator, for these personages are subservient to him. And, indeed, Phoebus' instructions to his son show him as a responsible deity, properly Stoic and Roman, caught in an irresponsible act that violates his own advice: pursue the middle way. Phoebus thus becomes something less admirable as an exalted administrator of the world's affairs. Thus by deviating from his proper role, he becomes a Stoic example of what not to do. The sun's scorching the earth is a warning about what happens when proper limits are violated and duties are abandoned: the harmony of discords is broken, and one element, divine fire, rages out of control.

The sun-god misbehaves again when his immoderate grief makes the Sun absent himself for one whole day, an amusing contradiction in terms. Also amusing, because ridiculous, is Ovid's optimistic comment that this darkness would have distressed the earth, had it not been burning and given itself light. The grief of Phaëthon's mother is more immoderate than his father's; but that of his sisters, the Heliades, is so extreme that they turn into poplar trees, whose tears become sap flowing down their bark. Thus Ovid embodies the idea that excessive grief destroys personality or drastically reduces one as a complete being. Even so, all is not lost, for these resinous tears, Ovid notes, harden into amber and in due time become ornaments for Roman brides. The amber pieces may be warnings or talismans against excessive grief, but they look more like a compliment to Roman men and women as Ovid treats them. Also complimentary to Italy is the fact that, after Jove struck him with lightning and turned him into his own aerial funeral pyre, Phaëthon crashed in the Italian Po. Unexpectedly, Ovid again produces reversals, turning tragedy into homage.

In northern Italy Phaëthon was mourned deeply also by Cycnus, a fond relative resident there. Grief changes Cycnus ("swan") into a swan. Thus Ovid links east and west, north and south, and shows that the Italians are as capable of a fine frenzy as the Greeks or anybody else. He is also giving the reason for some human and animal natures' preferring water to fire, a subject prepared for in Book I.

In Book II, Apollo, oddly, is not the young wooer of the Daphne tale, but a father in early middle age. Ovid emphasizes the difference between the two deities by using *Sol* and *Titan* in Book II. Thus he tends to call attention to the way in which myths about the same deity fail to agree and either evince change or call the veracity of myth into question. In the course of the *Metamorphoses*, the same thing happens to Cycnus: in all three of the stories in which he appears, he is changed into a swan (what else could happen with a name like that?), but his parentage differs in each tale and so do the circumstances of his change. Ovid does not bat an eyelid over the discrepancies; he merely presents the stories and lets his readers draw conclusions, all in all a favorite procedure of his, since his is largely a presentational technique.

But never was boy so mourned. Grieving Sol refuses to function. All the gods beseech him to go back to work, and it takes Jove, his governor, to force him back into cycle.

After this essential act, Jove, as good ruler, inspects the heavens for damage and the earth, giving Arcadia, the Ozarks of ancient Greece, especial attention for restoration. This inspection tour results in Jove's passion for Callisto ("fairest"), lightly clad in white hair band, gown, and clasp. Jove begins to seduce this nymph, one of Diana's attendants, by disguising himself as Diana. His approach gives this part of the tale the ambivalent naughtiness of a homosexual seduction that is not real, of course, but that is titillating and that could be regarded as a slur upon Diana and her troop. Jove does not stay long in drag; Callisto is unable to fight him off. He violates her and departs. As a result, Callisto experiences personality disturbance and disorientation. Ovid's sympathies are definitely with the girl Jove left behind. Afraid, ashamed, at length found out, for her pregnancy becomes apparent during group bathing, Callisto is excluded from the society. Until that moment, Diana, who is innocent, has not suspected the lack of innocence in another—a rather good insight on Ovid's part—but the other nymphs are not so inexperienced and guessed right off. Their reaction reveals much about Ovid's opinion of courtiers: they do not always follow the programs that they supposedly subscribe to.

Meanwhile, back at the palace, Juno has been waiting to get revenge and is moved to it by the insult of Callisto's giving birth to a son. She changes Callisto into a bear that retains human feelings, just as Io had. Callisto-bear moans and growls to her own grief, much like mooing Io, but unlike Io, she is not haunted by horrifying vision; she is pursued by deadly hounds, hunters, and wolves, one of whom once was her father, Lycaon. By mentioning Lycaon, Ovid encourages the reader to compare father and daughter, much to the daughter's credit. And he reverses the point made by means of Phaëthon, that children are not always as good as their parents. He is also preparing the reader for another hunter-hunted episode, the more famous Actaeon one of Book III, and for the Cephalus-Procris episodes, and he is adding to the hunt-and-cruelty imagery in general. All of this Ovid began with Daphne, who was also a hunter that became the hunted. There is a surprising amount of such imagery.

After fifteen years of living a beastly life, Callisto encounters her hunter son, Arcas ("bear"); she seems to identify him and frightens him by staring at him and moving toward him. Sensibly, he prepares to kill her: bear-hugs are notorious. The situation is fraught with horrifying possibilities: does she recognize her son? will he commit matricide? will she cuff his head off? The likelihood of a happy ending seems remote. But in the nick of time, Jove whisks the two off to become constellations, an act that elevates mother and son to the sphere of the gods. The question about this metamorphosis is, of course, would anyone want to be a star? One should remember this episode, too, for thus early does Ovid begin building support for the philosophic lecture in Book XV where the Sage preaches against killing animals on the grounds of the earthly transmigration of souls.

Juno is furious at the elevation: not only has she been insulted by Jove, but the insult has been made public and permanent. Her anger causes her to do something silly: she asks the sea-gods to ostracize Callisto and son by not letting them set in their waters. Her granted prayer makes her wifely wrath comic, because it means that, though the Bears cannot associate with earth- or sea-gods, they will always be visible in the night sky; and never out of sight, they will always call attention to her insult and her powerlessness.

Having her wish, Juno is carried off in her peacock-drawn car. And at this point Ovid creates a transition and maintains his chronology by waving his verbal wand and asserting that the peacock got its tail eyes at the same time the raven was changed from white to black. This claim to be moving back in time to a dated event is pure rationalistic humor and good spirits at the expense of myth. Myth time is often fluid time, and Ovid plays freely with it. He has already done so with the Bears, whom Phaëthon made hot in his erratic ride but who did not exist until Jove sent

21

Callisto and Arcas to the heavens, a later event in the *Metamorphoses*. Such play is another of his games, but one has to watch closely to catch him at it. He can do even better. When Phaëthon scorches the rivers, Ovid has him singe the river birds in the Cäyster, birds who had made its banks famous with song. Ovid does not say that the birds are swans, but the Cäyster was famous for its swans. Has Ovid committed another anachronism, writing of swans before Cycnus introduced that "strange new bird" by his change into one? Or has the reader been lured into making an unwarranted assumption? This is really putting the careful and well-informed reader in a quandary, that of options without certainties. The careless reader, of course, has been stung.

Another part of the link between Callisto's story and raven's is associative: similar objects (birds sacred to deities) connect each tale, as does the fact that Argus and raven both keep eyes on people.

As if this linkage were not enough, one blackbird recalls another, so that Ovid ingeniously presents his audience with a double flying gossip column of Raven and Crow. Crow is an incurable busybody who scoots after Raven because Raven has taken off in a hurry, and taking off in a hurry means that something is up. Raven gives Crow the news that Coronis (in Greek, "crow," or "raven") has been unfaithful to Apollo and that he is off to report her. For anyone who will trouble to visualize the situation, there is the comic reward of seeing white bird speeding off in full flight and blackbird slowing him down with conversation and advice. There is the added humor of confusion in the fact that Crow is nominally the person being reported on and, for that matter, because of noun meanings, Raven is also squealing on himself, as well as a namesake.

Not so comic is the moral point that the purity of the white raven is false because it is mixed with malice, is hardhearted, and does harm, general harm. Telling tales is a crime, according to Ovid's views about love, a view that makes one speculate about the reason for his banishment, which he said was something he saw but did not report.

Crow is not au courant in the gossip field and, as a windy has-been, is reduced to puffing herself up by moralizing on her own experience and advising Raven. And then, as if she had not amplified enough, Crow tediously preens herself by telling of her regal origin, suitors, the sea-god's attempt to ravish her, and her prayers for help, which were answered by the virgin goddess Minerva, who turned her into a crow. The reader has already encountered the maiden who prayed for metamorphosis in order to avoid the sexual advances of a god, once with Daphne and secondly with Syrinx, so that meeting the type again is a bit tedious, but it is nonetheless artistically effective in characterizing Crow as an insensitive pest who does not mind boring others.

Crow's story about the ills attending the practice of gossiping also reveals her as a dimwit. For, according to her own words, maiden Minerva had given three princesses a box containing her secret; one of the sisters opened the coffer and revealed Minerva's secret, a baby and a snake; Crow saw all of this and then told Minerva about the baby that the maiden goddess wanted to keep hidden. Of course, not only is Crow being ridiculed here, but the chastity of Minerva is also being questioned. In case the reader misses the point, Ovid repeats it by having Crow call attention to the fact that she has been replaced as Minerva's bird by the incestuous Nyctimene, an owl.

Crow's loss of job and status means nothing to Raven, who speeds on to no one's good. His snooping and truth-telling cause Apollo shock, the heat of anger, and the bite of remorse; Coronis, the pain of death; and Raven, banishment from whiteness. Coronis accepts her punishment as just, but regrets that the crime of passion affects her unborn child. A sentimental passage follows in which Apollo experiences revulsion, tries frantically to revive the dead girl, and ends by performing a posthumous delivery. In this myth, everyone is in the wrong, but Ovid presents Coronis, fickle in love, as least wrong. The only right thing is the production of Aesculapius.

Aesculapius' birth may support the idea that with Ovid myth is ameliorative, overall, but Ovid shows a tendency here in his treatment of Coronis to gloss over and prettify death, a characteristic that is more pronounced elsewhere in the poem, but reprehensible anywhere, because unreal, because it belittles the pain and the catastrophe, and because it makes death attractive.

The introduction of Aesculapius into the world and the story leads to his guardian Chiron and thence to a tale of the transformation of Chiron's daughter Ocyrhoë. She comes after Raven and Crow because, like them, she knows too much and talks too much and thereby causes pain. She sings sooth, but she is also revealing the mysteries of the Fates, and Jove shuts her up. Ovid here seems to criticize prophecy on the rational grounds indicated: foreknowledge causes pain. The closure is effected by turning Ocyrhoë into a horse, but this is only a partial silencing, for in antiquity horses were often credited with powers of divination. Ocyrhoë was not content with her father's gift, healing; hence, she typifies the woman who knows all the answers and can and will tell everyone what is going to happen to him. That she is right only makes it worse.

Her transformation, like those of Io into cow and Callisto into bear, is deftly recounted, and this sort of thing is part of the marvelous fun of the *Metamorphoses*. Ovid's using the analogy between human fingernails and the continuous horn of a horse's hoof is especially striking, partly because of the closeness of observation, which is one way of building up trust in the reader, and partly because it is a prototype of the sort of scientific thinking that traces functional change in the parts of an organism. If all this is not neat enough, Ovid ends the section by tickling our curiosity and jerking us alert a bit: he says that Ocyrhoë's new form gave her a new name, but he does not tell us the name, and so he leaves us with a riddle. This bit of game play seems unfair.

23

Then this wizard of sequences pulls a razzle-dazzle connective play, moving from Ocyrhoë to Chiron (her father) to Apollo (who is invoked by her father, but who is not at hand because he is off doing the pastoral scene as a result of being in love) to Mercury (who is rustling the cattle of absent Apollo) and Battus. The magic works thus: Ovid sets up a series (presences or absences—either will do) that the reader has to follow, but the series leaves Ovid free to pick which item he will really focus on and develop. The shell game provides an analogy. In any event, Ovid is master, for the reader can only follow fascinatedly, wondering what connection Ovid will be able to make, if any. This challenge Ovid always meets. Here he does so with an unexpected and annoying variation: the double bypass.

First Apollo is bypassed. Ovid rapidly passes over lovesick Apollo, describing him just enough so that we see what a hick love has again made of the lord of the lyre—getting him to dress up like a shepherd and play on the rustic Pan pipes, which Apollo will later snub—and moves on to the second bypass, a brief encounter between Mercury and Battus, a rustic who tattles for greed. All of the blabbers in this book expect some sort of reward, though thus far it has been moral or psychological gratification. Battus introduces a new one: material gain. Thus he prepares for the next tale. But in passing from man to flinty touchstone (an ironic transformation), Battus confronts a god who is also a thief, like himself, but, being an arch-thief, Mercury is not going to let some petty crook put one over on him. Hence, he transmogrifies the lout, smiling at his knavery, naturally. The tale is amusing, no doubt true of thieves' behavior, but unedifying.

For no reason at all after Battus' metamorphosis—hence, all preceding transitions were unnecessary—Mercury abandons cattle and all and flies off over Attica. In effect, Ovid has shown his mastery of transitions, or story-links, only to demonstrate with brazen effrontery that they really are superfluous and part of his sleight of hand, by means of which he can cause them largely to vanish. Thus he scores again.

Over Attica, Mercury sees pious maidens worshiping Minerva. From what we now know of Minerva, we wonder precisely why. Ovid describes Mercury hovering over the maids like a hungry bird of prey swooping around a freshly sacrificed animal but kept off by the presence of priests. This imagery is impressively ugly and uncivilized: sexual hunger here is grossly animal, pressing, spontaneous; its means is again the hunt; its gratification is implicitly compared with the gulping or rending of raw meat. Again Ovid faults the gods.

Mercury, of course, falls in love with the most beautiful of the worshipers, whose described loveliness contrasts markedly with the revolting bird-of-prey imagery. He lands, and, though he is confident of his extreme good looks, he tidies up and makes sure his hair and accoutrements are impressive. Without bothering to use normal means to introduce himself to his new love or to identify her—such are the advantages of godhood for an author—Mercury goes immediately to her home and, encountering her sister Aglauros, gives his pedigree, announces his intentions, and solicits her assistance. Apparently such are the disadvantages of godhood. Aglauros, whose greed had prompted the opening of Minerva's box, behaves in character and demands a heavy fee, thus making herself a bawd. Mercury leaves. Minerva, to prevent Aglauros from becoming a happy and wealthy female pimp and to punish her for prying into her secret, plagues royal snoop Aglauros with Envy.

This allegorical Envy is one of literature's more gratifyingly horrible bugaboos for adults and, as such, properly comic, somewhat after Joseph Conrad's grotesque villains. Further, Ovid says many true things about Envy: it is foul, distorted, perverse; it cannot see straight, is venomous and imitative, devours itself, and is its own punishment—a most pestilent, infectious hag who blasts everything: flowers, grass, nations. And, of course, she afflicts Aglauros with a most awful form of envy: envious visualization of the ecstatic copulation of sister Herse with the divine and beautiful Mercury. Envy's image of the union stimulates a frenzy of meanness in Aglauros. Then (in line 813) Ovid indicates that the love of Mercury and Herse is no crime in his eyes.

Because of the operations of Envy, Aglauros tries to block Mercury's entrance to Herse's room. The god turns her into black stone, for black was the color of her soul. What happens to Herse is omitted; in a sense it has already been described. Thus Ovid emphasizes the meanness of her sister in trying to prevent love, especially one that would confer distinction upon the family and unusual happiness on Herse. Oddly, Herse herself is never consulted.

It seems rather clear that members of a court should not be greedy or envious; they should not go back on agreements; they should not meddle in the love affairs of others.

The theme that heavenly minds know such loves is continued in the next story, begun with Mercury's returning to Olympus and receiving instructions from Jove to drive the cattle of the king of Sidon from the mountain to the seashore where the king's daughter and her maidens play. Jove has amour in mind, and Ovid comes forth with a sententia, a striking observation briefly expressed—he pops one out every so often, so that his is a pointed style: "Majesty and love do not go well together, nor tarry long in the same dwelling-place." Therefore, as a matter of principle or established law, the king of the gods looks for extramarital love, disguises himself as a white (and therefore pure-souled) bull, and joins the herd. He is the acme of white bulls: serene, peaceful, beautifully rounded and curved; his horns are so small and clean that they are obviously harmless; his eyes, gentle. He is so friendly, gay, and pattable that the princess no longer fears him and plays with him. And when she gets upon his back for a ride, he slyly edges out to sea and swims off with her. Thus is erotic foreplay presented in myth. Europa, who is not named in the passage, is afraid, but she is decoratively arrayed on the bull's back, and she is in Jove's power. And there Ovid leaves her forever fixed. Except as a link to Cadmus and equally brief mention of her in Books VI and VIII, Ovid never returns to her, and we see her forever on the bull's back, as she is represented in the plaza at Rockefeller Center, New York City.

This oddly cut story is clearly one about beauty and the beast and the way the two come to unite. But to one familiar with the consequences of this union, it is a lovely emblem of the event leading to the establishment of the royal dynasty of Crete, the births of Minos and Rhadamanthus, and all the good and ill that resulted therefrom. The picture omits all this, however, so that Book II ends with the prelude to a sacred marriage and on a gay and happy note.

In overview, Book II amounts to something like a mirror for magistrates and courtiers, for kings and servants. First, there is a warning against pride and ambition beyond one's condition and capacities, which is also a warning to an important power against giving a young demigod too much force and authority. These strictures are set in a tale that involves two courts, that of Merops and his wife, Clymene, and that of Apollo, so that the caution has to do with kings, princes, and power. The next major myth is that of Jove and Callisto, in which the unwilling sexual partner of the king of the gods is long and brutally punished by his jealous wife, is in danger of her life, and is finally exalted, in an ornamental fashion, to the highest level. This myth, too, smacks of court life and in general admonishes the high and mighty to go easy and to avoid causing inferiors trouble. There follow at least two tales condemning inferiors for gossip or talebearing at high levels because of the trouble it causes. Next comes the related one of Ocyrhoë, self-appointed court prophet who reveals things that the gods have not sanctioned for release and whose revelations cause pain. Her behavior is condemned by her being silenced. Then come two passages in which someone attempts to cheat a member of the sky court of Olympians, one a king's farm servant, the other an envious princess. Both are punished. Finally, there is the courtship of a princess by the ruler of the Olympians, the result of which will be a sacred marriage and the establishment of a new dynasty and court, that of the Cretan kings. Such alliances of greater with lesser powers or of godhood with mortal royalty are presented as the ideal.

Book II, whose settings have oscillated between palace and countryside, ends in an emblem that harmonizes both, as well as the primal and the civilized. The tones of the book have varied from the admiration of the splendor of the Sun King's palace, the nightmare quality of Phaëthon's ride, the lasciviousness and meanness of the treatment of Callisto, the comedy of Raven and Crow, the querulousness of Ocyrhoë, the knavery of Battus, the gruesomeness of Envy, and the contemptibleness of Aglauros to end with the courtship and carrying off of Europa, a passage in which there is no struggle, no alienation, no physical sexual act, but instead a gentle, fresh, lovely strangeness, all in cameo. Rather what a girl might like.

In general in the tales of this book, Ovid appears to advocate tolerance, gentleness, loyalty, discretion, avoidance of spite and greed, restraint of power, and consideration for the other person. It is difficult to read Book II and not feel that Ovid has been combining pleasure with instruction and that he has been playing with both his material and his readers.

METAMORPHOSES III: Dynasty

And now, since Ovid ended Book I with Phaëthon's arriving at his father's palace and immediately continued his story at the start of Book II, the audience expects Ovid to continue that of the Tyrian princess, for it is equally incomplete and entrancing at the end of Book II. And Ovid does—for two lines that focus on the bull—well, not really on the bull, but on the god, his arriving at Crete, and his setting aside the bull disguise to reveal himself as he is, an infinitive phrase that implies the consummation of his ardent desire and, hence, the presence of the princess. But, being only an implication, the lady has, in effect, been reduced to a nonentity, a condition that Ovid underlines by referring to her as an absence, the *"raptam,"* or "female that was carried off," and by making her the object of Cadmus' vain search.

What looked like a parallel to continuing the Phaëthon myth from one book to another has turned out to function as a brilliant, arresting, and tantalizing transition belonging to the genus red herring, or false lead. And as a transition from Herse's Athens to neighboring Boeotia, it is one of the longer doglegs in literature and worthy of Laurence Sterne. However, the story of the lady and the bull is not merely a tease; for, although Ovid does not immediately proceed to develop the fortunes of the Cretan royal house descending from Jove and Europa, he does present those of the dynasty of her brother, the culture hero Cadmus, founder of Boeotian Thebes. Since this ruling house, as Ovid treats it, lasts no longer than Cadmus' lifetime, the relevant Greek myths allowed the poet to construct a tightly knit book with a clear time sequence and major theme: dynasty, its achievements and misfortunes.

At the outset of Book III, Ovid puts a number of principles in presentational form. It is clear that mortals pay for the escapades of the gods: Cadmus becomes an exile as a result of Jove's abduction of Europa; Europa loses home and family. On the other hand, somewhat like Io, these mortals are rewarded by founding royal families, having lasting fame, and being associated with gods. Further, Ovid makes it clear that Agenor put an excessive burden on his son and threatened excessive punishment for failure, all the while being pious. The general principle here is that parental concern can be simultaneously right (pious concern for daughter's safety) and wrong (undue severity in penalty threatened son). Another point is that a boy of the right stuff, like Cadmus, will make good, helped Horatio Alger fashion by one of the high and mighty, of course.

Within the first one hundred and four lines of Book III, Cadmus consults Apollo, who aids him with an oracle; piously prepares to sacrifice to Jove; offends Mars; is given moral support by Minerva; and proves to be a chip off the paternal block. For Cadmus' behavior towards Apollo and Jove is pious, but his killing Mars' serpent so that he may piously avenge his comrades is hasty and impious. Piety provides dilemmas.

29

There are oddities within the serpent episode. For one thing, it is not clear that Cadmus knows the sacred nature of the beast, but he should have guessed from its size and splendor and from the unviolated condition of the woods, another indication that it is sacred. (Actaeon, a chip off the Cadmean block, will later violate another sacred grove.)

Ovid's loving description of Mars' beautiful and deadly serpent is most striking in the way the marvel changes size from huge to astronomically immense and back to proportions big enough to crush ordinary men and then to a size reduced enough so that Cadmus can cope with him. The size-shifting, of course, indicates psychological reaction to the beast: to Cadmus' Phoenician comrades, the serpent towers out of sight above the woods, he is as big as the constellation Draco; but to their avenger, Cadmus, he is only big enough to be pinned to an ordinary oak by an average spear, though his weight does make the tree bend. And to us readers the original enormity of this terrible beauty remains in our minds while Cadmus tackles it in its reduced dimensions. Ovid is playing with us again.

At this point in the narrative another oddity occurs. Cadmus hears a sourceless voice, a phenomenon much more awesome than that of ghostly Echo. Its message is worse: he who is staring at the slain snake shall become a snake for men to stare at. Cadmus is scared white, an indication of the dreadful nature of both the voice and the text. The prediction stresses the general impression already created, namely, that men are not masters of their fates, but are subject to unknown forces. It also focuses attention on a motif appearing throughout Book III: the slayer is or becomes the thing he slays (e.g., Cadmus slays the guardian snake and becomes the guardian of the land and will later become a snake; the serpent kills the Phoenicians and becomes the warriors who kill one another). Put in other terms, as T. S. Eliot might, the active is the passive, the doer is the sufferer. This idea was presented earlier, but more faintly, by Daphne and Callisto, huntresses who become prey. It dominates Book III. Actaeon the hunter becomes the hunted deer. Narcissus the lover is the object he loves. The repressor Pentheus is also the repressed.

There is something awesome about these reversals. They are not just dramatically effective. Ovid, like Sophocles and Euripides, seems to put his finger on some spot of horror hidden in the human psyche. Perhaps it is the realization that built into us is our destruction, that one's strength or major drive is his undoing, or that what one attacks outside himself is at the same time something within himself, or that because the personality contains poles, it is wretchedly divided and can be reversed. It may be that no one ever really knows who he is. But whatever the case, Ovid is here dealing with a theme that Hermann Fränkel called attention to, namely, that of identity.

But the message delivered by the unidentified voice is peculiar, too. It creates suspense, but that soon dwindles and has disappeared by the time it comes true, late in Book IV. What is more peculiar is that the prediction comes true, in a sense, almost immediately. The serpent is the protector of a place (the grove); he is destructive; he is intimately connected with war and with warriors. Cadmus becomes the serpent in that he replaces him, becoming in his turn the protector of the area, war lord and agent of destruction, and producer of warriors, who gaze on him and instruct him to avoid their fratricidal conflict.

As if the sacred monster and the sourceless voice were not enough, Cadmus now faces the horror of civil war fought out by the serpent's descendants. Because he has no part in the " 'fratricidal strife,' " he benefits by becoming king of the remnant. Harmony follows this discord, a situation represented allegorically by Cadmus' marrying Harmonia, appropriately the daughter of Mars and Venus. Thus conflict is resolved by patience, the need for leadership, and love.

Thus far in Book III Ovid has shown himself again a master at description and, though not averse to describing the terrifying, a man averse to bloodshed and war.

The happiness of Cadmus receives scant attention. It is covered in seven lines, two and one-half of which are a stereotyped Greek warning that Ovid himself might have heeded: count no man happy until he is dead. Ovid then moves to what he wishes to emphasize, the misfortunes of Cadmus, which strike him through his children and grandchildren.

The first of Cadmus' descendants to suffer ill fortune is Actaeon. What happens to him is a nightmare. Actaeon becomes deranged because the power that should have protected him turned on him and reversed his role in the hunt. He becomes a beast of prey, and as such, Actaeon can no longer communicate and is no longer recognizably human, and so he is attacked by those closest to him.

Ovid gives no rational explanation for what happens to Actaeon, calling it *"error"* ("going astray"), fortune, and fate. Thus he gives the reader two or three choices, since the words are not precise synonyms. The matter is further complicated because the narrative hints at various causes: Actaeon has hunted too long and perhaps has been excessive; he does not sacrifice to Diana or otherwise acknowledge her power; he is in an off-track area and should be wary; he is himself aware of the intensity of the sun's rays and may be verging on sunstroke, so that he seeks the woods; he takes no account of the ancient feeling that midday is a dangerous time; he is reckless in going into the woods alone. Furthermore, Actaeon moves into a valley sacred to Diana, a fact that he should know. If he does not, then he should be more cautious about entering the unknown woods, for groves are often sacred and, therefore, dangerous. He should be especially alert because the hunting has been so good, a fact that might suggest Diana's nearness.

31

In addition to Actaeon's carelessness and obtuseness as possible causes of his destruction, there is the overall situation. Actaeon and Diana have dropped their hunting roles and, therefore, their relationship as devotee and patron deity. They are now out of synchronization and are relaxing in their own ways, Diana in her own place, a realm of tree and water-nymphs into which Actaeon intrudes, a man in women's world, a mortal in the divine boudoir. He should have known better, for nymphs inhabit the trees and springs, but he leaves the world of the male sun-god and blunders into the women's shadowy bath.

In so doing, Actaeon moves from the known into the unknown and hostile and becomes disoriented. His being out of his depth reaches crucial proportions because he violates the women's sanctuary and because he stumbles upon a mystery, the arresting but to a degree unwanted womanliness of the chaste huntress, in itself a kind of reversal of roles. Diana's mystery is her person, which should not be seen nude by men, for being so seen shames her and she blushes, as Callisto did after her rape, and one should not shame a goddess. The mystery of Diana is that of being a beautiful woman and being unwilling to accept that condition as far as its heterosexual consequences go. Her attitude is completely in keeping with Diana's personality, but there is something sterile and hostile about it. And so Diana punishes Actaeon for this discovery, which amounts to her being hunted in her retreat, by reversing his normal role of hunter, and his hounds tear him apart. His metamorphosis and its results are macabre, pathetic, and gruesome.

But Ovid, for whom no situation is completely comic or tragic, injects some odd humor. He says that Actaeon's hounds are too many to name and promptly names about thirty-three. He even distinguishes them further. The list itself, of course, is a characteristic of epic, namely, the catalog, and it functions here to demonstrate further Ovid's ingenuity. Its length also gives a sense that Actaeon will be overwhelmed and that, savagely, as do some of the epithets and names, which are—according to the Loeb edition—"Seizer," "Gnasher," "Tigress," "Might," "Voracious," "Whirlwind." Other names, pedigrees, or descriptive phrases individualize each hound, reveal human patterns in naming dogs, and serve to make the animals horribly real. The horror is increased by having these faithful and well-trained servants perform their duties efficiently and unknowingly drag their master down.

The dogs' names are Greek. Xenophon, in his work on hunting, gives a list of proper names for hounds; Ovid uses only two of them. On the other hand, most of Ovid's names are short, a desirable quality when one needs to call to a particular dog—the criterion is Xenophon's. But Ovid does not always follow Xenophon's advice, for roughly a quarter of Ovid's names consist of more than two syllables. There is just a hint that Ovid is simultaneously following Xenophon and twitting him. Be that as it may, using Greek shows metrical cleverness and gives a touch of learned elegance to Ovid's verse, just as his using an occasional Greek case form does elsewhere. But the linking of savage nature with Greek makes one wonder just what Ovid's attitude towards the Greeks was.

In the Actaeon myth, Ovid consistently directs his readers' sympathies toward Actaeon, not as a hunter, but as the hunted and as an erring and tormented human being within an animal form. Ovid thus again foreshadows and prepares for the Pythagorean speech in Book XV, where the Sage argues against killing animals because they contain the souls of former human beings and because the butcher of animals deadens his feelings of pity and thus moves toward the shedding of human blood. (It should be on the forepart of the reader's mind by now that when he comes to a myth in which a person is changed into animal form, that tale can be directly related to the Pythagorean doctrine of the transmigration of souls and related ones in Book XV; hence, it is no longer necessary to make the point again.)

Ovid's sympathies with regard to Diana are not marked. Perhaps it is difficult to feel sorry for an immortal. However, Ovid does go out of his way to call the justice of Diana's punishment, or retribution, into question. It is typical of Ovid that he himself is ambivalent, as though he wished the reader to determine where the proper sympathies lie; yet, because of Actaeon's innocence and agony, Ovid manages to give the feeling that Actaeon was more sinned against than sinning.

The next myth, that of Semele, makes some points already presented by Actaeon's experience: do not trifle with power; that is, do not be casual about it, regard it as essentially human and thus underestimate it, or simply forget about it. Godhead is ultimate power. Do not be naive. Deities, especially the female of the species, can be extremely vengeful over petty matters. In addition, the battle-of-the-sexes motif emerges again, for once more Juno is irked by Jove's amours. And once again, the male (Jove) can be promiscuous, but it is the female (Semele) who pays. Incidentally, Semele pays for the same reason Actaeon does: she sees a deity stripped down.

Juno is unusually unpleasant here, for she is described as having transferred her wrath from Europa to all the girl's relatives, a deplorable practice today known as determining guilt by association. Jove's liaison with Semele and the consequent pregnancy naturally intensify Juno's anger. Characteristically, Juno feels that she must have revenge, in order to demonstrate that she really is somebody. Also typical of her is her foolishly calling attention to the irregularity of her own relationship to Jove: she is his sister as well as his wife. But her unpleasantness is most marked. She consciously works herself up into a very nasty state and descends to a deviousness that stains her majesty. Disguising herself as Semele's nurse, Beroë, she plays on the girl's vanity and tricks her into getting Jove to reveal himself to her in his essential form.

Beroë's speech is a small rhetorical masterpiece that reveals some of Ovid's early training. Indirectly the nurse's advice casts doubt on myth as a system of belief and on the sexual mores of those holding to it. Beroë allows that chastity is a virtue and adds that many men have overcome this obstacle to their desires by claiming to be gods. Then Beroë appeals to Princess Semele's pride and to her sexual curiosity. It is not enough, she says, for Semele's lover to be Jove; he should prove his love by loving Semele in all his splendor and with all his sexual power—as he does Juno.

Like Phaëthon, Semele gets Jove to grant her an unspecified request. Like his son Apollo, Jove is unwary and grants it irrevocably. Like Phoebus, he regrets generosity extended in a moment of emotional expansiveness. For the essential Jove, or Jove in all his glory, is lightning, and when as such he unites with Semele, he consumes her with his fire, thus warning all to avoid experiences of devastating intensity.

Semele's child, like Coronis', is snatched away from her womb just in time, but, more marvelous, it is grafted within Jove's thigh and deliverd after a novel gestation.

Once Semele's child, the "twice born" Bacchus, is safe, Jove spends some time at home, good-humoredly bantering Juno. His tipsy good humor is a bit barbed, for he unkindly declares that wives receive more pleasure from sexual intercourse than husbands do. Juno as flatly denies the assertion. This debate about the sexes between the pair submit to the arbitration of the Theban Tiresias, a contemporary of Cadmus. (Thus Ovid keeps the stories of Book III within the Cadmean framework, for the seer Tiresias was the family's most important associate.) A double standard seems to be involved; it seems to be acceptable for a man to enjoy copulation, but not for a woman. As far as the debate is concerned, however, Tiresias is an ideal judge, for he was changed into a woman and remained one for seven years. (Ovid does not say so, but this tale implies that as a woman, Tiresias naturally must have had sexual experience. Therefore, women are as immodest as men and may enjoy sexual activity as much as men or be as curious about it as men are.)

Tiresias' verdict is that women do indeed derive more pleasure from sexual intercourse than men do. His decision grieved Juno more than it should have, "They say." Thus Ovid escapes the onus for having indicated that Juno takes a very sour view of a benefit. Juno, presumably because her matronly modesty is offended, not that Tiresias is wrong, strikes Tiresias blind, a physical way of indicating that he perceives nothing. Jove cannot undo her act, for Olympian rules forbid one god's reversing another's judgment. But Jove counters Juno's by giving Tiresias second sight, or inner perception of what is what. Thus Jove demonstrates that Tiresias knows more than the ordinary man and that Jove was right.

Once again a mortal caught between contending deities suffers and is to a degree compensated; and again the reader is warned not to get involved in disputes between power figures if he can avoid it or if he does not wish to pay a price, and he is also cautioned not to offend the modesty of a great lady. And once again the male principle triumphs, as one might expect of patriarchal societies such as the Greek and Roman.

Tiresias' new capacity for providing a faultless answering service provides the link to the next tale, the famous one about Narcissus. He is a watery boy, son of Boeotian river-god Cephisus and a blue water-nymph named Liriope (akin to "lily"); and from familiarity with watery nymphs earlier in the *Metamorphoses*, the reader is prepared for Narcissus' coolness. Liriope, hearing about the seer's new powers, consults Tiresias about her son's future. The lasting fame of the tale, however, results from its psychological insights and not from Tiresias' accurate prediction. Not only has the myth given us the term *narcissism*, it also deals, broadly speaking, with the effects of perception on personality, an important motif in Book III. Actaeon and Semele saw something they should not have and, as a result, were destroyed. Pentheus, later in this book, will be so fascinated by what he despises that he will look on it—to his destruction. Narcissus is similarly destroyed by what he should not look upon, himself and his own merciless beauty. He is detached from reality by a mirror and by his own fluid nature. A watery lad, no fire ever warms him that would bring about procreation. And nothing can hold him except something watery like himself, the reflecting surface of a pool.

There is much more to his tale, for Ovid combines two myths that explore the self: self-absorption in Narcissus and in Echo what David Riesman labeled "other-directedness." The exploration begins with the proper combination of suspense and matter-of-factness. A mother is concerned about the future of her baby and consults a seer. The prophecy of Tiresias is cloudy, like all true prophecies: Narcissus will live long provided he does not come to know himself. For a long time the words seem meaningless. But Narcissus' progress to his doom begins when he is sixteen. By Roman standards, Narcissus ought to be putting on the toga of a man, but he seems neither boy nor man and lives in a state of unyielding conceit. He is, in effect, in a state of arrested adolescence, a condition, according to C. S. Lewis, characterized by a damnable preoccupation with one's own importance. It is also a time when personality development toward maturity, in Ovid's terms, means self-transcendence by giving one's self to others in order to exist more completely and more appropriately with regard to one's time of life. But this Narcissus refuses to do.

He meets his doom during a hunt. Ovid has thus far used hunting imagery often enough for love situations so that it carries over here a faint and an uneasy expectancy. And just two tales ago the hunt served as background for Actaeon's identity crisis, so that another overtone reverberates. Narcissus has become separated from his loyal companions. He is alone, and he is, we have been told, typically cold and unfeeling for others. He has already gone a long way toward his undoing, and, since the causes of his doom are built into him, Nemesis and her unspecified operations are superfluous. But, as though he realized his coming emergency, he calls for his friends.

By this point Ovid has prepared for the meeting of Echo and Narcissus and one of the saddest funny dialogues in literature. When Narcissus calls out to his comrades, they do not hear him. But someone does, someone who desperately needs him. Echo. She had been covering up for Jove and his inamoratas by babbling on and on to Juno and thus diverting her attention. Shy herself, Echo's behavior was directed by the actions and needs of others. Juno finally caught on and fitly punished Echo by making her conversation completely other-directed and brief. She is limited to repeating the last few words of what others say. When she sees Narcissus, she is inflamed with love, but too modest to come out from cover. She communicates with Narcissus as far as Juno has allowed, but though she repeats his very words, they mean one thing to Narcissus and another to Echo, and the dialogue constitutes a perfect example of semantic confusion and of dramatic irony. For when Narcissus calls, " 'Is anybody here?' " he is thinking of his companions. When Echo, who has to wait until he pops the question, replies, " 'Here,' " she means that *she* is and that, burning with love for him, she is very much " 'here.' "

This device is funny and very ingenious, but the wit glosses over the pain. And later, when Ovid runs over Echo's shame at rejection, her hiding, grief, loneliness, wasting away, and petrified bones, we understand what Narcissus' treatment of her cost her. Ovid's presenting her as living still, miraculously, as the voice one hears coming back from the mountainside when one calls, makes her a sad ghost forever haunting the world. This outcome, like the apotheosis of Callisto and Arcas and the efflorescence of Narcissus, is the crystallization of the dead in sucrose, a fine bit of ancient sentimentality. And so we have another effect of myth: it can act as a painkiller.

Ironically, Echo is Narcissus' verbal image. Fränkel says that she is a "symbol of those pathetic but annoying females who are extremely responsive but have no originality of their own." It is high comedy that Narcissus avoids this female pitfall for the wrong reason. He does not see that by rejecting her he is rejecting, or cutting off, part of himself, and by completing his isolation he is putting into operation that retributive justice (Nemesis) unnecessarily invoked by one whom he had scorned earlier. And so he moves to the place of destiny. Like the groves of Mars' serpent and of Diana, it is inviolate, and thus like Narcissus himself. It is also a beautiful never-never spot—never touched by man, beast, falling bough, or warmth; its never ruffled pool matches Narcissus' personality before he ever reaches it. Meeting it, he is truly coming to know himself.

Untouched geographic places seem to have been sacred among the ancients, so Narcissus might have been cautious. But he is hot and thirsty, that is, ready for or intensely desirous of his watery self. Naturally, that is, physically as well as psychologically, when Narcissus

36

faces the pool to drink from it, he sees himself and confuses an illusion with something real. Not even Echo could respond so exactly to Narcissus' desires and mood, be such a drain, or be so sterile. Narcissus is immediately entranced—mirrors are magic things—by his own beauty. But this love drains him, and he wastes away into a beautiful but short-lived flower. It is all very brilliant, lovely, sad, and, in spots, amusing. The moralizing is unmistakable. And Mr. Fränkel makes an observation that applies here, namely, that, although the ancients lacked the complex and precise terminology needed for a science of psychology, they could handle its phenomena in story form.

Ovid sees what is wrong with Narcissus, shows what it leads to, yet sympathizes with the youth and is able to see things from his viewpoint. He is compassionate and does not condemn. Indeed, Ovid gives Narcissus one of his best pointed, or aphoristic, lines, a line so compressed and antithetical or paradoxical that it seems to arise naturally from the emotional intensity and the agonized clarity with which Narcissus suddenly sees his predicament: " 'inopem me copia fecit' " (" 'abundance impoverishes me' "). And as he is dying, Ovid has Echo, still remembering that Narcissus spurned her and still angry, pity him. This ability to sympathize with an attitude one does not approve of—here Narcissus' rejection of love—is part of Ovid's make-up, and it is a characteristic that he shares with Virgil.

What happens to Narcissus is that he naturally becomes a natural aesthetic object. A law seems to operate; to paraphrase from Keats, a thing of beauty is a thing of beauty forever. Nature sees to that, and art, here Ovid's, imitates and intensifies nature. Both nature and art seem to conspire to alleviate pain, as a result of distancing it and beautifying it and commemorating its cause. If one is a moralist, art also lessens pain by teaching how to avoid it and makes one sympathize with the sufferer and thus wish to avoid causing agony.

The Narcissus story seems to be a rejoinder or an exception to one of the Delphic maxims, "Know thyself," and support of another, "Of nothing too much." It is likewise witty of Ovid to have Narcissus (lines 442 ff.) utter "a lover's lament" in order to woo himself, Mr. Galinsky notes, and thus adapt a literary genre to his own purposes. Mr. Wilkinson finds Ovid overflowing with wit in his comments on Narcissus' being spellbound by his own image: "He loves an unsubstantial hope and thinks that substance which is only shadow" (line 417); "Unwittingly he desires himself; he praises, and is himself what he praises; and while he seeks, is sought; equally he kindles love and burns with love" (lines 425-426). In this wit of the paradoxical and aphoristic, Mr. Wilkinson sees Ovid as a Narcissus who is "amator ingenii sui," a lover of his own wit. It is also paradoxically witty of the poet to have Narcissus show the power of love by denying love.

Because of its change of pace, tone, and mood, this story is equally successful, sensitive, daring—even brash—and typical of Ovid, because of its variations. The tale also brings to the fore a motif that will appear later, that of arrested development. It was a muted element in the narratives of Daphne, Syrinx, and Callisto, who would remain maids. Ovid now has applied the same motive to a male.

Storytellers recounting Tiresias' remarkable prophecy and its fulfillment in the lamentable end of Narcissus have clinched the seer's reputation. Only Pentheus doubts that fame and, therefore, Tiresias' clear warning that Pentheus will be dismembered if he sees the rites of Bacchus but does not worship the deity. The prophecy here, as with that for Narcissus, allows for chance or for personal decision on the part of the subject of the pronouncement. This allowance for the operation of free will is important in slanting the reader's reaction to Pentheus, as we shall see. Ovid keeps the traditional irony of the ignorant man with sight who taunts the blind man that can see the future, an irony effectively used by Sophocles in *Oedipus Rex*. And Ovid retains, too, the tradition that Tiresias is always right.

There is little bittersweet or delicate about the Pentheus myth of an austere and wrathful king in conflict with an effeminate demonic deity. Ovid focuses on a cultural change that, according to tradition, occurred at a given time: the introduction of the religion of Dionysus, or Bacchus, to Thebes, a detail that strengthens the illusion of a precise chronology in the *Metamorphoses*. But more important is Ovid's focus on the struggle between antithetical personalities or forces, Pentheus and Bacchus.

When Bacchus, the new god of liberating force for all and of frenzied, irrational worship, appears on the Theban scene, his worship seems soft, luxurious, senseless, riotous, and dissolute to Pentheus. As king, he angrily opposes it, praising the old virtues of the Boeotians: their daring in emigration, their martial prowess, their honor, and their homey old-time piety. But the Thebans are no longer under the control of their king. Ovid makes it clear that changes can occur rather suddenly in the behavior of a whole people (here the religious practices of the Thebans, which are also psychic experiences) and that one (here a ruler) cannot turn back the clock or reverse the process.

Next, like Euripides, who had treated the myth brilliantly, Ovid shows that both Pentheus and Bacchus, or Liber, manifest the same aspect of the human psyche, its dark, bloody, and irrational traits. These find their expression in the savagery of war and in outbursts of wildness in peace. Pentheus himself provides an example of the latter. When the normal pattern of daily life and worship is markedly broken by the egalitarian rites of Liber, Pentheus engages in a peacetime outburst of irrational violence against this rupture. In Ovid, he sees the change in exaggerated terms, namely, as the overthrow of the nation. In reaction he rages and irrationally prefers to see the city destroyed by war (another way of releasing such human energies, but much more destructive), rather than see it go under, a drunken and inglorious pushover. These, of course, are unrealistic alternatives. Pentheus does not realize that the virtues

38

that made Thebes possible are not appropriate now. Nor does he see that war frenzy and Bacchic frenzy spring from the same need for release of tension, for change, and for novelty and that Bacchic violence, recognized and ritualized, is relatively mild, but that repressed, it, too, can be destructive, bloody, and horrible.

Supporting these assertions is the fact that Ovid himself describes Pentheus as a natural phenomenon raging under repression when his counsellors warn him against offending Bacchus. His reaction to restraint shows the need for release. But he cannot see the fact. Once again implicit in Ovid's presentation is the idea that art allows the analytical intellect to operate because of the psychic distance that art necessitates; for the reader can understand what the participants in an action cannot, because he is not subjected to the blinding emotions that they are.

To return to the myth, Pentheus is warned four times to avoid impiety: once by Tiresias, once by the miracle of Acoetes' release from prison, once by Acoetes' account of his own piety and conversion, and once by Theban advisers. His stubborn refusal to heed the warnings is thus presented as Pentheus' own choice, and it makes Pentheus lose our sympathy because he seems to be asking for what happens. He comes to seem insensitive, violent, inflexible, and obtuse, and, hence, unlikable.

The longest warning takes up 109 of the 200 lines allotted to the Pentheus episode and thus has a prominence that invites investigation. Acoetes, who delivers it, warns against greed and trying to use a god for one's own purposes, but the gist of his story is much like that of the Pentheus tale as a whole: there are divine powers that are identified with religious and cultural trends; they do appear suddenly with new circumstances; they must be recognized and respected; they require sensitivity for their perception; they punish those who do not treat them properly. The warning is peculiarly egalitarian, for Acoetes, man of humble origins, is more balanced and more pious than a king of illustrious descent. In addition, it contains one of the most novel of the changes in the *Metamorphoses*, that of men into fish, and the most unusual details: the staying of the ship, the emergence of the vines, and the substanceless shapes of Bacchus' attendant animals. Pentheus rejects the warnings, views the rites, is dismembered. The Thebans worship the new deity. The tale is complete. The book ends.

All the substance of Book III is Theban. But the bulk of it is dynastic. What does Book III tell us about dynasty? First, that it must begin well. Second, that as a pattern it has real problems.

The book begins with the success story of Cadmus. He is the father of his country, the founder of the city-state of Thebes. He brings harmony to it. He gives it a ruling family for three generations. These accomplishments, especially his dynasty, should bring him security and happiness. They do not. For dynasty proves disastrous. It seems to have two flaws. Not all of the descendants may measure up to their progenitor's caliber. Not all of them may have his good fortune. Cadmus' children and grandchildren lack his prudence, restraint, or piety. They seem to intensify the culpable traits involved in his slaying Mars' serpent. As for good fortune, as well as character flaws in some instances, five of them run afoul of deities. Actaeon offends Diana; Semele calls down upon herself the wrath of Juno; Pentheus, his aunts, and his mother infuriate Bacchus. Book III ends with all Thebes worshiping a god who has caused Pentheus to be torn bloodily apart. Hence, the upshot of the book is that Cadmus suffers because of his progeny.

Considering what happens to the members of his family, one has no difficulty in deciding that dynasty teaches lessons in humility, on the limits of human power, about the likelihood of personal misfortune, about accepting unpalatable change, and about tolerance. The book is rich, noble in tone, although tone and mood vary, and, though it has its lighter moments and brilliant insights and touches, it is the most dignified and sober book yet. It is even a bit grim, notably in passages like the storm that blasts Semele with lightning and the rendings of Actaeon and Pentheus. But the greater grimness lies in the fact that even when one is right, one may be in some sense or in some other way, wrong. One may, like Cadmus, found the great city and bring the goddess Concord to the people only by offending Mars. Or one's particular strengths may cause one's undoing.

By the end of Book III, certain threads and patterns have appeared often enough so that one grasps the persistence of Ovid's interweaving of motifs. In effect it amounts to an insistence that it is the diversity built into the similarity of experience that keeps recurrent situations fresh, alive, and fascinating. The wrath of Juno occurs in connection with Io, Callisto, and Semele, and so does the love of Jove; each maiden is lovely; each is with child. But the experience of each is markedly different, and so are the forms of Juno's wrath and the fates of the loved ones. Other motifs, or threads, have appeared more than once: frustration, the hunt as an analog for courtship, the position of the courtier, the defiance of gods or a god, sex change, the watery personality, and many others. Yet each has been made fresh. One feels confident that these and others will recur in following books in one form or another. The effect of such recurrence and variation is somewhat like that of a fugue, but more like that of a tapestry, the fabric of life.

By now several of Ovid's game devices should be evident. One is taking a minor element in one or more preceding tales and making it major. Another is intensifying a situation or capping a story: Io is changed into a cow and tormented; Callisto is changed into a bear and hunted; Semele is struck by lightning. Another is repeating a basic situation and meeting the challenge of making it novel or effective. A fourth is providing transitions, the more surprising and the more baseless, the better. Still another is startling change of mood or tone, so that part of a myth is seen in a new light. Sometimes this effect can occur in a line, resulting from a pun or a paradox or the suggestion of a gulp inserted in the midst of burning mountains' majesty: *"aeriaequAlpes et nubifer Appenninus."* A sixth is failing to continue a story after it has been started or dropping a character whom one expects to learn more about, such as Europa or Herse. A seventh is doing one thing on the surface and another underneath. Another is having thematic unity in a book, but interrupting it.

In Book I all the material deals with discord and harmony, so that there is a thematic focus and clarity that is not present in Books II and III. In these books concord and discord remain functional and provide the conflict and resolution needed for Ovid's dramatic purposes and approach, but new major themes are dealt with. Book II is thematically consistent (if one views it as a mirror for magistrates), and in this way it is like Book I. But Book III has two episodes that interrupt the dynastic theme (the debate between Juno and Jove and the Echo-Narcissus myth), so that Ovid has a new structural, or sequential, strategy to throw the reader off the track. Yet another technique for unsettling the reader is that of created ambivalences. Phaëthon's epitaph is an example. Having characters or matters simultaneously right and wrong is another. Several of these have reared their lovely and enigmatic Januses. For example, myth is sometimes enjoyable *and* morally and religiously offensive. It is all right for Juno to be Jove's wife, but not to be his sister also. Jove may punish Lycaon, but should not punish all mankind. Agenor and Cadmus are simultaneously pious and impious. It is proper for Tiresias to prophesy, but not for Ocyrhoë. And yet another device is that of giving the reader two or more trails, only one of which can be followed—the options-without-certainties ploy, a very good trick for a fox to have.

In general, Ovid uses anything that he can to give the ancient tales freshness, color, life, meaning, novelty and surprise. Even the dull story and the fiddling and frittering that sometimes occur between interesting episodes have purpose and function. The result of his efforts, including his gamesmanship, is that, while everything needed for our success in the pursuit of Ovid is there, the aggregate is like Daphne and eludes our grasp until we properly adjust our perceptions.

And what surprises will our fox contrive now? Will he manufacture an ingenious transition and move to a completely new focus, as he did at the beginning of Book III, when he abandoned Jove's love for Europa and switched to the tribulations of Cadmus? Will he continue telling about Bacchus, as he did with Phaëthon at the start of Book II? Or will he introduce another descendant of Cadmus as his subject? He does the first and second. He keeps hostility to Bacchus as his subject, but replaces aggressive Pentheus with the passively resisting daughters of Minyas. And it is they who announce at the outset the first major theme—and it is a very broad one—that of deity denied. But Ovid has another surprise, one that emerges only when Book IV is almost complete: his subject now is not Cadmus and his dynasty, but the descendants of Agenor. The poet creates this more inclusive pattern of relationships by using *Agenorides* ("descendant of Agenor") twice, once of Cadmus and once of Perseus. Thus he makes us aware that all of the major figures at the beginning, middle, and end of Book IV—Bacchus, Cadmus, Ino, and Perseus—belong to the family tree headed by this Phoenician king. And he makes the awareness come in a flash of perception that extends and rearranges our apprehension of the subject of the book: a ruling family becomes part of a much larger pattern of relationships.

To return to the first major theme, in almost all of the tales of this book, some deity has or has had his or her powers refused honor or recognition, either by his being ignored, or by his being injured or insulted, or by having his powers rendered inoperative to a greater or lesser degree. Such acts deny the divinity of the personage involved. Because a god is a power figure, not just the representative of something (e.g., of love or of lightning), and because one who does not, will not, or cannot perform in his or her domain deserves little or no attention, a deity must respond to acts that diminish his powers or that frustrate them or that put them to naught. He must do so in order to assert his power and thus maintain his status, to say nothing of his existence. Hence, divine retributive reaction is—or should be—inevitable.

So it is with the Minyeïdes, who open Book IV. They flatly and explicitly deny Bacchus' divinity by refusing to worship him and even to believe in his divine parentage, a belief that would confer upon him at least the status of a demigod. Bacchus punishes them.

Elsewhere in the book the denial takes other forms. Venus' functioning as queen of love in the arms of Mars is stopped by Sol. Thus injured in her sex life and robbed of her divine function, she is, further, insulted by being made an object of ridicule. She retaliates by diminishing Sol's powers: she inflicts him with love so that he, whose gaze should inflame everything and everyone, is now burning because he would behold only one lovely princess. He finally, after suffering much and paling greatly, like any love-stricken mortal, secretly embraces her. But his joy is brief, for Clytie, a cast-off love, surreptitiously tattles on him and his new amour with the result that Leucothoë is killed by her irate parent.

As for Salmacis and Hermaphroditus, since both are divine to some degree, she as nymph and he as son of Hermes and Aphrodite, both are to a degree denied their individual godhoods by their merger. Salmacis vitiates Hermaphroditus' divinity by possessing him, and he retaliates by denying her the presence of virile men in her pool, for he makes it enervate them. So much for three of the tales told by the Minyeïdes, which, with the punishment of the ladies, forms the first major section of this book.

The second major section also deals with an affronted deity, Juno, and her wrath. Semele infringed upon Juno's rights as wife and as goddess of marriage when she supplanted Juno as Jove's sexual partner and thus held Juno's power and position as nothing. And Juno's legitimate role as wife and as goddess of marriage and as protectress of both was abrogated by Jove when he took Semele as his mistress. Juno punished Semele, but remained furious. Since Juno cannot attack either Bacchus or Jove, she vents her anger upon Bacchus' aunt Ino, who goes around boasting about her nephew.

The destruction of Ino and her family, as far as Cadmus knows, culminates all the earlier family catastrophes and crushes Cadmus, who realizes that he has injured the gods by his killing the sacred serpent and is suffering their vengeance.

The third major section of the book begins with the holdout Acrisius. He closes the gates of Argos and belligerently fends off Bacchus, rejecting his worship and denying his descent from Jove. He will not even admit that his own grandson was sired by Jove. But to refuse to believe, as Acrisius does, that Jove could impregnate Danaë is to deny his virile power and that of his fertilizing rain. To reject Bacchus is to refuse the grape and deny the awesome power of Jove's lightning. Who could refuse to accept such things? Truth, Ovid says, brings Acrisius around. He is not punished in the *Metamorphoses*.

Finally, there is the first interpolated tale of this book, that of Pyramus and Thisbe. Coming after twenty-two stories in which gods appear directly in the main action, this is a most curious one, for it breaks the pattern. No gods exist for Pyramus and Thisbe. Theirs is a love story with no acknowledgement of Venus or her powers. The lovers are adrift in a world where there is no patron deity to aid them and none to whom they pray, a world wherein parents disregard the efficacy of love and love itself is self-destructive. Vague and general gods enter the plot after the lovers are dead and grant Thisbe's prayer, which was made not to them, but to the mulberry tree. These deities are as contrived, colorless, and unconvincing as the god who began the creation, if "kindlier nature" did not. They are not necessary for the change in the color of the berries because Pyramus' blood had already effected that, and there is no reason to assume that the change would not be permanent. In sum, as far as mortals in the narrative are concerned, the gods, especially Venus, are ignored. Later myths in the *Metamorphoses* inform us what happened when Oeneus forgot to sacrifice to Diana and what happened to Atalanta and Hippomenes because they failed to thank Venus for her aid. In the tale of the Babylonian lovers, deity is not explicitly denied, but its lack creates an uneasy feeling.

The results of denying deity are mixed. Though Juno still feels slighted by Semele because Bacchus is so successful in punishing his enemies and because she is furious with Ino for glorying in her nephew's power, Juno does not cancel out the new god's triumph, nor does she effect complete vengeance upon Ino. The gods' revenge on Cadmus is offset by the comfort he receives from his divine grandson. Bacchus is not honored by Acrisius, who, although he regrets his behavior, is not otherwise punished for it in the *Metamorphoses*; Acrisius denies Jove's powers with no ill effect; and Perseus safely snatches Andromeda away from the vengeance of offended Ammon, an Egyptian equivalent of Jove. The evidence reveals, then, that the gods usually punish those who deny their powers, but that some people get away with such sacrilege; and, since some deities contend with others, to the frustration of some of them, these conflicts show that some gods are more potent than others. Furthermore, punishment for hubris may be doubtful, incomplete, or balanced by compensation. Thus Ovid's general game plan in this book is that of presenting a theme that has a number of qualifications.

This is true of other the major theme. Book IV, considered in overview, deals with the descendants of Agenor, who fall into two groups: Cadmus and his family (here Bacchus, Ino, and Ino's children) and Acrisius and his (Danaë and Perseus). (Incidentally, Cepheus and Andromeda are also related to Agenor, for they descend from his twin brother, Belus.) These extended and interlocking dynasties have problems, sometimes because a member is too severe, like Agenor, or unlucky, like Actaeon, or boastful, like Ino, but chiefly because someone offends one or more deities. Cadmus typifies this lot, and he is so blasted by dynastic tragedies that he slinks off. But his grief is more than counterbalanced by the comfort and glory of having a god in the family. One outstanding member of the dynasty more than makes up for all its setbacks. Perseus functions in the same way in his branch of the Agenorides. He is clearly the luminary of his family and, as we learn in Book V, the supporter and avenger of his grandfather, Acrisius. Hence, one might conclude from reading Book IV that ruling families cannot expect to produce consistently wise and able offspring. Nor can they guarantee success and happiness for their children. But they can hope that every now and again they will produce someone of the caliber of Bacchus or Perseus. And then everything is all right.

Of course, the theme of love is present. The novel treatments are the vigorous lust of dainty Salmacis, the sentimental account of the frustrated love of Pyramus and Thisbe, the exhibitionism of the Mars-and-

Venus encounter, and family love. The devotion of Harmonia and Cadmus is obvious enough. Less clear is the implication that Ino and Athamas love the children that they are driven to destroy, but if they did not, Juno would have no basis for her revenge. In twentieth-century America, where the family seems to be a dispersal device and where generation gaps have received such publicity, it may be difficult to take ancient family love as axiomatic. But one should. John Buchan's opinion "the family always meant much to Rome" indicates the ancient complex emotional commitment to the family and to relatives that involves love, pride, sense of status, the drive to perpetuate one's self and one's family name, the need for support and security, and other drives and feelings.

There is at least one more innovation in handling the love motif. All of the stories told by Minyeïdes are about love, just the sort of thing a group of women, especially if young and unmarried, might amuse themselves with. But the tales all present love as bittersweet, if not rowdy or coarse, as in those about Mars and Venus and Salmacis. The choice of tales, then, shows the Minyeïdes to be an odd mixture of the curious and reluctant, the bawdy and fastidious, the emotional and restrained. For the tales are all, roughly, against love because they demonstrate how unfortunate or ridiculous it is to be possessed by an outside force, namely love, or by another person. This selection, therefore, suggests that the Minyeïdes, while they enjoy hearing about the love pains and embarrassment of others, are not disposed to experience them themselves.

Other motifs reappear. Here Sol is the tattler; Clytie is another. The divine sex comedy, exemplified earlier by Apollo and Daphne and the Jove-Juno-Tiresias exchange, here takes the form of Venus' adultery with Mars. Snakes of various sorts repeat the motif introduced by Python in Book I; Serpens in Book II; Mars' serpent and the copulating snakes of Book III. In Book IV there are the snakes of madness that Tisiphone thrusts into the bosoms of Ino and Athamas, the friendly dynastic serpents that Harmonia and Cadmus become, the Gorgon's tresses, the poisonous snakes that Perseus inadvertently populates Libya with, and the dragon guarding Atlas' golden fruit. The beautiful death figure, represented by Narcissus, occurs again in Ino and others.

As if this interweaving of themes and motifs and of juxtaposing one tale after another did not provide a sufficiently complicated structure, Ovid puts four of the narratives into a frame in which they function. This frame he inserts in a longer frame, whose headpiece is Cadmus' encountering the serpent of Mars and whose final piece is the metamorphosis of Cadmus and Harmonia into serpents and their having the comfort of Bacchus.

The Cadmean frame makes two points, one already mentioned: one's family may be stricken with one catastrophe after another, but one brilliantly successful offspring will more than compensate for the rest. Second, Cadmus is a just man. True, he is a bit slow in coming to the realization that the serpent he slew two generations ago was sacred. It takes him a lifetime, when he should have known the fact at once, if not from the size and splendor of the beast, then from the miraculous warriors that sprang from its teeth. But ripeness is all. Finally, in old age he sees and admits his fault and calls down upon himself the doom foretold him in his youth.

Like Cadmus are the Minyeïdes in that they fail to recognize the sacred, but they are unlike him in that they cannot or do not ripen. In these respects one frame throws the other into relief.

Within their own frame the stories told by the daughters of Minyas function in two ways. For one, they deal with the tragic or comic consequences of frustrating a release from tension. For another, they have an ironic dimension: the parents of Pyramus and Thisbe fatally frustrate their union, though the parents have theirs; Sol thwarts Venus' affair, yet has his own with Clytie; Venus foils Sol's liberally bestowing his favors, though she passes hers around; Salmacis refuses to be like the other nymphs, namely, athletic, but she will not allow Hermaphroditus the same right to his individuality; Hermaphroditus revels in Salmacis as cool and soothing pool, but he does not want her to enjoy him in her way. Thus the stories tell not only of frustration but of the hypocrisy or ambivalence of those who do the frustrating. To put the matter in a different perspective, the frustraters prevent something that they themselves do or want. They do it to others. But the Minyeïdes do it to themselves. They frustrate their own very human desire for release from tension and tedium by rejecting what Bacchus provides, never seeing that the release from the mundane that storytelling and the imagination provide is akin to, but less basic than, the emotional, nervous, and muscular release and novelty that the democratic rites of Dionysus provide.

As for the ladies, they can handle the release if their persons are not involved physically. They are aloof. They hold back. That is the reason that all their stories show love as either ludicrous or dangerous. Their unwillingness to become involved with Bacchus suggests a similar reserve and also an unwillingness to be possessed psychically.

But they cannot prevent being overwhelmed by the power of the god. This power is given impressive treatment when the presence of Bacchus takes over the Minyeïdes' apartment. His music and odors fill the room, the weaving turns into his vines and grapes, the house trembles, lamps blaze, his phantasmal beasts howl, and the house fills up with smoke. Then the Minyeïdes are mocked. They are turned into bats, shrivelled squeakers that flit in the shadows.

Their understanding is also ridiculed. This impression results partly from the unevenness of the stories they tell. Out of four, only one is excellent. But more serious is their refusal to engage in the ritualized release provided by the Bacchic orgy when at the same time they characterize their routine as boring and tedious and want relief from it. In other words, they feel to a degree the need for the Dionysian, but they

47

understand neither the need nor the Dionysian. The means of relieving tedium that they choose is storytelling, a sublimation which they regard as mere pastime. Hence, they do not understand the tales they tell. Unfortunately, the tales are about them. The tales all deal with frustration and with change resulting from it. And the princesses, on their part, are frustrating their own desire for relief and frustrating a god. They do not apply the narratives to themselves. From the stories, moreover, one suspects that the ladies are in for a change. They, however, do not.

The first storyteller knows a great many tales, but as she runs over a few in her mind for purposes of selection, the headings seem incredibly dull; more important, they suggest that she categorizes them as mere plots dealing with marvels. That the marvels might have significance for human beings in everyday life does not occur to her, nor does the fact that all the tales deal warningly with physical change from clearly defined causes that the narrator would tell about. To her the tales are merely pastimes. And so, with perfect intuition, she picks a tale in which the physical change is minor (white mulberries become red), but the human frustration causing the change is given overwhelming attention. Even the warning of a fatal misunderstanding is glaringly present in the narrative —for the teller and her listeners to ignore.

The story, of course, is that of Pyramus and Thisbe—romantic, tragic, sentimental, pathetic—just the sort of thing to make a girl release a tear. The lovers were young and beautiful; cruel parents kept them apart, though they lived next door; love drew them together; they burned; they communicated " 'by nods and signs.' " They discovered the crack in the clay wall separating their houses. The narrator rather dwells on that crack. It was all they had, their only means of communication, but how it frustrated them! Because of it, however, they were able to plan their union. They would meet at night in the country by a tomb, under a tall (phallic) tree that is most fruitful (" 'uberrima' "). The word for "most fruitful" also suggests the Latin word for "breasts." This tree with white berries (female symbol, possibly male in conjunction with the phallic tree)—mulberries are terribly sweet—is near a cool spring, just the thing for hot and thirsty people, and a tomb (female symbol). It seems that some ancient discovered more Freudianism than merely Narcissus.

When the lovers left the restrictions and protection of home and the walled city, they exposed themselves to the wild. It intervened. But the intervention took the form of a maw-crammed lioness, representing the benevolent Cybele or mother-goddess and, hence, the generative forces of nature. The lioness intended no harm, but it frightened Thisbe away and bloodied her cloak, acts also liable to a Freudian interpretation. Pyramus found the cloak, thought it told of Thisbe's death, and holding himself responsible, committed suicide—pathetically. His spurting blood turned the white mulberries purple. Thisbe, upon her return, correctly interpreted the situation and resolved that death, which had separated her from her love, should be the means of their union. She called upon their absent parents to bury them in the same tomb and upon the tree to memorialize their deaths. These desires were granted.

If this story causes the gentle heart to shed a tear, it also teaches several lessons: parents should not repress their children's proper desires; love cannot be thwarted; it can be fatal to act hastily, that is, without full knowledge of all the facts; love can be true to death and even beyond; and nature is on the side of love. Although the Minyeïdes consider some of these things and although they see that Love is a mighty force that will be obeyed, they fail to come close to the idea that Liber might be similar in power, in release, and in compelling reverence.

After a short silence, sister Leuconoë expresses the tenor of their thoughts: Love is so powerful that even the Sun, who surprised Love in a shockingly illicit situation, has felt her power in retaliation. It was the Sun, Leuconoë recounts the old myth in the *Odyssey*, who first saw Mars and Venus coupling, was pained, and revealed the facts to Venus' husband, Vulcan. This tale against tattlers has a new twist. Vulcan catches the embracing lovers in his subtle net and exposes them to the other gods, thus disgracing them. But one of the gods, who are not pained by the sight, turns the whole affair into a laugh by saying that he would like to be disgraced in just this way. The passage does not say that the cuckold is also the butt of the laughter, but it seems that anyone who uses his art and craft to reveal his wife's unpunishable infidelity and to advertise her availability is also an object of ridicule, a voyeur and shameful exhibitor.

Despite the guiltiness of her behavior, immodest Venus is offended, and so she strikes back, inflaming the blazing Sol with love of Babylonian princess Leucothoë. Again a male deity disguises himself as a woman, this time to protect the maid's reputation, for Sol appears as Leucothoë's mother and kisses her chastely. Then he dismisses her attendant slaves and resumes his own shape and brightness. Dazzled, the maid submits. Jack Lindsay is of the opinion that there was no privacy in the ancient Roman house and that anyone who wished to draw near could hear enough. Be that as it may, someone knows of Leucothoë's seduction and tells Sol's cast-off love Clytie. Envious and spiteful, Clytie makes the affair public knowledge and then proclaims the scandal to Leucothoë's father. Sol still rejects Clytie, who pines into some kind of sunflower. The deeply grieving Sun, like the Apollo of Book I, behaves like one who fosters plants and turns his lost love into frankincense.

This, too, is a very tear-stimulating, emotion-releasing story. It is also collaterally Cadmean: Ovid has been careful to point out that Leucothoë's father is descended from Belus. Now, as noted earlier, Belus is the brother of Agenor, and thus the princess and her father are related to Cadmus and his house.

Motifs in this tale repeat ones earlier in this book and in preceding ones: talebearers, cruel parents, and the envious come in for contempt; Sol's loyalty to his dead mistress and his memorializing her are admired.

On the other hand, it is not to be expected that one will not play the field, for Jove, Coronis, and Venus have. New, however, is the suggestion, made through Orchamus, Leucothoë's father and king of Persia, that the Persians are barbarians who would sacrifice a sunstruck girl and who could not see the honor of a sacred marriage. Further, Orchamus' behavior resembles that of the repressive parents of Pyramus and Thisbe, his neighbors, and the severity of his brother, Agenor.

As for the change of Leucothoë and Clytie into plants, some of the Minyeïdes simply do not believe these marvels; others say that real gods can do anything. But Bacchus, they opine, is not one of them. The princesses do consider the right question, namely, what should one believe about the gods? Their answers, however, are snap judgments, and with regard to Bacchus, whom they reject out of hand, they are dead wrong. They might have engaged in some firsthand observation and experience before they reached a decision. Nevertheless, the marvelous tale about Leucothoë holds their ears. For a time, caught up in what are for them the brightness, novelty, and emotions of its wonders, they suspend their disbelief. When it is over, they weigh and doubt. Ironically, they are unable or unwilling to do this much for Bacchus, that is, to experience first and then judge.

The storytelling continues, Alcithoë being called upon. She searches audibly through her repertory for something that will give pleasure because of its novelty. Once again the theme is physical love, but this time the story is a superior one.

Unlike other water-nymphs, who are or pretend to be Diana-like, Salmacis was completely feminine. She refused to follow Diana and to run around hunting with bow and arrow. The water of her pool was clear as glass; no reeds, rushes, or spiky grasses grew in or around it, but it was edged with soft turf and grass forever green. Frequently she bathed in it; frequently she combed her hair; and she used the pool as a mirror so that she could look her best. No Narcissus she. In a see-through gown she rested on the turf, or she picked flowers, a pastime chastely sensuous that draws attention and suggests that picker and plucked are somehow alike.

Then one day the extremely attractive Hermaphroditus—his name indicates his parentage—wandered by. He was fifteen and a bit, not quite a man. But Salmacis wanted him badly. Nonetheless, she calmed herself by composing her person, fixing her dress just so and getting a serene and dignified expression on her face. Then she sallied forth and began a dignified speech, really a courtship one appropriate for a man—as a matter of fact she sounds a bit like Odysseus addressing Nausicaä, as Mr. Galinsky points out. She told Hermaphroditus that he was godlike, a Cupid, and that if he were a human being, then happy and blessed were his father, mother, brother, sister, and—here she reveals her physical yearnings—the nurse who gave him the breast. Far happier, however, would be his wife. Salmacis then offered herself to him as wife—or anything. Ignorant of love, Hermaphroditus blushed attractively and refused emphatically. (Since his name suggests a person with nicely balanced masculine and feminine components, perhaps the aggressive female was not the right sort for him.) Salmacis pretended to leave, but from hiding she saw the lad strip, dive into the pool, and swim about, ivory under glass. At this point she lost control, jumped in after him, caught him in an amorous embrace, and, as the result of an unfortunate prayer, their physical beings merged, and an androgynous one was the outcome. Hermaphroditus' mind remained dominant, however, for he prayed that the waters of the pool would ever make men half-men, and they do.

The character of Salmacis is a triumph of observation. She is the markedly demure, neat, composed feminine type who is unexpedctedly aggressive and impossible to fend off. Furthermore, her aggressiveness makes the male of her choice impotent. Her choice is interesting, too: the epicene, not fully matured, innocent, beautiful. Both Salmacis and Hermaphroditus bear witness to the Jungian idea that men have feminine components in their personalities and women, whatever their appearance, may have very strong masculine ones.

When Alcithoë's story ends, manifestations of the power of Bacchus fill the room. Here, as in the Pentheus tale, the epiphany is indirect; the god does not appear, only his adjuncts. This absence makes him seem a force that operates behind and upon phenomena. Earlier (lines 18-20) matrons and young women describe Bacchus with sensuous aesthetic approval. Now in lines 391-407 the poet seems to describe the hallucinatory effects that would be the ones desired as the responses to the ritual of a mystery religion. The description is remarkable in itself. It is also noteworthy for its unqualified approval of what is so awesomely presented.

As for the frightened Minyeïdes, their being turned into bats evaluates their character and behavior. Their fate, paralleling that of Pentheus, convinces all Thebans that Bacchus is truly a power to acknowledge.

In contrast with the Minyeïdes, Ino reveres her divine nephew, as well as being proud of her husband and children. But having the good will of one deity does not save one from the enmity of another. Ino's happiness, the success of Semele's son, and the power that his revenge demonstrates—all make Juno feel slighted, and she behaves worse than ever. She had turned Io into a cow and Callisto into a bear. Then she lured Semele into suicidal love. Now she decides to incite a father to kill his child. In an impressive, somber-sounding passage, Ovid has Juno descend to the Underworld and stimulate one of the Furies to carry out her plan. The result is that Athamas smashes the child against a rock. Ino, also maddened, jumps into the sea with their second child. But Venus intercedes for these two, so that they are changed into minor marine divinities. Juno has not had her way completely. In the *Aeneid*, Virgil had

51

dwelled upon the wrath of Juno, showing it to be awesome, even though wrong. Ovid in the course of four books has made it despicable.

Cadmus, despondent because of the disasters plaguing his family, concludes that Thebes is an unfortunate place and flees. After weary wandering, he reviews his life and, reversing the Socratic maxim, decides that only the examined life is not worth living. He, therefore, prays that, if he has so long been punished for his youthful slaying of Mars' serpent, he may be changed into a snake. His prayer is answered, and the prophecy of Book III comes true, so that Cadmus' supposition is correct. Behind the individual catastrophes brought about by Diana, Bacchus, and Juno, a larger, less apparent design of divine retribution has been working. Yet it is not certain that the process is just. By accepting his fate, however, Cadmus acquires a nobility of a sort that the gods do not share, that of being just. He rises above the contradictory pulls that surround a good man.

All is not defeat for him, however. Harmonia becomes a snake, too, and though their transformations frighten her and her husband, they glide off into the woods, innocuous creatures, and Bacchus gives them comfort. Thus in their latter days they are consoled by one another's companionship and become the emblem of the happiness of a marriage of compatibility and long duration. They are more than just an ancient married couple. To the Romans, snakes represented the genii of a husband and wife. To the Greeks, the spirit of a dead man became a snake that developed from his spinal marrow. Bacchantes fearlessly handle snakes. So there are many appropriate aspects to this benevolent transformation that points most obviously to a lasting relationship. In this respect, Cadmus and Harmonia are a variation on the Deucalion and Pyrrha motif, so far given consistently favorable treatment.

The transition to the next story is a variation of the missing person device used in Book I. Here Ovid uses the exception to the rule. There is one holdout against Bacchus now, namely, Acrisius, king of Argos, but he even disbelieved that Jove sired his grandson, Perseus. In this fashion, Ovid slides over Acrisius, who becomes a way of getting to Perseus; hence, he perpetrates a double transition. Thus adroitly does the poet move from the god to his relative, the hero, whom he introduces in spectacular midflight over the Libyan desert. Perseus is carrying the Medusa's head, which is dripping blood all over the place. Where the blood falls, a snake comes into being. Thus Perseus becomes the agent in an aetiological myth. Obviously the head has sensational powers. Also sensational is Perseus' flight, the length and extent of which outdoes Phaëthon's. It also gives Perseus an overview and an elevation that, coupled with his successful coping with the winds, suggests that this unusual young man may have an equally unusual career, one of extensive imperium. That he finally tires of being wind- and wing-borne indicates that even he is mortal.

Alighting in the far western kingdom of Atlas, Perseus politely and succinctly craves hospitality, a valid request, and points out that he is one of Jove's sons, as well as laying a vague and general claim to impressive deeds. Atlas at this point unfortunately recalls a cautionary prophecy and tries to shove the lad out. Perseus pushes back, all the while talking rapidly and respectfully. But Atlas is too strong for him—Atlas is, after all, Titanic. Not to be repulsed, Perseus resorts to showing Atlas Medusa's head and thus performs the second or third greatest geological event in the *Metamorphoses*, for the giant becomes a mountain. The gods second the event by making the mountain an even greater one. These effects, as I recall, were used in a movie cartoon in which the comic hero's brute antagonist was transformed into a jagged mountain, which immediately became an even larger one. The same sense of the appropriately ridiculous and the marvelous existed in both ancient poet and modern cartoon maker.

With the morning light, the proper and imperturbable Perseus heads east and encounters a maiden in distress because of a garrulous mother and an unfair Libyan deity. Perseus is so touched by her beauty that he "almost" forgets to fly. (The word *almost* gives the situation a light and deliciously humorous touch.) Characteristically, Perseus does not lose control. Lighting beside the stunning young woman, he pays her a suave amorous compliment, namely, that she should be putting chains on lovers, not wearing them, and asks her name, address, and cause of confinement. Perseus is nothing if not prudent; he does not wish to get involved with juvenile delinquents. Andromeda proves that she is none such, for she is much too modest to talk to a man and wants to cover her face with her hands, but, since she cannot, she cries, a perfect model of propriety and pathos. However, she has been pressed for answers, and, wanting to clear herself of wrongdoing, she reveals how much boasting there has been about the maternal beauty, for which offense Andromeda, not her mother, must pay the price. Ammon, who imposes the penalty, is unjust. Andromeda is worthy of aid, so that Perseus is justified in helping her.

At this point Ovid produces the victim's mother and father, who weep and wail and cling to her chains as the sea monster booms along toward his tender prey. It all sounds like *The Perils of Pauline*. Perseus, never at a loss for words or the wit to make the best of a situation, brags a little on his own about his parentage, his killing Medusa, and his flying ability and allows that these entitle him to Andromeda's hand. However, since the title is no good without the girl, he magnanimously offers, without acknowledging this minor fact, to try to save her, provided that she is promised to him. The parents, finding themselves over their own barrel, promise and throw in a kingdom to boot.

The monster now surges up, and Perseus takes to the air. The beast attacks his shadow on the water. It is not very intelligent, for it operates indiscriminately on a stimulus-response basis. It is up to devouring immobilized maidens, but not to besting heroes. Perseus executes arabesques with which the stupid monster cannot cope and handily slays

53

him, though a bit discommoded by having his wings wet. How much of a contest is this?

Men and gods applaud. Andromeda is unchained and comes forward. Forward to what? Not to the center of the stage, for that is occupied by Perseus, who is washing his hands and, by bedding down Medusa's head on seaweed, is in the process of unconsciously originating coral, as he had unintentionally populated the desert with snakes. Andromeda may be beautiful and well born, but she can never compete with Medusa, who is absolutely petrifying, nor with Perseus, who is always in control of things. Her passive nature makes her the reverse of Salmacis and, hence, unfit for dominating the scene. Perseus, in contrast, could be Salmacis' brother.

Perseus weds Andromeda after properly sacrificing to Mercury, Minerva, and father Jove. At the wedding banquet, he and others drink wine and thus accept the power of Bacchus. He is asked to tell how he slew Medusa, what wonderful courage and craft enabled him to do so. It would be very impolite for Perseus to deny such a well-phrased request, and so he complies and in the process neatly crosses up Ovid. Either Ovid is nodding in order to imitate Homer, or he is trying to catch his reader doing so and is playing the fox with him. For Perseus here describes Atlas as a rocky mass existing before Perseus cut off Medusa's head, whereas earlier Ovid had Perseus turn Atlas into a mountain by showing him that very head. If Perseus is lying, another possibility, then he is prudently concealing the full power of his trophy. He does reveal, however, that Medusa has created her own monumental sculpture works of men and beasts, a fair warning of her ability.

His narration ends with explaining, again upon request, the origin of Medusa's snaky locks: most beautiful Medusa, whose hair was her crowning glory, was ravished by Neptune in Minerva's temple; the goddess punished the deed, but her retribution, the writhing, poisonous hair, fell on Medusa, not her ravisher. Thus another maiden goddess has been most unjust, as Diana was with Actaeon. The core of Medusa's story is found in those of a number of girls who are unfairly treated and for whom beauty has proven perilous.

At the end of Book IV, Perseus dominates the scene as the power of Bacchus had its beginning; one seems to balance the other. Bacchus is the mysterious liberator from the monotony of daily routine. His means are violence, irrational behavior, and languor. In contrast, Perseus gets away from the everyday into the excitement of meeting challenges, doing the unusual, and receiving the attention of an after-dinner celebrity or the roaring approbation of the crowd for slaying the dreadful beast. He is the adventurer of youthful dreams. He is improbable, but there is nothing mysterious or maddening about him, and he has all the charm of combining the exciting with the efficient and the conventional.

An overview of Book IV suggests that although mortals and even gods themselves have denied deity, Ovid does the most to deny the absolute power of the gods; but he does not deny that they do have power; and Bacchus receives impressive homage.

As for love, there is much of it, for it motivates Pyramus and Thisbe; Mars and Venus; Lecuothoë, Clytie, and Apollo; Salmacis; and Perseus and Andromeda. But it is given less weight than the god and the hero. Somehow erotic love is not as important. It lacks high seriousness. The love of Perseus for Andromeda is aesthetic, not erotic, and it is submerged in the hero's exploits. Indeed, this love motivates one of his major deeds: Andromeda is important as the cause of heroic action and as the spouse of a future king. Thus she is part of a serious action. The other love stories are pastimes, whereas hers is most like Harmonia's. For the love of Cadmus and Harmonia is one that lasts beyond death and is a much more sober, stable, dignified, and important relationship than the brief candles of Pyramus and Thisbe and the other lovers about whom the Minyeïdes tell.

Book IV ends with an up-in-the-air conclusion; that is, it leaves Perseus still sitting at his wedding feast, but he has finished the tale explaining how Medusa acquired her snaky locks.

METAMORPHOSES V:
Artists—Destroyers and Preservers—and the Sexes

The fortunes of Perseus continue. In Book IV he was the naive hero on his initiatory quest. He had obtained the Medusa's head and made a marvelous flight, changed a Titan into a mountain, and won a bride. Though he could not have prevailed without supernatural aid, including his wings and the dreadful head, his own daring and resoluteness made him heroic. His killing was limited to Medusa and to the sea monster (Atlas' change being another matter) and was done with the sword by his own hand, so that it, one, was minimal and, two, showed his prowess. Perseus was also characterized by complete poise and by a social artistry. There was something ritualized and conventionalized about the politeness and courtesy of the young prince. These qualities might result from his belonging to the naive art form of the fairy tale; nevertheless, the detailing of his politesse and chivalric behavior individualized him as one who had carried good manners to the heights of art.

These strands Book V develops further. Perseus continues to display his sang-froid and courtliness when he allows his rival Cepheus first throw and when he warns all present of the power of Medusa's head. His artistry, however, is extended into a new area, death. For reasons that will be apparent later, death is stressed in the first part of the book in the heroic slayings of Perseus, in the suicide of Pyreneus, and in Hades' ravishing Proserpina to the kingdom of the dead. All these acts involve sudden death in unusual ways. But Perseus is the true artist in the field, for, paradoxically, he now kills and preserves simultaneously. To perform as death artist, he again relies heavily upon supernatural aid. This time it is the ultimate weapon, a kind of death ray or infallible evil eye, Medusa's head.

The blandly self-assured and, one assumes, handsome young hero who acts swiftly, accurately, and effectively and who has incredible abilities and the best credentials, manners, and assistance, Perseus emerges as a death artist in two ways. First, one has only to remember the deaths of heroes in the *Iliad* or the *Chanson de Roland* to appreciate the fact that Ovid wants us to admire the deaths that Perseus creates with ordinary weapons: a torch, a scimitar, a wine urn (large), a spear. Ovid has others in the fray create spectacular demises so that the reader does not forget that the ultimate artist is Ovid and that Perseus is but his beau ideal.

Second, Perseus' artistry reaches its climax when he uses the Medusa's head to turn enemies into statues of men forever preserved at the moment of death, somewhat like the *Dying Gaul,* but more amazing because the moment when time ceases in a life is caught and preserved eternally. The whole situation is paradoxical. It is part of Perseus' excellence as a creator of mortuary statuary that his work is done effortlessly and that its fidelity is perfect down to the smallest detail. It is also part of his excellent technique and sensibility that the victor always possesses his opponent at the instant when his power over his victim was greatest, namely, when the victor had the power of life and death over his foe. This point is made fairly clearly in lines 210-235, where Perseus turns cringing Phineus to stone and says that he will keep the statue as a memorial so that his wife can see the sort of coward she might have married. Finally, not only is this metamorphic statuary realistic, it is as close to the real thing as one can get in art.

By means of its spirited artistry, the whole fight-in-the-hall passage suggests the point that art, like Medusa's head, is itself metamorphic and that it can change, as it does here, the gruesome into the entertaining, the exciting, the aesthetically viable, the pleasant, or the beautiful. Perseus has created his everlastings in marble. Ovid has created his in words. Both are masters in the realm of the marvelous and its art.

Within this smashingly sensational opening of Book V, Ovid manages to get a number of good touches. First, he manages to be unexpected: the wedding feast is disturbed . . . by a disappointed suitor (not mentioned before) . . . who turns out to be a close relative of Andromeda's . . . in fact, a bit too close, for he is her uncle. He is an excellent foil for Perseus, for uncle is dull witted, unsure of himself, blustering, craven, and ineffective.

Next, there is a sort of parody of the heroic exchange of words before battle. Phineus' words are necessary to clarify his motives, else his behavior would seem completely irrational. As it is, it is merely irrational. Phineus, the uncle, regards Perseus as a wife-snatcher, which he is not. Fighting mad, Phineus announces his intention to annihilate this criminal. He does this in three lines with appropriate brevity. He then cocks his spear. But he keeps it in throwing position while his brother tries for thirteen lines to reason him out of revenge. Even granting the ancient love of argument and rhetoric, this is a bit much. Worse, all that the brother's speech does is to confuse Phineus, for at its end, he cannot decide at whom to throw the spear, Perseus or brother Cepheus.

The characterization here is good, too. Whereas Phineus is hot-headed and not very intelligent, Cepheus is ready of wit and word, and he makes a number of good points in his response, such as, first, that Phineus had really given up any claim to Andromeda when he failed to show up for a showdown with the sea monster and protect his fiancée. Second is the neat, pithy distinction with which Cepheus ends his speech: I did not choose between you, Phineus, and Perseus and give him the preference, but between Perseus and death. Anyone would have chosen the frog-king under the circumstances, and Phineus' vanity should have been soothed.

But Phineus sees nothing clearly. In his confusion, family feeling apparently wins out, either that or instinctive self-interest, for Phineus throws at Perseus and misses. Perseus, who must have heard all of the brotherly exchange and seen the hesitation and the cast, gives Phineus a free throw. This admirable bravery is like standing fast and letting one's opponent shoot first in a duel. Only after the cast misses him does Perseus leap up and fire back with deadly accuracy. Phineus, in contrast, ducks. And thus the fight in the hall begins.

It is a gorgeous fight, worthy of, but antedating, Hollywood. Perseus is alone except that his sister Minerva is said to be on the scene shielding him and giving him moral support. No particular acts are attributed to her, however, so that the good she does seems merely nominal, rather than real. (Her actual function is to provide a transition to the next set of stories.) The cast of combatants, including as it does warriors from India, Syria, Assyria, Babylon, Bactria, Greece, Libya, Ethiopia, and the Caucasus, makes it seem that Perseus is standing off, if not the world, a goodly cross section of northern Africa, Greece, and the Near East. All sorts of deaths are covered—pathetic, ironic, sensational—in a word or in detail. Perseus does not do all the killing, for accidents occur, innocents are laid low, and, surprisingly, Perseus does have a supporter or two. And blood frenzy seizes the men in the hall so that they begin killing at random, as though in a Western-movie saloon free-for-all.

The fighting becomes very difficult for Perseus to manage. Phineus has a thousand followers. The spears fly too fast and furiously. Forced to drop gallantry, Perseus, nevertheless, warns any friends present not to look before he displays the Gorgon's head and ends the battle. Ovid names a number of those who perished by it and then gives the casualty data: two hundred turned to stone; two hundred survivors. The thousand plus fighters of a few lines before have become, now that the frenzied action is over, a somewhat more modest four hundred plus a few.

Phineus, however, is alive. Though he pleads for mercy, Perseus shows him none. A hero cannot tolerate a coward. Besides, Perseus wants his cringing statue around to remind Andromeda of the man she almost married. This reminder, of course, would increase Andromeda's prestige and self-esteem, and it would reflect all sorts of glory on Perseus, but there is also something very grim about it. It seems to be a warning.

The last two episodes dealing with the prowess of Perseus—his righting a wrong done to his doubting grandfather Acrisius and his putting doubting Polydectes in his place—show the hero winning victories so casually that they merely etcetera him off the scene. Even Minerva is bored with the Medusa routine and departs. Perseus has had his day, and his latter efforts, though just, do not measure up to those of his early career. So much for that Greek.

Perseus is the first of the destroyers of Book V. Paradoxically he reaches the ultimate within his power when he also attains the heights of art, when his killing itself commemorates. One should recall that Perseus had described Medusa's naturalistic sculpture display, produced in her natural habitat, and compare it with the one that Perseus produced with her aid in Cepheus' palace: the two are so alike that Perseus and Medusa become interchangeable. Both are frights. Thus in another way, Ovid undercuts the Greek hero. He does so further by having him, as the myth insists, procure fame largely by means of another. Nevertheless, he remains the killer par excellence: handsome, courteous, unruffled, efficient, and deadly.

(One ought to consider, moreover, whether Perseus is not a perverter of art, as Ovid is here, in that he derives an unwholesome and unnatural pleasure from pain and deprivation of life. His artistry turns pain into its opposite, aesthetic pleasure. In the deaths produced by Medusa, the victim dies feeling nothing at all. Thus death has no sting; it is not horrible; ergo, it does not matter. No doubt Ovid has created a miraculous harmony of opposites, but his aesthetic triumph is a moral disaster. For if human beings are to remain compassionate, they must always remember that the pain of others and their feelings are real and that life is something to preserve. This ethical battle has had notables on the other side from Ovid, for example, Flaubert and Hemingway. It is to Ovid's credit that he discountenances Perseus, but his means are so subtle that they are easily lost in his sensationalism.)

Minerva, not conspicuous in Book IV as a companion, has accompanied Perseus until his immobilization of Polydectes at the end of his tale in the *Metamorphoses.* Apparently she is bored by his effortless wins, for she wants to see something novel, a spring created by Pegasus with a blow of his hoof. Seeing the act might be something, but there is nothing unusual about the spring after it has been created. Thus the goddess turns out to be the usual tourist and novelty-seeker. How could seeing the spring compare with witnessing the birth of Pegasus from Medusa's blood, an even greater marvel that Minerva had seen? But the goddess makes the trip, like the average marvel-seeker gawking at the humdrum testimony of the miraculous event. She has little discrimination.

At this point Ovid refers to Minerva as *"Iove nata"* ("born from Jove"), as indeed she was. But the phrase is customarily used of a hero; for example, Aeneas is frequently referred to as *"nate dea"* ("goddess born"). To adapt the phrase to a deity brings the divinity down a peg, especially after the *Aeneid,* and to apply it to a female makes her seem muscular, tough, and masculine. And to underline the masculine in Minerva's nature by alluding to her sole parent, a male, is slightly brassy.

However, as mentioned above, the goddess is a transition device, and even though she is a more prominent figure in the remainder of Book V, she is still merely a means of keeping the narrative going. But as she does, the goddess moves the narrative from destruction (the acts of Perseus) to creativity (those of the Muses), which includes fertility (the spring). Even so, Minerva is one of Ovid's major personages who are reduced to playing very minor roles, and so diminished, she becomes a slightly comic figure.

Minerva is met on Mt. Helicon by the Muses, admires the new spring and their habitat and special skills, and is told the Muses' latest traumatic experience. Indeed, the Muses, though generally happy, feel insecure, a fact to take note of, because this last two-thirds of the book belongs to women and their viewpoints, and they suffer from a great deal of insecurity. As far as the Muses go, they are upset because they have been challenged by a military monarch and by nine ladies of royal birth. From this point on, Minerva becomes progressively the listener.

According to the Muses, the bold, bad Thracian tyrant and conqueror of Daulis and Phocis thought he could also take learning, culture and art —namely, the Muses—by force. He irrevocably wrecked himself in his attempt to soar like them. Thus his metaphorical rape is thwarted. Since Minerva is here heeding the Muses, we have a minute allegory in which wisdom pays attention to learning and experience; in the Perseus story, wisdom (Minerva) supported heroic valor in the form of Perseus. The upshot is that wisdom is not an end in itself, but something intermediate and intended for use. More conspicuous, however, is the fact that by means of the Pyreneus episode Ovid pats true artists on the back, as he does at the end of the *Metamorphoses:* kings may conquer, but poets rise above them. Brute force, Ovid implies, is inferior to wit, and, further, art involves wisdom, as well as learning, for the Muses find Minerva suited to be one of them. In addition, art requires security and serenity, for the Muses should not be upset or made captive and controlled or brutalized by tyrants like Pyreneus.

At this point in the Muse's discourse there is transition to others who make life miserable for the Muses, namely, the imitators. The woods are full of them, even on Mt. Helicon. In the present instance they are magpies imitating speech, and they require explanation, which the Muse gives in an indifferent recapitulation of their origins and behavior. The magpies used to be the nine daughters of Pierus, king of Pella. They thought that they were better than the Olympian gods. (Ironically, these princesses are the *Pierides*, a patronymic not used in the *Metamorphoses*, but one at times used to denote the Muses themselves.) This raucously ambitious group of mortals, the Muse relates, after touring the provinces, worked their way to the top and challenged the Muses as frauds. The result was a singing contest somewhat like those that occurred in ancient Greece and are exemplified by the part of a parthenion, or contest between choruses of maidens, by Alkman. Ovid gives this sort of contest novel treatment by having it partly recapped by one contestant and partly repeated and by having single contestants represent their groups. Since the point of a literary singing contest, whether pastoral or parthenion, is that one singer or side should surpass the other in poetic composition, Ovid has to write for both sides and top himself. His putting himself in this position amounts to his giving himself a dare and thus adding to the drama of the situation and to his fame.

The first song in the contest, that of the daughter of Pierus, is given in suitably inferior summary by one of the biased Muses. Then the Muse's

61

reply is repeated verbatim. It is prosaic at the outset and is verbose in passages and does not adhere to its ostensible, or declared, subject, which is to sing of Ceres. It is clearly superior to the princess's song, but it is not a perfect work of art, and in this way Ovid meets the dare: the Muse is good, but imperfect, and Ovid, who is writing for her, composes better than she by not writing well, for that is what his purpose requires. A similar but simpler form of the situation occurred in connection with the Pan-Syrinx tale of Book I.

Ovid, as one might expect, does other clever things in detailing the contest. He has the mortal nine show their presumption by not drawing lots and by singing first, as though the contest would end with their song, their opponents overwhelmed. They are, of course, foolish in other ways: they pit their mortality against acknowledged divinity; they give the Muses a standard to go beyond; and they are notably nasty in their choice of topic: Typhoeus' alleged driving the Olympians to Egypt, where they took animal forms to hide from his wrath. Further, anyone with any background or education would have known the tradition that Typhoeus and the giants were defeated by the Olympians, and the Muses are living proof of the fact. The recap of the nine's song shows that it was nothing much, merely an insult to the Olympians, to whom the Muses were closely related. Oddly, the daughters of Pierus feel that they are the equals of the Muses because of their voices, skill, and numbers, though why numbers should be important, except for volume, is not clear. They have obviously set themselves up for the kill.

This demolition the Muse performs at length. Indeed, her song is so long that she warns Minerva of the fact. Minerva would not miss this humbling of the presumptuous and makes herself comfortable in the shade, asking the Muse to repeat the song in order, and thus calling attention to the sequence of the song and its possible inclusion of the minor or ostensibly irrelevant. Ovid thus alerts one that something may need explanation.

The performing Muse then sings Calliope's original lyric. Several interesting things are going on at this point. First, a Muse is represented not as inspiring poetic composition, but as composing it herself. Second, her song is repeated by another Muse, who appropriately has an excellent memory, but who is inappropriately a complete imitator. Third, in reality, Ovid is the Muse, for he is doing the composition. He is both an imitator, relying on the works of others in a number of ways, and original in his adaptation. Hence, not all imitators are reprehensible. And, as noted earlier, Ovid is indirectly complimenting himself. Fourth, the Muse is singing a particular kind of classical composition, a Homeric hymn. Of those extant, two deal with Demeter, the Greek Ceres, and of these, one is a long narrative dealing with the rape of Persephone. Ovid's account differs markedly from the Homeric one. Finally, the Muse sings of Ceres the sustainer, whereas her opponent sang of Typhoeus the destroyer. Since the Muse wins, it is not hard to tell where Ovid's sympathies lie and why he whisked Perseus off the scene. Not only does Ceres preserve life by sustaining it, art also preserves life in other ways, by recording what is noteworthy and by presenting wisdom.

More important to notice about Book V is the fact that it divides into two distinct but unbalanced parts: two hundred and fifty lines deal with a hero; four hundred and twenty-seven have to do with goddesses. The first section treats of killing and presents the male attitude; the second gives, for the most part, the women's interests and views. These center on love of various kinds, by far the most common topic of Calliope's song. However, before the Muses reach this song, they tell Minerva of their insecurity, which results from the attempt of a vile king to ravish them and from the competitiveness of nine royal hussies. This insecurity pervades the women's world of Calliope's hymn to Ceres, and it is caused mostly by men.

Venus is one exception. Her having Cupid inspire Dis, or Hades, with love of Proserpina causes a great deal of trouble, but she is not just territorially ambitious. She is concerned about a trend among the goddesses, that of rejecting heterosexual relationships. Proserpina, presented as wishing to remain perpetually virgin, consorting with other maidens and dwelling in a place of perpetual spring—cool, well-watered, luxuriant in flowers, but fruitless—is a teenage girl still a child. To escape stasis, she must marry Death; that is, she must change her form from that of unripe girl to that of mature woman, matron, wife, and become her mother, who is a different stage of the same person. She, and like her the plants, must grow up and ripen, else there will be no fruit, no harvest, no continuation of life in its cycles of generation. Indeed, Venus is aiding Ceres by helping Proserpina mature, an area that Ceres seems to neglect. Perhaps she does not wish her daughter to grow up. When her daughter does and is taken from Ceres, Ceres is distraught. The trouble ends, however, with a balanced solution brought about by the moderation of Jove, one of the two good males in the hymn, the other being Triptolemus, emissary of Ceres. Venus has contributed to this solution by changing Proserpina from maid to wife and putting her in cycle. Proserpina is no longer the personification of a part of the year; she has become a fertility goddess in her own right and now represents the dying and resurrected vegetative cycle, as well as the human parallel to it.

Part of the parallel explained and celebrated by the myth of the rape of Proserpina is a *rite de passage*, the reaching the state of wife. The myth is also indoctrination for another *rite de passage*, death, and instills acceptance of the phenomenon. Death is not so horrible in the story, for it is an integral element in the change that makes life possible. Indeed, death entails another sort of life, and the love in Hades, where Dido walks with her beloved Sychaeus and Orpheus with Eurydice, promises what earth cannot, and thus the myth dispels the traumatic effects of the fear of death.

Thus Venus' act has results that transcend her avowed intent. It also causes a peck of trouble, for all the other major females in Calliope's song are disturbed by it. But, since the agents of rape are men, men are directly responsible for it and for the suffering of the ladies. Cyane tries to stop Hades' rape of Proserpina and is inflicted with incurable grief. Her view is that a male should woo, not force, the woman that he desires. Ceres, full of motherly love, suffers extremely because of the loss of her daughter. In reaction, she becomes very angry and vengeful. Proserpina is hurt psychologically more than physically. She is frightened by what is happening to her and grieved by her being torn away from her mother and her girlish playmates, and even as queen of the Underworld, she is fearful and sad. Because of devotion to their friend, the Sirens not only search everywhere for her, but give up their human form in order to continue the quest. Arethusa has experienced the panic caused by attempted rape and is supportive of Ceres. As a follower of Diana should, the nymph has always avoided heterosexual relationships, and when she was an oread or tree nymph in Arcadia, once preferred strenuous hunting; but as a naiad, she has a new love, that for her new land, for whose plight she is concerned. Thus the rape of Proserpina affects her. The friendly and compassionate old woman who gives refreshing barley water to a Ceres parched and weary from searching for her lost daughter is affected in another way. She weeps for the nasty boy who sneered at the distraught mother and who was changed into a lizard. In all these episodes the female personages are either appealing, sympathetic, innocent, or beneficent.

The offensive characters in Calliope's narrative are the nasty boy; Ascalaphus, who tattles on Proserpina; Lyncus, who tries to steal credit from the grain-goddess; Alpheus, aroused to lust and attempted rape by female nudity; and Hades, stimulated to love by Venus. The response of Alpheus and Hades to erotic stimulation reveals their natures; nudity and Venus are not responsible for the form their reaction takes, namely, impetuous assault.

The qualitative differences between the sexes becomes most obvious when Ceres appeals to Jove concerning Proserpina. Though Ceres refers to herself as a suppliant, she speaks like an estranged wife or an abandoned woman, one no longer pleasing to the male who once found her attractive and got her with child. To this implied wrong has been added the abduction and sexual forcing of her child. A single parent, Ceres is utterly devoted to her offspring. Now, in order to make a case before the highest tribunal, she feels that she must momentarily waive her parentage in favor of Jove's, paradoxically, so that she can make her case and regain Proserpina. In her mind, men are unfair to women. They desert them; they neglect their offspring; they are interested only in their own relationship to the children; and they resort to sexual violence. Ceres will not leave her child in the clutches of Hades, that criminal. But she has power only as she moves Jove to act.

Jove is calm and thoughtful. His position is that Proserpina belongs to them both, and they both care for her. However, he represents the rape in a practical light: the aggressor is kingly and is Jove's brother. He was not motivated by a desire to harm Proserpina, but by love. There has been no crime of violence here. On the other hand, Jove unequivocally acknowledges Ceres' right to have her daughter returned and respects her strong feelings on the matter. But there is also the Fates' decree about Proserpina's taking food in the Underworld; that he can arbitrate, but not eliminate. Jove's statements reveal a masculine bias and also flexibility and fairness and a tendency to compromise and to accept *faits accomplis*. He expresses no guilt about having loved Ceres and left her. He does uphold Ceres' maternal rights, as modified by the Fates' stipulation. But being a wise judge, he makes both Ceres and Proserpina happy by providing for their reunion for half of each year. Despite Jove, Calliope's song in its entirety gives the impression that the fair sex is the admirable one, relatively weak, but goodhearted. It has rights, but these are often violated. And, regardless of Jove's opinion about rape, the song gives the impression that women are revolted by being forced.

Something more emerges in the Muse's narrative, a sense that there is a women's society. This sense is given not only by the song's contrasting with the fighting, flying, and adventure of the Perseus material, but also by the indications of women's congregating—Diana's nymphs, Proserpina and her girlfriends—and by the fact that Proserpina likes the idea of spending half the year with her mother, leaving her husband behind. Her mother feels similarly. The feeling that a women's culture exists is augmented by the fact that the female characters have a single view about rape, as though it were disseminated in a subculture. The contrast between the violently aggressive Typhoeus of the princess' song and the gentle women of the Muse's indicates another attitude learned from members of one's own sex: men are traditionally violent, and women are not.

It is the contrast between violent or militant males and the supportive, gentler women that makes Minerva, who combines warrior characteristics with feminine ones, the appropriate bridge between the two major sections of Book V. Her figure stresses the contrasting elements of the book by combining them.

Ovid's gamesmanship in this book relies, of course, on producing the unexpected. He does not fail to foil and delight his audience. One would not expect the engrossing career of Perseus to trickle away in minor repetitions of his greatest triumph, so that he becomes tiresome. One might expect, at least, to leave such an amazing conqueror in love and arms in possession of his north African kingdom, not slip away from him forever on "Little Seriphus." One would expect Minerva to be more discriminating in her choice of tourist attractions or marvels. One would not expect the Muses to be suffering from severe anxiety, but to be serenely studious or engaged in performing the arts and far removed from the reach of militarists and traveling sister acts. Even given the foreseeable bias of a Muse's summary of her competitor's song, one might expect that song to amount to more than the one the daughter of Pierus sang. But one would certainly expect Calliope's lyric to be the acme of heavenly composition. Though very good in spots, it is, overall, disappointing.

The major problem with it is that Calliope, Memory's child, remembers too much. She strays from her subject, Ceres, benefactress of mankind. The Sirens, lovely and novel though they are, are dragged in by their heels. The common boy who ridicules thirsty Ceres is a clumsy intrusion and mars the hymn by being out of tone, too insignificant for a goddess to bother with. The love of Orphne and Acheron is inconsistent with Venus' earlier protest that one third of the globe, the Underworld, is deprived of love. And Arethusa's autobiography, engaging as it is, is neither clearly relevant nor about Ceres. Indeed, it puts Ceres in the subordinate role of listener, and after hearing it, Ceres simply flies away without comment. Apparently the account meant nothing to her, nothing worthy of mention, not even thanks. Was Arethusa's tale a diversion for Ceres? Did it, because of Arethusa's dependence upon and devotion to Diana, recall Ceres to an awareness of her obligations to her worshipers and dependents? Calliope does not explain. To sum up the problem in another way, the trouble with Calliope's song is that it has a major theme, namely, women's attitudes about men and sex, but Calliope thinks that her theme is Ceres and her beneficence; hence, she ends her narrative with Ceres' commission to Triptolemus. The best that one can say for her song is that it uneasily straddles two themes, one major, one minor.

In contrast with Calliope, whose uncertain focus was mentioned above, Ovid knows what her major theme is and makes it an integral part of his book, for he uses her song as part of the material focusing on women and contrasts that material with the earlier heroic portion of his book. Thus Ovid establishes his own superiority to the Muse by having her composition appear imperfect and then using her imperfect work to function perfectly in his overall plan.

There are other flaws in Calliope's song that should be noted. There are two very good metamorphoses that the Muse describes in detail, those of Cyane and Arethusa, and five dull or perfunctory ones, those of the rude boy, Ascalaphus, the Sirens, Lyncus, and the daughters of Pierus. Lyncus gets shortest shrift of all, as though the Muse had run out of inspiration. In addition, though Calliope does some well-constructed and interesting character sketches of female figures in her song, she includes a grain of silliness in some of the most important. Cyane's matronly sentiments that it is wrong to terrify the woman one wants and to carry her off by force and that a male should woo instead are certainly right and decent. But she is silly to think that she can stop Hades and dead wrong to say that he cannot possess Proserpina without Ceres' consent. Her grief at the rape, which violates her pool by plunging through it, is folly through excess. Arethusa's silliness is sunnier. She gives Ceres important information and pleads for the relief of agricultural Sicily and was a proper and strenuous devotee of huntress Diana—all good acts. But she stresses too much the beauty that irked her and that she did not wish to share, so that her pride in her looks comes through. She cannot put

66

them out of her mind. Furthermore, though she avoided the pursuit of the river-god Alpheus, she had had physical contact with his waters, and her status as maiden, therefore, is ambiguous. Also, she has been changed into a spring, and water is a fertility substance. In addition, it is Arethusa who prays for the return of fertility to stricken Sicily. Whether Arethusa knows it or not, she has turned into something of a fertility deity herself. This change she is happily unaware of. Venus just as illogically ignores the fact that love already existed in Hades' realm and decides to conquer it. And the Sirens, utterly devoted to their dear Proserpina, laudably sacrifice human form so that they can search for her over the sea. Alas, the impetuous ones, they are on the wrong track. She has gone underground. Even Ceres, goddess of fruitfulness, seems foolishly inflexible about her ravished daughter's condition and wishes her returned at once, so that when she accepts the Fates' decree and a six-month visit each year, Ceres seems too easily gratified, hence, silly because quickly changeable.

The way in which Calliope presents the female personages named above makes them heroines, for they are bold, staunch, faithful, persevering, beneficent, responsive, beautiful, and severely tested, and all are doers of noteworthy acts and the heroic figures of their own myths. All are impressive and arresting characters. Yet all have about them this touch of the silly. Because of their virtues and their traces of foolishness, they balance Perseus, whose character displays a similar combination. The total result is an urbane, light-handed version of the comic-heroic.

Despite the imperfections noted earlier, there is much that is good about Calliope's performance. It is interesting. It does not drag. It has variety. And there are many good touches. For example, after following good Homeric practice and dedicating her hymn to Ceres, the goddess deftly picks up where her opponent left off and properly disposes of that lady's monstrous protagonist, Typhoeus, by burying him under Sicily. Though suppressed, he still troubles the earth's crust. Thus Calliope snubs the upstart diva and provides a neat transition into her own lyric, for one of Typhoeus' earthquakes gives Hades, a responsible king, cause for an inspection tour of his upper boundaries, and it is then that he falls in love with Proserpina. And so one sees that transitions are important, even to the Muses.

Another pleasing aspect of the narrative is its delicacy, seen in the handling of the physical assault of Proserpina. Raptus is ambiguous, and Ovid's use of the word could be taken to refer only to the abduction, not to forced sexual union. The Muse, however, indirectly indicates that sexual relations occurred, using Proserpina's loss of flowers, her torn gown, and the mute testimony of her girdle, floating on Cyane's pool, to suggest that Hades had committed some loving act upon her. Arethusa also tells Ceres obliquely that physical union had taken place when she describes Proserpina as being sad queen and wife of Hades. It is also decorous that Cyane, when she rises from her pool to stop Hades in his kidnapping, exposes herself only as far as her waist.

67

Amusingly, Arethusa is less modest than Cyane, for she describes herself sporting about in the waters of Alpheus and standing naked on his bank, and her flight from the river-god produces some heavy breathing. There is something unconsciously sensual about her, but, then, she was ambivalent before. It is also entertaining that both water-nymphs are colorful.

The general tone of Book V is that of elegant, sophisticated comedy with serious undertones or implications. We have learned by now to expect that this book might repeat earlier motifs, and so it does. Tattlers are nasty, for example, and the pursuit of a woman is again presented in images of predator and prey. Metamorphoses abound, of course. And love is once more a major topic. But Ovid's originality and versatility never flag. Continuously he makes the ancient material new. Love is now seen extensively through the women's eyes. From this viewpoint, love frequently turns into a battle of the sexes: Hades' indifference to women annoys Venus, who retaliates; Arethusa rejects males; Jove philanders and Ceres takes a dim view of his behavior; Hades stirs up feminine resentment by abducting Proserpina.

Calliope's views on the sexes, which seem to correspond with Ovid's elsewhere, are that it is difficult for a male or a female to avoid the power of Venus. Her story implies that a woman will rightly make sexual choices in accordance with her constitution, or temperament. There is nothing wrong about her rejecting men. A man, following the example of Hades, may ignore love. That is his right. But Venus may interfere. That is her right. Male philandering has the sanction of Jove. But it may be inconvenient or distressing for the female. Women are to be wooed, not raped. But there are different kinds of sexual force: one, an act of violence; the other, an act motivated by love. However, the woman's feelings should be respected. If they are violated, wintry sterility results. Resentment does not promote fruitfulness. And males who cause it will, like Hades, have to pay a price, in his instance, a half-time wife. Males fare best in their relationships with females when they are considerate of women's feelings, like Cyane's wooer, or when they serve fruitfulness, like Triptolemus. Rape as a crime of violence is despicable.

The preoccupations of the 1970's and 1980's with rape and with women's rights and the earlier but continuing American interest in the battle between the sexes, exemplified by Thurber and Hemingway, make it likely that current readers of Book V will be more responsive to its treatment of love than to its treatment of the artist. They will be happy to find that here, too, Ovid favors women, not because they are perfect, but because they are more defenseless, more loving, more self-sacrificing, and more concerned with fruitfulness.

Book V does deal with artists, its other important theme, with Perseus, whose art preserves by killing, and with the Muses, who preserve in the living, breathing sequence of song. Both commemorate, but the subjects of the Muses are more meaningful and varied than those of

Perseus, whose subjects are mostly men—dead ones. They glorify him and his cold blood. The goddesses are more charitable and less self-centered, for their verses exalt others than themselves; and even their enemies, when they are not self-destructive, become living memorials. Both kinds of artist demonstrate that a career in the arts is demanding, strenuous, and precarious. Ovid seems to find that of the Muses more worthwhile. Whichever one chooses, artists are outstanding because of their products, whether they be realistic, like the statuary of Perseus, or imaginative, like the pious and soothing song about the forces of nature that energize crops and springs or cause them to disappear. These products are marvels of their own peculiar kind. They arrest attention. They keep alive, or preserve, by stopping the flux of phenomena, that is, by stopping the change that makes life possible. They teach by making one think and ponder. They make life interesting because its details are meaningful. In this respect they depart from the broad sweep of heroic kings and mighty nations presented in histories and from the lofty generalizations of philosophy to occupy the middle ground of the Alexander mosaic and Horace's song to Phidyle, the middle ground where individuals do and feel and respond to one another amid natural phenomena whose underlying forces they somewhat comprehend. Of the art forms, Ovid suggests that sculpture is less interesting and less alive than poetry because it lacks the sequence and movement of poetry and because it is less ambiguous and engages the mind and feelings less.

On the subject of art in social situations, Ovid is unequivocally on the side of good manners. Perseus, Minerva, and the Muses—all display them.

On the matter of supernatural aid as part of the artistic process, the stories of Book V indicate that without such assistance, one cannot excel. Perseus has it. Pyreneus and the Pierides lack it and cannot soar. The Muses and Minerva may give it, but oddly, their own discrimination is not always perfect. The Ovidian resolution of this paradoxical situation is Ovid, the poet with the inspiration and the devotion and also with the innate talent and the facility acquired by hard work. The myths may be the products of the daughters of Memory and inspire the poet, but he is the performer of the moment, and credit is due him for using what they have provided and whatever support they may give and for his working through and beyond these.

Book V finishes with a full stop at the end of the Muse's song.

METAMORPHOSES VI: The Inordinate in the Revealing Web

After the full stop of Book V, now what? Will the fortunes of Ceres continue? or those of the Muses? Will the Muses praise another deity? Or will there be a tale about Alpheus, Triptolemus, Venus, or someone not even present in the preceding narrative? Ovid is disappointingly conventional. Book VI grows directly out of Book V: the Muses' experience with the daughters of Pierus sparks Minerva into an active concern for her own affairs.

Pallas-Minerva also has a detractor, Arachne. Although the basic situation of the Muses' story—conflict between deity and mortal over a shared skill—is now reused, the two tales are distinctly individual. The Muses competed with the coarse daughters of Pierus, presented as the nasty over-privileged who do a royal sister act. Arachne, their thematic counterpart, is the nasty underprivileged doing a solo. There is a gulf in refinement that separates the Muses from the rival nine, whereas Arachne and Minerva are equally feisty and down-to-earth. Therefore, one feels that Minerva is competing with herself, and so is Arachne. But one does not sense this about the Muses' rivals. The contest between the aristocratic nine and the divine ennead is given a lopsided presentation. That between Arachne and Minerva gives each contestant comparable coverage. Finally, to a modern, the background given the Emathian sisters seems commonplace.

In contrast, Arachne receives a perceptive, somewhat unusual biographical sketch. Lowly born, married to an ordinary man, living in an insignificant hamlet, she is yet so famous throughout Lydian cities that vine-nymphs and naiads leave their abodes to watch her ply her one skill. She has no other wealth. And so she is tensely wrapped up in this aspect of herself. She is the female hero of daily routine elevated to almost Olympian heights. Remembering that the Minyeïdes used storytelling to alleviate the tedium and tension caused by weaving, we have another reason for Arachne's being wound tight. Whereas Perseus completely upstaged Andromeda and everyone else in his story, Arachne obscures the males in her family and anyone else around: her husband is an anonymity; her father dyes wool for her; her mother is dead; the rest are spectators. Arachne is the big frog in the small pond. But she is an even more interesting sort of talented person. The victim of her own pride, limited, arrogant, mean, quick to anger, astringent, gifted, marveled at, and kowtowed to, Arachne cannot relax and sport in the mancipiary possession of her genius. She cannot, through Minvera, identify her gift with something larger in the cosmos and transcend herself. If anyone is caught in the web, Arachne is. It is the web of personality, ability, and circumstance. At the end of her story, Ovid adds, using the spider as her emblem, the web came from herself. In other words, Ovid discounts the part that surroundings play in her downfall and stresses her character as paramount. But, as Ovid wrote elsewhere, *"Abeunt studia in mores"* ("Pursuits turn into character"). Furthermore, like the hunter who

71

becomes the hunted, the weaver becomes the inhabitant and, in that way, the captive of her web.

Ovid, of course, is too much the weaver himself to keep to one thread, and as he develops Arachne's character and situation, he presents the woman in motion as having grace and sensuous or aesthetic appeal (lines 17-22). To this he adds his sympathy for Arachne by making her almost heroic in her defiance of Minerva. Arachne thus becomes the protagonist of a dramatic genre, domestic tragedy. But Ovid goes beyond all this. Like his gods, he is too democratic to be a respecter of either the wealthy, well-born Pierides or the lowly Arachne. Like his gods, which are those of a legalistic Roman, he is just. Thus he puts himself between the pole of sympathy, pity, and understanding on the one hand and that of justice and sentence on the other, so that he must perform, because of his temperament, both roles and yet maintain balance. This act is a difficult one, indeed. Ovid performs it fairly, well, and surprisingly. For when one finishes Arachne's story, one realizes that it is not about a contest. Ovid has had the reader engrossed in finding out who will win. But that is not the point. There is no clear win. The tale is not about a skill, then, but about an attitude. Arachne is out of tune with the powers that be, the something in the universe that had the skill to separate the warring elements and so shaped the orb of earth and ordered the waves, woods, plains, valley, pools, and mountains and that appeared in human form in the household arts and crafts. Understanding her and sympathizing with her because Ovid has led us to, one comes also to pass judgment on Arachne: her crime of hubris occurs because she is small and mean. She is not big enough to be with Minerva, that is, to glorify the goddess and to participate in the expansiveness and grandeur of the universe through her divine gift.

That Arachne may be alerted to art as a dimension of the universe, Minerva takes the form of an old woman and warns her to pay Minerva proper respect. Thus the warning comes from the human level and from one entitled by her age and experience to Arachne's respect and consideration and by her sex to Arachne's receptivity. In a way, the old woman is the mother Arachne lacks. However, Arachne, who had scorned the goddess earlier, spurns the human as well, giving the old woman proud and bitter words and repeating her earlier challenge to Minerva. It is accepted, and the true goddess stands revealed. Even faced by such an epiphany, Arachne remains rebellious, wavering only to the extent of reddening slightly.

The contest, a novel one, begins with serious but also mock-heroic bustle: the setting up and working of the looms. This passage has analogs in the early epics: the how-to-summon-the-dead section early in Book XI of the *Odyssey* and the passage in the *Iliad* in which Hephaestus readies himself and his forge in order to make the new arms of Achilles, for example. Ovid also has the contestants gird themselves for the weaving as warriors might for the fight. Part of the novelty here comes from the fact that a male writer knows enough about or cares enough about a kind of work peculiar to women to write a somewhat technical and sensuous appreciation of it and to use it tellingly in his narrative. The passage may tell something about Ovid's audience, for giving weaving this much attention is a tribute to womankind, domesticity, and Minerva. (If the double-entendres about wool working used in *Lysistrata* carry over here, Ovid may be directing attention to frustrated sexuality.)

Next the weavings themselves are described, Ovid creating another of the major examples of meaningful ekphrasis in Latin literature, for the pictures woven give the combat at least two levels of significance: they reveal the personalities of the weavers, and they form a morality contest. Minerva's pride, competitiveness, and benevolence are revealed: she contests with Neptune; she gives the olive; she is proud of her victory and her city. On the moral level her tapestry represents peace (the border of peaceful olive), power used to humble hubris (the corner medallions showing the punishments of those who defy the gods), justice (the central scene in which Jove holds a court on the Areopagus, site of an ancient Athenian court), the benevolence of the gods (both Neptune and Minerva bestow gifts on men), order and protection (implied by Jove's court). These are Minerva's values and a pictorial warning to all like Arachne.

Minerva's effort is modest in comparison with Arachne's. In a frenzy of artistic production, the cottage craftsperson produces at least twenty separate scenes—a bit much—plus a border of flowers and ivy. The flowers suggest the weaver's affinities with that unwilling bride Proserpina; the ivy, with the Dionysiac and the unrestrained, or inordinate. Each scene within that border contributes to a mass of evidence that the male gods are beasts and fornicating deceivers, abusers of women and goddesses alike.

Not only is Arachne proud. It is now all too clear that she hates the gods, she hates shape-changing, and she hates maleness. She is clearly a complete egocentric, rejecting all that differs from her. So much for the imbalance in her personality. But it has another dimension, a fascination with sex, and since one presumes that her pictures are beautiful, she is latently lascivious and lickerish, delighting in and absorbed by what she abhors. Arachne's morality is as limited and warped as her personality. It is all concerned with sex, and it is the morality of insult and hypocrisy. As with her pride in weaving, she takes everything to mean extremes.

Minerva cannot fault Arachne's work; it is flawless. But she can condemn it for impiety, just as she condemns her failure to give Minerva due praise. And so the goddess slashes Arachne's tapestry and its *"caelestia crimina,"* a neatly ambiguous phrase, for it may denote crimes committed by the gods or slanders of the gods. Ovid leaves us to make the choice that will reveal our own personalities.

The story ends with Minerva's striking Arachne four times with her shuttle and marking her forever. Because Arachne cannot resist or retaliate, she tries to commit suicide, but Minerva in pity saves her and transforms her into a spider. If anyone is caught in a web of her own making, it is Arachne. (Unfortunately, surveying Ovid's life, one has the feeling that Ovid ignored his own perceptions and became trapped in his own web.)

The next tale in effect answers the question, can a queen who has everything—impressive ancestors, rule in a famous city, health, wealth, beauty, a husband who is a wizard of a musician, and fourteen children—learn anything from the fate of a poor but talented childhood acquaintance? The answer is, no, not if she is Niobe. Even though she grew up with Arachne and heard about her downfall, proud Niobe learns nothing from common humanity, or, for that matter, from some of her vaunted ancestors—Tantalus was a caution and nothing to model oneself on, and the Pleiades, of whom her mother was one, died of grief. Yet Niobe repeats the family pattern by feeling that she is on a par with the gods. There is, therefore, no reason for her to reverence them. Indeed, she feels that she is better than one of them, Latona, who has only two children to Niobe's fourteen, and so she stops the rites of Latona on the grounds, partly, that Latona is a hearsay goddess, whereas fertile Niobe is a divinity that everyone in Thebes has seen.

In this passage Ovid not only returns to Thebes and its impious royalties; he also picks up the thread of its prophets by using Manto, daughter of Tiresias; and in Niobe's self-admiration, he is redoing Narcissus, for Narcissus and Niobe are both impoverished by their wealth and by their knowledge of themselves. Both Tiresias and Manto irk Theban royalty, but Tiresias tried to use his foreknowledge to warn the doomed Pentheus, whereas Manto, equally prescient and, therefore, knowing that a warning is useless, merely sets Niobe up for the kill.

Niobe, of course, acts foolishly; and her stressing her fertility, though in her eyes it is her strong point, exposes her and her Achilles' heel. It is true, as she says, that Leto was sired by minor Titan Coeus (on old-fashioned divinity Phoebe) and that the goddess has known some very hard times, but her two children, Diana and Apollo, are much more important than their mother and are very lively. They are only too ready to uphold their mother's status and the family prestige. Apollo immediately begins shooting down Niobe's sons. The killings are varied, detailed, sensational, and moving, and one follows the other without cease, but they are also painless and artistic, a sort of aesthetic acrobatics, and not nearly so bloody as the ones done in Cepheus' hall. Amphion kills himself out of grief, a warning, no doubt, to husbands who fail to restrain their wives properly.

Niobe goes wild with grief, but she has learned nothing, not even from direct experience, and she blindly boasts of her seven remaining offspring. She cannot escape her character or its consequences. The seven girls are struck down one right after the other. Niobe sits down and grows rigid because of her misfortunes. She turns into weeping stone and is whirlwinded off to a mountain top in Lydia. There she remains a weeping statue.

Niobe fits into several patterns that Ovid has been weaving. For one, her children are displayed as better than their parent, just as Callisto was better than her father, Lycaon; and later Jove will be said to surpass his father, Saturn, and Augustus, his. Niobe's sons are properly riding and exercising and are not impious toward one another or toward the gods. They are presented simply as decent kids, and so are their sisters. For another, Niobe belongs with those who grieve excessively: Clytie, Pandion, Cyane, Phoebus (for Phaethon), the Heliades, and Cycnus. For a third, she belongs to a much larger group comprised of those experiencing the results of hubris, Pentheus or Lycaon, for example. Of herself, she represents the proud woman who destroys her family. Not all of these threads are given equal emphasis, but they are present here and are part of the overall tissue. At the end of her career, Niobe is mute testimony to the unending grief that pride can cause.

As a result of Niobe's spectacular passing, piety increases. So does telling stories about Latona. An anonymous fellow tells a plain, unvarnished tale of striking realism, rather like one of Defoe's. His old dad had to send him off with a guide to drive some cattle down from Lycia. Coming to a reedy lake with an old, fire-blackened altar in its midst, the Lycian guide whispered, " ' "Be favorable to me!" ' " The narrator echoed him and then asked for the story of the place. Here, said the Lycian, Latona came with her newborn twins, worn out with fleeing the wrath of Juno and weak with thirst. She stooped to drink, but the local louts stopped her, and she pled with them.

The guide makes Latona's sufferings very real and her speech very human. Indeed, it is surprising that a goddess should be so human. The result is that her plea touches the chords of common decency and its rhetoric is truly moving. Latona says, for example, " ' "These children too, let them touch your hearts, who from my bosom stretch out their little arms." ' " But Ovid cannot resist ridiculing rhetoric, regardless of the situation, for he adds, " 'And it chanced that the children did stretch out their arms.' " There is more to Ovid's observation, however, for it suggests his feeling that art is superior to nature because nature sometimes imitates art.

The local boors, unmoved by humanity, suffering, rhetoric, or children, find pleasure in torturing Latona further by muddying the water. This is sadism. Latona, who seems here and in the Niobe episode a goddess of low power, appeals to heaven, and the result is that the peasants are turned into very realistic frogs.

Notable in the myth are the sympathy for the suffering, the assumption that children are appealing, the realism or everyday tone and circumstances, and the meanness of the peasants. There is no idealization of the countryside here or of its inhabitants. Ovid has, in effect, created a counterpastoral. The telling also demonstrates what the gods look like to people with agricultural backgrounds like the narrator's. For a moment Ovid becomes the George Crabbe of antiquity.

If it is democratic to have an occasional anonymous storyteller and characters from the lower levels of life to show that men are much alike regardless of level, Ovid is not democratic enough to want to abolish class structure. The myth of the satyr Marsyas shows that even the lesser deities cannot compete with the great ones and that the gods' class structure is ultimately based upon force. Because Apollo has the loser, Marsyas, flayed alive after the competition, the god appears even crueler than the Lycian rustics. In the scale of things that can happen to a person, metamorphosis is many degrees less horrible than being skinned alive. The storyteller of this tale, also anonymous, is a seeker after ghoulish sensation. He has no difficulty in topping the sadism of the boors, for he merely follows the realism of the preceding raconteur and describes in detail what a flayed person looks like. The multitudinous tears shed by nymphs, sylvan deities, and rural people because of Marsyas' horrible change and their change into a clear stream are so much an improbable anticlimax that only the cruelty and the man-goat changed into a single enormous wound seem real. One feels that one has once again reached the nadir of beastliness.

After the stories about Marsyas and the Lycian rustics, people turn to feeling sorry for Amphion and his children. For Niobe they have only reproach. Yet her brother, Pelops, weeps for her, too, and cryptically displays his ivory shoulder patch. The gesture is not without its significance, however; for, as Pelops' weeping shows family grief for more than his sister, Pelops' gesturing shows familial understanding: Niobe alone is not to blame; she suffers from a heritage of impiety that Latona called attention to earlier, when she said: " 'This daughter of Tantalus has added insult to her injuries: she has dared to prefer her own children to you [i.e., Apollo and Diana], and has called me childless—may that fall on her head!—and by her impious speech has displayed her father's unbridled tongue.' " Pelops' shoulder is concrete proof that he, too, bears the consequences of his father's impiety. Yet Pelops, as Ovid presents him, is guilty of nothing. Pelops, however, extends the web. With Arachne and Niobe, the entrapping web is one they seem to weave themselves. Pelops shows that the web may include one's parents and that one may be the victim of a genetic wound. Latona had said this, but Pelops validates her assertion. Since Tantalus tried to deceive the gods by feeding them stewed Pelops and since Niobe gratuitously insulted deities, one might think that the web stopped with Pelops, but Ovid's readers probably knew that Pelops himself committed crimes and that he passed along to Thyestes, Atreus, and Agamemnon the criminality, impiety and inordinateness of Tantalus. Pelops' tears, therefore, are also prophetic: he grieves for his own misdoings and those of his descendants. And his ivory patch is the emblem of the genetic web—past, present, and future—that human beings cannot escape.

The Pan-Hellenic mourning for the royal family of Thebes now provides Ovid with a transitional device, first used in Book I to move from the myth of Daphne to that of Io: the device of the conspicuous absentee. He is Pandion, king of famous Athens, who cannot join all the other kings of Greece in offering condolences to the Thebans—the civilized thing to do—because he is beseiged by overseas barbarians.

Tereus ("watcher"), wealthy and powerful Thracian king descended from Mars, relieves Athens, and Pandion finds him an eminently suitable son-in-law and marries his daughter Procne to him. But the politically advantageous union is accursed. Not only are Juno, Hymen, and the Graces absent from the wedding, but the Furies being bridal torches snatched from a funeral and make the bridal bed. The screech owl of bad omen hoots above the bridal chamber. In this jolly atmosphere a child is conceived. As far as mortal Thracians can tell, however, the atmosphere is jolly, and so they celebrate.

Looking at the nuptials of Tereus and Procne thus, one is tempted to dismiss the situation and its disastrous consequences as destiny. But looking more closely at the beginnings of their married life, one may reach other conclusions. First, the wedding was clearly a political matter arrranged by a king who was not too sure of his ability to keep his realm. It was not one based on personal relationships. Second, even though the mating was biologically effective as far as reproduction was concerned, it was not effective in another way. The nuptials did not bring about the emotional and psychological joining of the two involved. As for the wedding passage, Ovid was careful to construct it so that there is a facade, a public celebration antithetical to what is occurring behind it. And when he ends the episode by saying, "even so is our true advantage hidden," he implies that what is advantageous is not the political marriage, but the sound, viable human relationship, which is lacking.

In order to understand one reason that this marriage did not take, we should remember that it occurred in Thrace. That is why Ovid writes that the Thracians were happy and sacrificed on the day of the wedding. But Procne was far from home, family, and familiar customs when she married the son of Mars.

What is wrong with the situation and the relationship is indicated by the deities who are lacking. The Graces are absent, which means that at the ceremony and the sexual union, there are neither beauty nor mirth nor grace. Both affairs, then, are clumsy, ugly, and somber. Juno *"pronuba"* ("who prepares the bride") is lacking; that is, Procne has not been properly prepared for and led into her new state in life. (The situation makes one think of the wistful bride in the ancient painting known as the Aldobrandini wedding.) Nor is Hymen, the spirit behind the wedding song, there to excite the bride about her new role in life and to urge her to accept it.

The elements that are present symbolize the feelings of Procne: the owl of ill omen, her sense of being doomed; the funeral torches, her lifelessness. The Furies suggest her resentment because of the pain of losing her maidenhead or her distress at being married to a barbarian, and they indicate her desire for retribution. All of these lacks and presences haunt Procne's marriage day and her psyche. Procne is, to simplify matters, the lonely young woman who leaves her home and native land to go off to marry a coarse and unrefined husband in a strange and barbarous country.

She submits, initially, at least, but this is not the life she wants. She is homesick and longs for her sister, who represents unmarried womanhood, her family, Athens, and civilization. Her wishing to go to Athens *or* to have Philomela, her sister, come to her indicates her craving for contact with all that she has lost. It is significant that her request for a visit is couched in wheedling terms, which indicate her working at pleasing her spouse and her doubts about doing so. It is also a bit intense. The visit, then , is seen as a recompense for being good. That it leads to a greater wrong than any Procne has yet felt and to a greater revenge than she could anticipate, is one of the ironies that her own discontent did not even vaguely apprehend.

Irony after irony unfolds in the story. Procne's wheedling her sister's visit as a wifely reward is ironic, and so is Tereus' unquestioning, unthinking cooperation. So are the hearty felicitations that begin Tereus' visit to Athens to effect the sisters' reunion, and so is his statement of the object of his trip. For when the object enters, Tereus' object begins to change. Philomela is a gorgeous girl in gorgeous attire, a refined naiad-dryad type: natural in her refinement, but also wild and woodsy and having the added allure of flowing water. At once we begin to know Tereus' nature, and he, to know himself. By national temperament he is easily set on fire; by his own he is even more inclined to burn intensely. Seeing Philomela, he ignites and can hardly contain himself. He wants to bribe her servants, corrupt her nurse, tempt the girl herself with lucre, or ravish her and go to war. Although he is like an overstimulated jumping bean, he does none of these rash things, but diverts his sexual excitement into eloquence, reiteration, and tears (he pretends that Procne has told him to illustrate her tears). Such a dissembler is this rutting Thracian that everyone at the Athenian court thinks him the kindest of husbands. This irony is followed by another, for Philomela wishes, in all innocence, to visit her sister and urges Pandion to let her go. Here Tereus suffers an even deeper burn, for when Philomela hugs her father, Tereus burns to be her father. Ironically, Pandion gives his second daughter into Tereus' keeping and urges his son-in-law to protect her. He accepts Tereus' displays of family feeling as natural, counts on his piety and family loyalty, yet has misgivings.

There is no amorous pursuit in this myth, because Philomela knows no reason for running. But Ovid continues the predator-victim imagery that is part of the chase, for aboard ship en route to Thrace, Tereus watches Philomela like a hungry eagle eyeing a caught coney. Once ashore, he drags the maid off to an isolated mountain hut and ravishes her. Her reproaches and threats to reveal all, contrast ironically with her name, which means "sweet melody." They anger Tereus, who cuts out her tongue, but before he does, Philomela makes the essential point: Tereus has laid waste all the familial relationships. This point is underlined by the earlier images of husbandry that Ovid uses in connection with the Tereus-Philomela relationship—his love is a fire burning ripe grain, leaves, or a hay mow—and intensifies by the feral ones—Tereus and Philomela are eagle and hare, lamb torn by wolf, dove bloodied by talon. Of course, these are also all images of destruction, of feeding on something and devastating it, not ones of love or creativity. The dramatic and ironic reversal of loving family relationships is thus accomplished. Tereus confirms it by again and again forcing the mutilated girl.

But just before this beastliness occurs, Philomela's excised tongue quivers, murmurs, and tries to return to its mistress. This detail is pure melodrama, of which there are other traces in the story. But it is also a sign that Philomela's every fiber is bent upon revealing Tereus' vicious acts. Guarded, immured, and silenced as she is, Philomela yet manages to catch Tereus in her web, for she weaves her story into a fabric. (This act is another Ovidian indication that his art is the craft of verbal weaving, even of revealing what cannot be uttered; it is the combining of many threads, colors, shadings, and signs and, if one recalls the story-picturing done by Arachne and Minerva, of scenes and deeds into a continuous, meaningful, interconnected whole.)

Until Procne receives the fabric, she has believed her sister dead and, ironically, has properly mourned for her. (There seems to be a double irony here: Procne mourns for a sister who is not dead; yet Procne has reason to grieve.) Once informed, Procne takes advantage of the women's mountain revel in honor of Bacchus, rescues her sister, and with her plans and executes an inordinate revenge. After Procne slays her son, the two sisters cook Itys and serve him to his father as a sacred meal. Then they tell Tereus what he has eaten. Enraged, he tries to kill the sisters, but all three are changed into birds.

There are more ironies in the tale than indicated above. Ovid's striving for—and producing—the sensational as heavy as the irony. As heavy as either is the use of earlier threads: the inordinate passions dominating Arachne and Niobe reappear here, as does the eating of human flesh, implicit in the Pelops myth and almost brought off in that of Lycaon. There are also the revenge motif of the Latona, Minerva, and Apollo stories of this book and of those dealing with the offenders of Juno and Bacchus and the cruelty that so far has pervaded much of Book VI, as well as the rape motif in the earlier Proserpina story.

Looking at the Tereus episode with regard to identity, one sees that Philomela's identity has been destroyed. Once raped by her brother-in-law, the maiden Philomela is dead, and she can never again be the woodsy-wild princess, chaste daugher, or gentle, loving sister. Her identity and those of Tereus and Procne are changed by various passions into those of subhuman creatures.

Looking at the episode from the perspective of the web metaphor, one finds that part of Tereus' web is ignorance of his own nature, an ignorance shared by Pandion and his daughters. Tereus is also the victim of another kind of entanglement, that of national characteristics. He cannot avoid either, for they are fated, or given, but he will inevitably pay for them. It is part of the irony of fate that this good-neighbor king, winning general, and willing husband and father is a villain caught in the toils of uncontrollable desire. Ovid makes the terrible action gripping and, through the distancing of art, entertaining.

Like a good and also foxy storyteller, Ovid knows the need to vary mood and subject—indeed, he revels in it—while keeping the tapestry intact and the reader off balance. The need now is for a breath of fresh air to sweep away the hectic passions and the blood stench of the Tereus episode. It is provided by Boreas, rude wind-god and tyrant of the north. After being frustrated in his suit for the hand of Athenian princess Orithyia because of Tereus' abominable deeds, Boreas, a somewhat windy rhetorician, carries off his bride. *Orithyia* means "she who rages on the mountain," so that if names indicate character, she is a fit mate for a boisterous wind. In any event, though the carrying-off is a rape, it is not like that perpetrated by Tereus upon Philomela, but one of love, like Hades' of Proserpina. Venus is complimented again. And the resultant marriage is apparently a happy one, for evidence to the contrary is lacking, and one feels that Ovid would have supplied any lurid brutalities had he found them to his purpose. Instead, the outcome of this relationship is not a cannibal meal and three birds, but two heroes who go on the first Greek legendary voyage of exploration, that of the *Argo*.

For variety in treatment of material in Book VI, Ovid relies heavily upon literary realism. The lower class Arachne and the Lycian peasants, the anatomy of Marsyas, and the tabloid affairs of King Tereus make Book VI the most realistic yet. Furthermore, at the end of this book Ovid has moved his chronology to a roughly datable period, a generation before the voyage of the *Argo*, an event that occurred about a generation before the Trojan War, that is, 1250 B.C. or thereabouts. This chronology, whether legendary or not, increases the sense of being told about real events without dispensing with the marvelous that is part of legend. And merely having Pandion, Tereus, Procne, Philomela and Itys play out their roles without any deity at hand makes the story seem radically real.

Neither gods nor men come out with flying colors in Book VI. They seem to be equally proud and mean. The gods have more power, however, and, therefore, must be respected. But, on the whole, the effect of Book VI is leveling, as far as men and gods go. On the purely human level, arrogance is ruinous; crafts per se are admired; rape is good or bad, depending upon whether it can be classified as *amor* ("love") or *inuria* ("harm"); meanness and cruelty are deplorable, but fascinating; and intent seems to be more important than means or act.

When considering the structure of a book of the *Metamorphoses,* one becomes aware, first, that each book has an overall, or major, theme. Next, one notices that there are secondary themes, or motifs. In Book I, for example, discord and concord constitute the major motif; love, love as a chase, marital jealousy, and the punishment of mortal for offending a god are secondary ones. Further, to complicate matters, a book may contain two themes looming so large that they seem almost equal in importance. This happens in Book V, where the theme of the varieties of artist is paralleled by that of the contrast between male and female. In addition, the major theme of a book may be interrupted, as the Tiresias and Narcissus tales interrupt that of Book III; a theme may be repeated with variation in order to make various points, as the love-pursuit is in Book I; and a series of tales may be set in a frame that qualifies their meaning, for example, those of the Minyeïdes in Book IV and those of the Muses in Book V. The preceding are all possibilities in a game one of whose rules is that a rule or procedure may be suspended or changed at any time without notice.

As book follows book, one finds that major and secondary themes reappear. And as one picks out these threads and compares their use in the related tales, one learns something about the way that constants—the motifs or themes—vary with changing circumstances. In Book I the love-chase varies thus: Apollo's of Daphne is elegant and rustic, breathless, comic and serious, gentlemanly, and memorialized in a plant; Jove's of Io is suave, rural, relentless, and effortlessly effective rape; Pan's of Syrinx is rustic, frustrated, sentimental, and memorialized in a plant and an ancient musical device; in Book II, Mercury's pursuit of Herse is one of animal lust, urbane elegance, and bribery in order to obtain sexual access; Jove's of Europa is that of disguise and animal allure at a beach party; and Jove's of Callisto involves rusticity, disguise, homosexual advances, struggle, and rape. From these variations one learns something about the love-chase itself, and one finds oneself preferring one male's behavior over the others and thus makes moral decisions. One learns, too, that style in love is important and that even losing in love has rewards. Apollo's experience is not Pan's because the quality is different, and Apollo's laurel wreath is more to be prized than Pan's simple pipes. Neither lover wins his love, but each has something to cherish even though he loses.

One becomes aware, too, of the complexities arising from something apparently as simple as stringing a series of tales together. Ovid is not simply following one myth with another, merely stringing them together; he is weaving, developing patterns. And from the patterns and the consequent comparisons, significance is discernible, as it is with the love-chase motif. The poet-as-weaver is admittedly a metaphor, but is seems to fit the facts better than Mr. Otis' viewing Ovid as architect or muralist. Thus, whatever its limitations, it is less likely to lead one astray.

81

To return to Book VI, the major theme here is that of the inordinate, or those who lack proper balance or restraint. Arachne and Niobe are unable to restrain their pride; the Lycian peasants, their meanness; Marsyas, his self-confidence; Tereus, his lust; Boreas, his violence. Only Pelops interrupts the thematic pattern, for he does nothing but weep and, emblem-like, bare his shoulder. However, even this anatomical display alludes to his being the victim of an inordinate parent who could not restrain his cunning, and it is Pelops who helps to call attention to the web that no one can avoid. That these personages are caught in the web is the point that Ovid makes about the inordinate. The web itself is composed of one's heredity, one's culture, one's temperament, chance, and the circumstances in which one happens to find oneself. For Pelops, the web is heredity, a genetic wound. For Arachne it is her personality and talent, both given to her and thus inherited—but also matters of chance—and the conditions inherent in weaving, as well as the effects of receiving general admiration. That Minerva descends upon her when she does, is a matter of chance, as is the fact that the Muses happened to have been affronted just before Minerva visited them. Tereus' lust is innate and also a national characteristic, according to the ancients. His clumsy wedding, like all wedding ceremonies, is partly the product of a culture. Niobe's pride is enhanced by the circumstances of her being the queen of an important city and of her fecundity. Along these strands of the webs which define their lives and make them possible, the men and women act and are displayed and revealed.

On the whole, the men and women are caught in these revealing webs and have only a little control over their destinies, because circumstances, chance, character, culture, heredity, and ignorance interact and largely determine what they do. In short, these components constitute fate. One may be fated like Boreas to be successful and happy by letting one's nature prevail, assuming the happy chance, as in his case, that one's mate is of like nature, but the conspicuous and memorable events and personages are the catastrophes and the tragic failures. Ovid does not protest against the scheme of things. His sense of the web phenomenon allows him to be sympathetic, and his acceptance of the scheme of things allows him to enjoy the passing parade and, surprisingly, still retain values, even though his characters seem to be largely fated to be right or wrong, pious or impious, loving or hurtful. Fate, in his understanding of the scheme, does not eliminate the categories of right and wrong. A twentieth-century sociologist might believe that criminals are the innocent products of heredity and environment, but not Ovid. For him, what is, is. And beyond his own game-playing, he presents a broader game that men do not control.

METAMORPHOSES VII: Pure Joy

In the opening lines of this book Ovid, follows the lead given at the end of Book VI. He takes the first famous Greek voyagers across the sea to Colchis, giving a brief salute to the sons of Boreas, and summarizes the heroes' exchange with barbarian king Aeëtes. Of the trip, Ovid mentions only the exploit of Calais and Zetes, a minor one, referring to the others in a vague, general way, and he largely ignores Aeëtes and the Greeks. The results are that the Greek hero Jason and his illustrious crew are reduced to something approximating nonentities and that the focus is on Medea. For Ovid, the significant result of this famous voyage is the discovery of a woman, for it is she that the rest of his tale renders fascinating.

For one thing, Medea is one of the most romantic and complicated of Ovid's heroines. There has been little romance in the *Metamorphoses* since Pyramus and Thisbe in Book IV, so that the appearance of Medea is refreshing. She continues, of course, the preceding theme of the effects of love on personality; for near examples, there are the cruelty and lust it produced in Tereus and the boisterous actions of rude but husbandly Boreas. Here again Medea is refreshing, for she is neither inclined to rape, like Tereus or Salmacis; nor to bluster, like Boreas; nor to flightly relationships, like Jove; nor to ineffectual planning, like Pyramus and Thisbe. She is a thoughtful and passionate person who, when she first appears, gives a detailed account of her feelings and analyzes them. In addition, she seems precocious, for she approaches her new and disturbing condition, first love, as though she were a scholastic philosopher: the whole matter is a contest between reason and appetite. Her account of her inner conflict is engrossing because of its detail and thoroughness. This close scrutiny is itself something new in the *Metamorphoses*.

Ovid lays the background for Medea's introspection by labeling her amorous feelings "strong fires" and a "fury" that Medea cannot overcome by reason, though she struggles long. Taking a calculated risk as author, he presents the conflict immediately after its climax or crisis, and Medea knows this, for her first words to herself are, " 'You are fighting back in vain, Medea.' " These words and the following analysis, then, constitute a paradox: Medea has given in to her condition, yet she continues to fight against it. Her reasoning in what follows, operates as effectively as ever, though it may be that only after the overmastering passion has conquered, can Medea be rational enough to talk to herself and reason so clearly. Such a sequence seems a possible inference from Ovid's presentation, and if this interpretation is valid, then Ovid's psychological perception is unusual and worthwhile of itself. He has again surpassed his audience. In any event, Medea is a passionate and imaginative thinker. She is well informed, analyzes and reasons well, and in general is well versed in rhetoric, elocution, moral philosophy, and geography. For example, she knows all about Greece and its civilization and culture. There is a bit of the bluestocking about Medea and of the self-preoccupied teenager. This combination of qualities makes her usual, especially for a barbarian.

The emotions and attitudes in conflict in the princess are love of or sense of duty to country and parent, love of culture and civilization, love of Jason, love of the ideal or a tendency to idealize, a desire for adventure, and love of self. All in all, this heady mixture is clearly an unbalanced *discordia concors* because motives two through six all direct Medea in the same way, towards Jason. However, Medea would be merely a shallow late adolescent if she were only infatuate. She is not. Not only is she intelligent and knowledgeable, she does have values, and she does resist her feelings. She does not rationalize or deceive herself completely. Hence, if one inspects her character at this point, one may conclude that she has many admirable qualities. However, there is a dark side to her personality, one inherent in her rank, parentage, culture, ability, and training: Medea is an apothecary and occultist of formidable power. The word *witch* does not do her justice. Her history is that of the conflict between her ethical reason and her desires and sinister powers.

Taken as a whole, Medea's story in this book is that of the tragic deterioration of a woman's character. This fact is most easily perceived if one looks at its initial presentation and then moves immediately to its final one. At the outset, Medea is a maiden of indeterminate age—presumably young, since she has until now not known love, though this fact also indicates a certain fastidious superiority to the local youths —who feels all the force of first love and is yet not without reason, restraint, modesty, and feeling for her family and its status and for her own honor. She is aware, passionate, compassionate, discriminating, well-informed, and analytical. This barbarian princess ends as a jilted wife and criminal flying away to evade punishment for attempted murder. Ironically, she is saved by the magic that destroyed her career in a world she had admired for its civilization. She leaves it literally under a cloud. She whose struggle between love and duty had engaged the reader's interests and sympathies at the outset is dismissed from the scene without a jot of regret.

Because Medea's downward progress constitutes almost exactly half of Book VII, it deserves detailed consideration. First it should be noted that Medea's decay is described in terms that a Christian moralist of a century earlier than ours might have found completely comprehensible. At the start, Medea—inexperienced, emotional, and confused—senses that she is overwhelmed by a strange superior power, love. She feels oppressed, burdened, and borne down by the passion within her, and, therefore, unhappy. She is aware of a violent conflict between this longing and all of the conscious content of her mind or intellect or reason. Under this pressure she enunciates an aphorism that accords well with one Christian definition of sin, namely, that it consists of choosing a lesser good instead of the greater one: " '*video meliora proboque, deteriora sequor!*' " (" 'I see the better things and approve of them; I go after the worse.' ")

At this point Medea is keenly aware of her royal status and the resulting identification with a particular country and of her virginity and, therefore, of her worth and honor. And so she thinks of marriage, a permanent and honorable personal and sexual relationship. But she also feels the attraction of the exotic. Marriage to Jason means union with an alien world. At the moment she doubts the propriety of such an alliance and thinks that her own land can provide someone for her to love. The tension between these opposing drives, roughly the appeal of the novel and the restraint of prudence, is so balanced that there is nothing for Medea to do, and so she thinks that Jason's fate is for the gods to decide. Her emotions, however, will not let her rest, for she wants Jason to live, and she says so. Then she adds more temperately that she does not have to love Jason in order to pray for him. Her statement is literally true, but it is not that of a disinterested party; it indicates Medea's emotional involvement. Since Medea is wrought up, she is not capable of being very objective. Hence, she is arguing emotionally. First, she begs the question by asking, " 'For what has Jason done?' " (that her father should demand tasks certain to lead to Jason's death). Jason, in fact, has not done anything yet. The point of the tasks is that they are aimed at stopping Jason from doing what he wishes, namely, from removing the precious fleece. Hence, the proper questions for Medea to ask are ones such as these: is Aeëtes' title to the fleece valid? does Aeëtes have justifiable grounds for trying to eliminate a contender for the fleece? does Jason have any valid claim to the fleece? does Jason have no choice but to undertake the tasks? are Aeëtes' means of keeping the fleece unduly cruel or unnecessary? is the fleece needed for the welfare of the kingdom? It may be to Medea's credit that she has earlier found her father's stipulations, or conditions, too severe, but she fails to see that Jason does not have to accept them or that, short of a curt refusal, her father has to propose extreme measures, if he wants to keep the fleece. In short, Medea is arguing from her heart in favor of a handsome man who would have her father's treasure just for the asking of it.

Medea's next reason for praying that Jason may live is an *argumentum ad hominem:* he is young, noble, manly, and, most important, he is beautiful. At this juncture, Medea declares that because of these qualities, Jason has touched her heart, and thus she admits that her argument is emotional, not logical. All along she has been confessing her love through her lack of logic. Now she rationalizes semantically and calls her love compassion. It also becomes apparent that in this area of experience, Medea is responsive to sensation, not to prudence, principle, or reason.

Having now justified to herself Jason's right to her sympathy, Medea becomes aware that being touched is not sufficent for the situation. Jason requires help, her help, she says, as she lists the formidable tests that he will face.

At this point one should note that Medea does not doubt her ability to help Jason and should conclude that she must really possess unnatural powers, unless she lies or is deluded. One should also notice that there is an element of magic in the tasks that Jason faces. One might dismiss the bulls as an exaggerated presentation of savage beasts dangerous to yoke and difficult to plough with; the dragon might be merely an exaggerated python; but men springing from sown teeth are magic, as are sleepless dragons and golden fleece. Medea's aid, then, is something beyond the heroic; and given the circumstances, it, too, must involve magic. The real contest, then, will be not between the magic-possessing king and the hero, but between the magic-possessing father and his magic-performing daughter. Thus Medea is an ancient illustration of what twentieth-century Americans have called "the generation gap." However, a Roman used to the patriarchal system know as the *familia* or a person familiar with Virgil's pious Aeneas or Plato's Euthyphro would be likely to identify Medea's first sin, or downward step, as filial impiety.

And so the new woman, Medea, rejects the iron and stone heart of her father for greater humaneness, or so she says. And she again blandly indicates that she can change the course of events when she says, referring to Jason's impending destruction, " 'If I permit this.' "

Medea next reacts against the barbarity of exposing Jason to what amounts to a sensational variety of gladiatorial combat against brazen beasts and armed warriors. She is here objecting to something in her culture and, by implication, something potential in herself, for she can conceive of looking on Jason as he dies and of urging the bulls and the armed men to kill him. (Incidentally, Medea here seems to be voicing Ovid's veiled objection to barbaric cruelty.) She then proceeds to pray that the gods send better things, but again decides that the situation requires her action, not her prayers. When she says this, she is in effect guilty of hubris and impiety toward the gods because she is asserting that her desires are more important than the will of the gods and her powers are more effective than theirs. (In this connection, it is interesting that no god punishes Medea, nor is one needed; Medea carries her punishment within her.)

Next Medea surveys what she plans to do and what may be the consequences, seeing that her plans entail treason and aiding an alien. One possibility is that Jason might abandon her, either sail away or go off to another woman; another result, dependent upon abandonment, could be punishment by her own people. Abandonment for another woman bothers her most, and she decides ominously that if Jason could ever prefer someone else to her, he should die. At the moment, however, Jason appears so handsome, so soulful, and so physically attractive that she cannot believe that he would be deceitful or forget her aid. Medea's prudence dominates now: she determines to make him pledge his faith and—here hubris emerges again—to make the gods witness these vows. And so Medea has Jason all neatly packaged, in her mind, and the future, too, for she sees herself acclaimed by the women of every Greek city as savior. Considering what she is leaving—sister, brother, father, gods, native earth—in short, her roots—gives Medea a moment of hesitation.

She decides that there is little to detain her: her father is a fierce, cruel, stern barbarian; her brother is a child (why his age should make a difference, except in lack of understanding, is not clear); her sister would sympathize with her; and as for the gods, Medea is carrying off the greatest one within her: Love. (Here Ovid's impious Medea seems to invite comparison with Virgil's pious Aeneas, who left Troy carrying with him his native gods.) As for Colchis, uncouth and barbarous, it is far out of the main stream of civilization. Medea says of it: " 'I shall not be leaving great things.' " In exchange for leaving Colchis, she sees herself being given the honorary title Preserver of the Young Men of Greece, the benefits of a world-famous culture and refinement, and the incomparable Jason. As for the sea journey, whose dangers she has heard of, she cannot fear them with Jason's arms about her.

Suddenly her reason is stronger than her wish-fulfilling imagination. Medea herself stops her fantasies, realizing that they are based on semantic delusion, that she is calling wickedness by seductive names. She advises herself to do what is right. Thus her soliloquy ends. Ovid stresses his view of her condition at this moment: Rectitude, Family Loyalty, and Shame are so real and prepossessing that they materialize before her as allegorical figures; she can perceive them with her senses; and Love, beaten, is about to retire.

Medea continues her way to the grove of Hecate, the sinister Underworld goddess and patroness of black magic. Ovid does not state the reason for Medea's visit, but the possibilities seem limited. Because Medea is a witch, she may be going to worship one of the sources of her power. Or she may be going to Hecate to obtain something that she wants. Just now, if Medea wishes to be good and proper, she does not have to do anything. However, her soliloquy began with her on the way to the grove and her asserting that she could not resist her love. Therefore, although Medea's mind has told her to be good, her feet are taking her to a place of wish fulfillment, and her wishes have been clearly indicated.

Unaccountably, Medea's dubious dilemma is solved for her. Jason is not so passive or helpless as Medea thought. He appears so opportunely that his arrival seems more than sheer coincidence. Seeing him, Medea is again overcome by love and gives the proper signs thereof: blushing, paling, and being unable to take one's gaze away from the beloved. She is absolutely and helplessly enchanted and completely gives herself away.

Thus far in his overall presentation of Medea in love, Ovid has shown that, although reason can overcome the emotion of illicit love and the support given it by the imagination, reason and principle, even when supported by the imagination, are powerless against sensation, here the sight of the loved one. Even Cupid, the personification of love, cannot operate as strongly as the sight of the beloved.

Jason then does what Medea had not even imagined his doing, for in her daydreams, she was the aggressive, active person, not Jason. He takes her by the hand, asks her aid, and promises the bridal bed. He does not mention love. Indeed, since he comes to Medea suddenly, after having Aeëtes set forth the tests, Jason seems to have scouted out the situation, determined who was likeliest to give the kind of assistance needed, made up his mind to offer himself in return, and found the proper occasion. Hence, one may conclude that Jason is no romantic teenager, but a man on the lookout for the main chance.

Medea bursts into tears.

Hers is just the right reaction. Though Ovid does not analyze her tears, they flow from the release of the tension that she has suffered and because of the solution now provided her. But they are not tears of romance, gratitude, or amorousness. They come not only from release and relief, but also from a clear realization of the actual situation, and that is not all light and loveliness. Medea realizes that she is not in control of the situation, and this fact may hurt and shock her. She should be aware that for Jason, this marriage is one of convenience. She should see that he is not in love with her. She may even see that his dependence upon her makes him less a hero. In any event, Medea herself puts the worst interpretation on what she is about to do, not the best. She knows what she will do and, presumably, the damnable nature of those acts that she has just reproached herself for giving fair names to. She is ensnared not by ignorance, but by love. She says this clearly and concisely and matter-of-factly. She is remarkably levelheaded at this point, knowing that she is doing wrong and going ahead with it. The situation is tragic. It also has something of the nightmare about it because Medea sees herself doing things that she does not want to do and doing them because she has the wrong kind of control over her own actions, one dictated by that alien, love.

Tense once more, Medea is terse and practical. She tells Jason that she will preserve him and commands him to live up to his promises. Jason swears an oath so appropriate that he must know that Medea is a witch, for he invokes Hecate, goddess of black magic; the Colchian sun-god, from whom Medea inherited one portion of her fund of magic; and Jason's own success and dangers, which are partly dependent upon magic. Medea believes him and immediately makes Jason happy by giving him the proper protective herbs and instructions for their use. The fact that she has been prepared for just this occasion comes as a shock because it reveals the grim characteristics of her personality that have been latent: her calculation and her deep commitment to her course of action. In short, Medea is not simply a girl stricken by love.

Thus far in this book, Ovid has handled his narrative in a fashion peculiar to some operas, ballets, and musical comedies, those in which the librettos are rather sketchy in continuity or connectedness and in which the attention is directed toward the fine costumes, scenery, dancing, music, arias, duets, choruses, or moments of high emotion. Steps, in short, are omitted. For example, the reader is not told that Medea saw

Jason and wandered off to meditate on her reactions; he is left to infer these matters, just as he is left to decide why Medea was on her way to Hecate's altars. He is not prepared for Jason's appealing to Medea. Jason is simply on the right spot at the right time with a proposal prepared for the one person likely to give him aid for the obvious reasons. Medea's having the right herbs so readily available is surprising because it is unprepared for. Just how Jason and Medea first sized one another up so precisely with practically no contact is not explained. The effects of such omissions—and there are important ones later in her biography—are brevity, apparent disjointedness, novelty, indirectness, and a sense of intense focus on areas to which attention is not usually given. (To have a clearer idea of what Ovid is doing, one should compare the narrative techniques of the Medea story with those of the *Iliad*, wherein the events leading up to the wrath of Achilles are given and the consequences are traced in detail and any expansions of this plot line—divine intervention and the exploits of other heroes—are clearly relevant to the eminence of Achilles and to the results of his withdrawal from combat. The devices and continuity of the *Iliad* are full and normative. Those used by Ovid in telling Medea's story are not. To find a somewhat similar progression by use of thematic groupings, that is, by presenting juxtaposed passages, by omitting introductory and explanatory material, and by practically eliminating connective devices, one might turn to Ezra Pound's *Canto XIII*. There the modern poet constructs a portrait of the good man by presenting a collection of Confucius' acts and sayings. The major difference between the two biographical sketches is that Pound does not need narrative progression because Confucius is consistently admirable, whereas Ovid does, because Medea deteriorates.)

The next focus in the tale of Medea, true to the Ovidian principle that the reader is to be played with, is unexpectedly normative: Jason confronts his adversaries in the arena. Though everyone there sees his exploits, the reader knows that they are only partly his and that Medea provided the magic that made them possible. Among the spectators, the princess is now the helpless witness of events. She fears for Jason when he faces the sown warriors, for she is not certain that her charms to confer invulnerability will work. As a result, she sings a spell. But it is Jason who saves himself; he throws a stone that sets the warriors fighting among themselves. Medea is reduced to discreet inner rejoicing at his triumph. Public opinion forces her to remain a background figure, and Jason not only stars, but shows that he is not without intelligence and ability. (The whole episode suggests a Roman spectacle put on before a vast audience, with Medea a partisan in the stands.) Ovid further puts her in her place by referring to her as "barbarian." After the bold deeds in the arena, Jason's rendering the dragon powerless and returning home with his two prizes are trifles recounted with dignified brevity and with focus upon Jason.

Thus far, then, Medea has been presented as a nubile adolescent who has a conscience, which she has overcome, and unusual powers, which she has exercised to obtain her desires. She is desperately in love. She is also, deep within, calculating and determined. But at the outset of her career, she is relatively pure and inexperienced. Certainly she is not a hardened criminal. Hence, Ovid can trace her degeneration, as, centuries later, Defoe did that of Moll Flanders. To this downward progress Ovid now devotes his attention.

For the moment all goes well. The Thessalians celebrate the return of the heroes and bring gifts. Perhaps Medea receives the fame and recognition that she dreamed of, but since she is not named as the recipient of the gifts and since the context includes sacrifices to the gods, perhaps the gifts fulfill vows to the gods. Ovid leaves the matter to the reader's choice. Medea is not honored with the title that she expected, so perhaps she is merely a conspicuous part of a celebration that does not quite live up to her desires.

Jason's first concern in all the homecoming hubbub is his aged male parent. Medea is touched by Jason's pious tears for a father brought to the verge of death by old age and by his willingness to give some of his life for his parent, so that even with her very different sort of sensibility, she thinks of the father she abandoned. Ovid does not tell us what Medea thinks; once again the reader can decide for himself. It may be that she is in an expansive, sentimental mood and that, loving Jason so much, she imitates him. Such doting might prognosticate the reformation of Medea's character, and, indeed, her next act is a good deed.

Out of love, Medea undertakes the rejuvenation of Aeson, a complicated affair that falls into two parts. The first is a night ritual. It requires a particular night and time and dress, water sprinkling, and ululation. Certain deities are invoked. Then Medea lists her areas of expertise, among them weather magic, earthquakes, ghost-raising, eclipses, sun-dimming, poison, and counter-magic. She calls upon the powers invoked for something new, an elixir of rejuvenation, for which she needs magic transportation. It is provided in the form of a dragon car that enables Medea to travel through Greece, mostly Thessaly, gathering herbs that give long life. The itinerary makes Thessaly seem a most salubrious country. Even the winged dragons become younger from merely smelling the herbs that Medea collects.

Second come the rites of rejuvenation. The witch does not enter a house or engage in sexual intercourse. She builds a turf altar to Hecate and another to Youth, with ditches for the blood of a sacrificed black sheep. Wine, milk, and incantations follow. The youth-giving fluid is brewed from appropriate herbs and animal substances. The uninitiated are warned off. Then alone with a hypnotized Aeson on a bed of restorative herbs, Medea drains his aged blood and fills him with her concoction. Aeson awakens forty years younger.

Bacchus is so impressed by Medea's mixture that he requests some for his nurses. This is an Olympian compliment paid by a deity to a divinely descended personage of lesser stature. Since Dionysus is famous for his own beverage, the compliment is no mean one, and it functions in a number of ways. For one, the female confers a more precious gift than the male. Another point implied is that the Olympian is inferior to the mortal, for so Medea appears in Ovid's treatment of her. The Bacchus-Medea situation is a loose parallel of the Athena-Arachne one, the difference being that the god is perfectly willing to give credit where it is due. Medea is again shown, as with Jason, superior to the gods and the Fates in power; hence, hubris is again implied. She stands out as an individual beyond the restraints of nature and of the gods, a law unto herself. Ovid is also undercutting the power of Dionysus' wine to rejuvenate, the temporary illusion that Cadmus and Tiresias experience in Euripides' *Bacchae*. Further, Ovid here briefly anticipates the later uproar (in Book IX) among the gods concerning the rejuvenation of their favorites. Finally, Medea is clearly doing something constructive and receiving recognition for it.

Though the lady could now claim title to being the savior of the human race, she does not continue such beneficence. Success merely allows her to be vindictive. Having deceived her father, she decides to deceive both Jason and the daughters of Pelias, Jason's uncle and disinheritor. She engages in something like black magic, turns the rejuvenation process into a farce, and has Pelias's daughters commit the worst act of filial impiety, patricide, out of filial loyalty. Though the act is motivated by a desire for revenge or justice in some accounts of the myth, Ovid seems to attibute it to pure meanness and impulse, in short, to a desire to see what lengths Medea can get away with.

It is logical that, after causing the death of Pelias, Medea would be obliged to flee in the most expeditious way possible. But her taking an extended trip at this point has no logic at all. No one knows just how rapidly a winged-dragon car traveled, but by devoting forty lines (about ten percent) of the Medea story to the excursion, Ovid makes it seem lengthy. It is long enough for Jason to leave the locale of Aeson's restoration and move to Corinth.

Medea's journey itself is an epic catalog of places famous for various marvels, many of them metamorphoses. Its effect is to make Medea seem like a tourist. If she is satisfying her maiden desire to see Greek culture and civilization and great cities, she settles oddly for myth and for minor places, for the most part.

There can be no question, however, about the deterioration of Medea's character. She has become a powerful person who does not think ethically at all, for she schemes and acts on impulse, receiving gratification from deceit, the employment of magic, and touring the third rate. On her tour, she becomes something of a fantastic grotesque, for she is one myth looking at mementos of a lot of other myths.

Ovid covers Medea's stay in Corinth with such brevity that she seems to land, find Jason remarried, burn his new wife and the palace, kill her sons for revenge, and resume flight. Only mention of the children indicates that the interval between Medea's arrival in Corinth and her departure must have lasted several years. Ovid may rely here and elsewhere in the myth of Medea upon his readers' knowing details that he does not mention and thus their filling these in. But this assumption is shaky. It is a rather common phenomenon for myths to have variants. In folklore the differences may occur because of local interests and experience. When known writers, such as Aeschylus or Sophocles, used myth, they felt free to adapt myth to their artistic purposes. Even the *Odyssey* contains variants of the tale of Agamemnon's death. It may be assumed, then, that Ovid wanted his readers to note what he did in his telling of the Medea myth. One result of his rapid coverage of the stay in Corinth is the belittling of Medea's loyalty to Jason and the ignoring of their reduced circumstances and of their quarreling. Another result is clear focus on Medea as a vindictive murderess whose passions know no restraint and whose impiety, still characterizing her, reaches its nadir in her killing her own children.

There is another important effect of the way in which Ovid tells Medea's story: novelty. Ovid constantly throws his readers off balance. Book VI ends with Calais and Zetes joining the crew of the *Argo*, and the expectation is created that Book VII will tell of that glorious adventure. It does for a few lines, but disappointingly. Then the narrative concentrates upon Medea. Blocking out the major episodes thus far in her tale shows its eccentric nature: Medea's struggle with her love for Jason and her compact with him; Jason's day in the Colchian arena and Medea's responses to its events; Aeson's rejuvenation (Jason's request for it, Medea's long prayer, Medea's herb-gathering journey, the rituals and preparations for the cure, the cure itself); Medea's deception of the daughters of Pelias and his death; her subsequent flight, another tour, which brings her to Corinth. Medea's career in Corinth, as passionate and sensational as any part of her life, is not treated in detail, but merely ticked off. Ovid has not made Medea's history dull, but neither has he dwelled upon portions of it most obviously suitable for artistic use, especially if the writer wanted to handle strong emotions and sensational situations. In avoiding the obvious and exercising his ingenuity, Ovid has played games with his audience by showing it that he could disappoint its expectations, that he could find unexpected areas to develop, and that he could develop these in novel, engrossing, and spectacular ways.

As noted above, Ovid is further disconcerting in that he does not always flesh in parts of his narrative where material is needed. As additional examples, there is no reason for the extent of Medea's flight from Iolcus; Medea never explains to Jason the reason for her pretended break with him; the reasons for Jason's marrying another woman are not stated. All of these matters seem to require explanation and need to be fitted into Ovid's perception of Medea's life. That they are not causes unnecessary irritation to and confusion of the reader. Ovid has, on the other hand, given the reader the necessary major information needed to convey Ovid's assessment of Medea. The total effect, then, is one of reader gratification and frustration, of completeness and incompleteness. In short, Ovid is playing games with his audience.

Even in the Corinth passage another sort of distraction occurs. I have referred to it elsewhere as clutter. When Ovid has Medea land at Corinth, he interrupts her activities with an apparently pointless observation that seems a bad joke, a gibe at superstition, or an interesting bit of folklore: "Here, according to ancient tradition, in the earliest times men's bodies sprang from mushrooms." Since mushrooms were known to be both delicious and dangerous—Pliny regards eating them as risky because they are poisonous—the association of mushrooms with Corinth and with Medea, who will soom be using poison, is not unfunctional or inappropriate—both are delightful and dangerous in their own ways—but the relevance of the remark is tantalizingly obscure and also superfluous.

(As additional distractions, Ovid earlier inserted at least two inconsistencies. Professor Anderson has pointed out that it is paradoxical to have each daughter of Pelias doing her father good by shedding his blood. The passage is also logically inconsistent, for it runs thus: "as each [daughter] was filial she became first in the unfilial act." Since only one of the sisters could be first, the statement is an amusing illogicality. It is, in addition, apparently inconsistent with tradition to have Medea poison Theseus' cup with aconite brought from Scythia, presumably picked up on the return voyage of the *Argo*, since aconite grew from the foam Cerberus spewed on upper earth when Hercules dragged him up as his twelfth and last labor. But Hercules joined the *Argo* after his third labor, and, though he did not stay long with the crew, Hercules' remaining labors seem to have taken longer than the voyage of the famous ship. Hence, it seems unlikely that the aconite would have been growing on Scythian shores when Medea coasted by.)

After arson and murder in Corinth, Medea once again has to use her serpent chariot to flee. She soars to Athens, which has known fliers of greater purity—Phene, Periphas, and Alcyone—so that its citizens need not always be afraid of fliers. Aegeus, blameless except in this, receives her. Worse, he marries her. In return, Medea, whose son by Aegeus is not mentioned and who, therefore, has no ostensible motive for her crime, tries to dupe Aegeus into poisoning his son, Theseus. Had the crime occurred, it would have been a violation of the host-guest relationship and the impious murder of an offspring, hence, doubly heinous. As with the daughters of Pelias, Medea, who is not reluctant to commit crimes herself, vilely wishes to degrade others to her level. Fortunately, Aegeus identifies his son in time. Medea is not all powerful. Yet she escapes death by conjuring up clouds that carry her off. She leaves the scene once and for all. No one regrets her departure.

As female hero, Medea is the inverted equivalent of Perseus. She is the feminine killer par excellence, but unlike Perseus, she is underhanded, deceitful, and spiteful. Through her, Ovid seems to indicate that to pervert nature is evil, that evil is unstable, and that it, therefore, destroys itself, driving itself from the civilized human scene. Ironically, either Athens or Corinth should have been the cultural epitome and zenith of Medea's earlier dreams, but her impulses and abuse of power ruined her chances for life in either city. As for Jason, whose dependence on Medea Ovid has him freely admit, he is largely a beautiful prop.

Aegeus is very happy to have his only son with him at last, but he is also appalled that he almost murdered the youth. Pure joy he does not experience. However, he is mostly happy and gives gifts to the gods and offers sacrifices, which are accompanied by the usual public feasting, merriment, and song. The song celebrates the exploits of the young Theseus by cataloging them. The list is impressive, presenting Theseus largely as benefactor and peace-bringer. Even though it is an epic catalog, it is merely a list, and it is about as much fame as Ovid will allow this Athenian prince and major Greek hero.

At this point, in an aside, Ovid produces the sententia that seems to provide the point of the whole book: "so true it is that there is no pleasure unalloyed, and some care always comes to mar our joys." Considering the whole of Book VII, one sees that when Medea was happiest, she also realized that she was evil and dishonored. While rejoicing at the recovery of his son, Aegeus must face a war. Minos, that strong king, cannot enjoy his strength; he must avenge his son and face rejection by some whose aid he seeks. Aeacus, of many warriors king, bears the sorrow of loss of friends and subjects through a vindictive plague. Cephalus, charming and beautiful, will always be saddened by his accidentally killing his wife. There is no pure joy.

But there is a sufficiency of epic catalogs in Book VII, and now Ovid adds one more, that of the realms Minos visits in his search for military aid. Minos at the moment is a thematic and a transitional device, but he seems very real as he scours the Aegean for allies, sailing to Anaphe, Astypalaea, Myconus, Cimolus, Syros, Seriphos, Paros, and Siphnos and getting aid there and going to Oliaros, Didymae, Tenos, Andros, Gyaros, Peparethos, and Aegina and failing in these places. In the process Ovid gives us the sense that populations in the eastern Mediterranean have vastly increased since the times of Daphne, Deucalion, Io, and Cadmus; that warfare has developed more; and that life is generally more complicated. The list ends, of course, with the place in which the next two tales are told, Aegina. Here Ovid meets reader expectation. In Aegina the good king and staunch ally of Athens turns down Minos' request, is not moved by Minos' threat, and openly receives Cephalus, the Athenian emissary.

In the real world, treaty nations have business to talk over, and so it happens here. Cephalus asks for troops and pertinently opines that Minos' real motive is to gain control of all Greece. Aeacus gladly pledges the troops requested, having plenty of men for both Athens and Aegina. Cephalus congratulates him, but adds that he misses old, familiar faces, and thus he mars Aeacus' joy by recalling the plague that decimated his people.

Angered by Jove's affair with Aegina and by Aeacus' naming his island kingdom after his mother, Juno afflicted the island with pestilence. Aeacus tells the whole gruesome story, complete with causes and the ghastly results, for some ninety odd lines. Mr. Anderson finds the account so overdone that it is "spectacularly amusing," but "exercises no hold on the audience's emotions." Less discriminating readers, one suspects, may find the narrative of the plague appallingly real and moving. Whichever is the effect upon the reader, Juno further loses respect, for she is seen now not as just the bane of this nymph or that princess, but as the scourge of a whole nation. And Ovid has added a new kind of sensationalism to his masterpiece. He also returns to an earlier motif found in the Flood of Book I: the miscarriage of divine justice. Here, as there, his major point about a disaster wrought by a god to right a wrong seems to be that when the gods are excessive or undiscriminating in their punishments, they are unjust and subvert piety.

It is easy to give credence to the plague, but it is difficult to accept the idea that Jove replenished the population of Aegina with men metamorphosed from ants. This bit of folk fantasy explains the name of a people and their characteristics by means of a bit of folk etymology. They are Myrmidons because they, like their name, came from the *myrmex*, Greek for "ant"; hence, they are hard-working, hard-fisted, hardy. Psychologically, however, one accepts the happy ending. The ending of the next tale is just the reverse.

The successful, handsome, and charming Athenian diplomat tells a story revealing that he, too, has past experience that makes present happiness bittersweet. There are several things of a general nature that one should note about his narrative. One is that its subject is that of the Tereus-Procne-Philomela myth: love after marriage, complicated by the presence of the other woman. Two, this story, however, is a romance, but a relatively unusual subtype, because ordinary romances tend to deal with the period before marriage, the problems of the young lovers, and the obstacles to their union, marriage solving all. Like Jove, Ovid knows that after marriage the difficulties continue; therefore, so can romance. In marriage, the titilating problem is to keep the union intact or at least functioning and to introduce uncertainty, variety, suspense, amorous conflict, and excitement into a stable relationship usually of a more moderate and even pace than courtship or amorous pursuit. Romance is not romance without obstacles or blight; continuous pure happiness is unthinkable because of the itch for something new and different. Such are the implications of married romance.

Third, Cephalus is not Tereus. He is not to be inflamed by some sweetly flowing dryad, for he regards his wife as the Athenian beauty of the age. Since Ovid has presented Cephalus as the beau ideal of Athenian nobility, since he and his wife are bound in mutual love, and since wealth and social position do not lure them beyond their condition, their marriage seems impregnable.

Fourth, Mr. Brooks Otis has an excellent commentary on the marriage: the relationship is that of mutual true love lasting as long as life, but also self-destructive because it leads to jealousy and suspicion, marital separation, and finally Procris' death. To this Mr. William Anderson adds that Cephalus' account is a delicate retelling of the story handled more lewdly by Apollodorus, Hyginus, and Antoninus Liberalis. Ovid keeps the crudeness in the background for the knowing reader to fill in, but Cephalus' reticence shows his refined feelings and his loving concern that Procris be seen in the best light.

Both views are valuable. It should be added that Cephalus still loves Procris after her death and treasures her memory. Further, he is, if looked at in a certain way—and that is the way many Romans might have looked at him—elegantly comic, not everywhere and always, but on notable occasions. For one thing, he is uxorious. For another, though ostensibly or avowedly faithful to his wife, he has a very strong sensual and erotic streak. In his imagination Procris is the focus of most of this, but it comes out in his amorous address to the breeze. His marked sensuality makes one think that he might be unfaithful and is one of the foibles that make the comedy.

The organizing principle of the Cephalus-Procris story is the ambiguity or ambivalence of love, for it is an emotion that may entail possessiveness, suspicion, jealousy, and inconstancy of object, as well as devotion, affection, and fond passion. Built into the story are other ambiguities. Because Cephalus is reticent, the reader does not know just how far Aurora's rape of Cephalus progressed or how long he remained with the goddess. If he stayed with her for a short time, perhaps there was no sexual relationship. But if he stayed away long enough to have someone try to seduce Procris, then Aurora was probably being gratified by him and that not through conversation. If he did bed down with Aurora —and his reference to his own "deserted bed" may imply that he had—then he would have another reason to suspect Procris, and, of course, he does suspect her. Whichever is the case, Cephalus may be burnishing his own image by being reticent. Cephalus interprets Aurora's angry prophecy— that he will regret his relationship with Procris—as a prediction of her infidelity, but the prophecy itself is ambiguous and turns out not to mean what Cephalus thinks it means. There is a further ambiguity in the story in that Cephalus's life is not single valued: Cephalus desires to be with Procris, but he does not wish to be with her all the time, for he has another desire. He wants to hunt. Even hunting is ambiguous. Hunting imagery has appeared repeatedly in the *Metamorphoses* as a metaphor for erotic pursuit. Literally, hunting is an appropriate male activity after marriage, for it provides manly exercise and excitement and may replace amorous pursuit. But in a myth context it may not be limited to bagging animals, for the woods can be full of attractive nymphs and, hence, may be a place of erotic adventure. And so it turns out for Cephalus—with a difference: the beautiful and erotic male, comically, becomes the prey of a goddess and is raped.

These or similar ambiguities can and do cause tension in married life. A loving wife who does not mind her husband's hunting and does not nag, can, by her very forbearance make a true and loving husband feel guilty. A guilty person may suspect another of his crime on no grounds whatsoever. In other words, the cause of tension may itself be ambiguous.

In the end, Cephalus causes Procris to be suspicious of his fidelity by using ambiguous language while hunting. Like a lover, he calls upon the breeze, or *aura*, to come to his bosom and gratify him. Since *aura* can also be a woman's name, one suggestively close to *Aurora*, and since his language is open to erotic interpretation, Procris spies upon her husband once she is told of his invocation. In her leafy hiding place, she observes her spouse and inadvertently moves. Thinking that the rustling bushes conceal a quarry, Cephalus responds to the ambiguous sign, throws his unerring spear, and mortally wounds his wife. Only their true love removes the misunderstanding, but it operates too late to save Procris. Thus ends the comi-tragedy.

The whole episode is full of humorous touches. They begin with Cephalus' explaining to Phocus why Cephalus wept when asked about his beautiful javelin. The tears and their cause are not comic, but Cephalus addresses his explanation to Phocus by calling him " 'nate dea' " (" 'goddess born' "), which is perfectly true, for Phocus is the son of sea-nymph Psamathe. But the phrase is also slightly ridiculous courtly hyperbole, because both Phocus and Psamathe are small fry. The comic results because the situation lacks the grandeur requisite for the honorific phrase. This lack is intensified because *"nate dea"* resounds through the *Aeneid,* where Virgil applies it to Aeneas, son of Venus, founder of the Julian line and venerated ancestor of the Romans. Ovid's Roman audience would be likely to recognize this echo. Such recognition in turn intensifies the marked insignificance of Phocus and also calls into question the taste and integrity of Cephalus because he overdoes his courtly flattery. (Incidentally, Virgil is thus put into the company of a maladroit courtier.)

There is something unintentionally humorous about a tearful Cephalus' insisting to young Phocus that, really, of the sisters Orithyia and Procris, the latter was the one worthy of rape. Even if the *raptus* were only a kidnapping by a rough deity, it was still violence done to person and feelings. And if Boreas, by implication, had poor taste in preferring Orithyia, Cephalus has uttered a tasteless brag.

There is humor in a man's being raped, because men are supposed to be aggressive and women, modest. Even more ridiculous is Cephalus' protesting his love for Procris while perhaps being physically loved by Aurora. In any event, Cephalus prattles about Procris uncontrollably and incessantly while in the clutches of Aurora, retailing especially the joys of love with Procris and of their wedding night. About these lines (709-710) Mr. Anderson is more delicate than Cephalus, for Mr. Anderson says that the list has "to do with the marriage bed" and is Ovid's "delicate way" of indicating that Cephalus did not have sexual relations with the goddess. Starting with line 707, the Latin indicates something like this (Cephalus is telling Phocus of his stay with Aurora): " 'I was loving Procris: / Procris was on my mind, "Procris" always on my lips. / The secrets of the bridal-bed and new sexual unions and fresh bridal-beds / and the first compacts of the deserted bed I kept recounting.' " The only thing delicate about these lines is that Cephalus does not here go into erotic detail, but he apparently did for Aurora. The passage indicates a broad, earthy, and indelicate babbling on the part of Cephalus that is part of a restrained but clearly suggestive humor on Ovid's part. (There is, incidentally, a terra-cotta relief in the collection of the British Museum of Eos "carrying off Kephalos." In it a fifth-century Greek seems to have caught the humor of a huge rather tense-looking Aurora's carting away a stiff and expostu-lating Cephalus the size of a large doll.)

Another delightful touch on Ovid's part is the fact that Cephalus himself has no sense of humor.

Cephalus' silliness—he sounds almost frightened when in Aurora's clutches—makes him such a bore that the goddess releases him, telling him that he will regret having had Procris. This is the prophecy of an angry goddess and a hint that she will have her revenge; hence, when Cephalus brings about his wife's death by using a name so close to the goddess', one almost feels that she has been functioning sinisterly behind the scene. At this earlier point in the tale, however, Cephalus's thinking about Aurora's words leads him to suspect his wife's fidelity. He weighs the pros and cons, thinks of Aurora's own inconstancy, excuses himself on the grounds that all lovers are suspicious, and blames Aurora for encour-aging his fears and disguising him. He then proceeds to test Procris, though there is nothing at home to make him suspicious. The testing leads to a rupture; Procris is justifiably hurt and runs away. Now she goes hunting with Diana and her entourage, a haven probable only in myth.

The breach is healed after a suitable passage of time and appro-priate apologies by Cephalus. Years of married bliss follow. Though her return was gift enough for her spouse, Procris gave her sportsman the unerring javelin admired by Phocus and a hound that could catch anything, sure signs that Cephalus has Procris's permission to hunt once more.

There is a story about that hound. Cephalus tells it for his listeners to marvel at. He gives no sign of understanding it.

Once when Thebes was afflicted with a terrifying beast of unspecified species, the youths about decided to hunt it down, but it proved uncatchable, so Cephalus unleashed the hound that could catch anything. The result was a stalemate, an unsolvable problem: the beast could not get away; the dog could not catch the beast. What Ovid has done here, of course, is to present his readers with a dramatized logical fallacy, that of contradictory premises. The familiar from of this fallacy is to assume that there is an immovable object and then assume that one can logically postulate its opposite, the irresistible force, and, having made incompatible assumptions, then ask, what happens when the two meet? The logical answer is, nothing. Ovid's answer is, art. It takes a god to solve the problem, but the solution is the marble statues of beast and hound frozen forever on the verge of catching and being caught.

Just as Ovid created an emblem with Europa on the back of the bull, so he has made another here. This one, in contrast, is open-ended. Ovid does not say what his emblem means, but ideas cluster about it like seeds atop a dandelion stem. Since the statuary was brought about by metamorphosis, one may assume that Ovid is saying that art is metamorphic and is giving readers another function of metamorphosis. Ovid may be indicating that art preserves the memorable but transitory in an enduring form; that it is a divine power that enables the artist to effect such metamorphosis; that art imitates nature; that logical fallacies appear in actual life; that there are eternal principles, such as predatoriness; that man, represented by Cephalus, exists in and witnesses patterns he does not understand; that life is neither victory nor defeat, but pursuit; that life results from the simultaneous co-existence of opposing forces. The statues may emblemize Cephalus marriage: the partners possess one another and at the same time do not. Barbara Knowlton, a student, suggested that the pair of animals symbolizes marriage as the chase, the freezing of it, and the memorializing of it. Another suggestion is that the marble animals indicate that the pursuit must go on in order to keep the excitement of courtship operating within the stability of marriage. The point is not that any of the preceding interpretations must obtain the reader's agreement, but that the statuary is a device with which Ovid confronts the reader and which he uses to involve the reader in the material by teasing him into thought or speculation. It is one of the means that Ovid uses to make his poem a game in which reader pursues writer. It also has a very modern effect, for the open-ended image is what Ezra Pound called the "vortex," the luminous image that draws ideas into it and spews them out full of its force.

In the Procris myth, hunting is not used as erotic metaphor, but in a fashion closer to that of the Actaeon myth. Although it is a suitable aristocratic way for Cephalus to have variety and male excitement away from the city, social life, and wife and although it is a way of life that protects Procris from mean men, it takes both to the wild, uncultivated countryside, to the uncivilized and un-marital, and to killing. As in the Actaeon episode and in the later Pythagorean injunction against killing animals, Ovid here again gives evidence that hunting causes harm because it is wrong. With Cephalus and Procris, it represents the dark side of their personalities, showing them both as hunters and hurters, as well as lovers, and of this combination the magic javelin of phallic shape—the love gift, the hunting weapon, the cause of the death of the loved one, the desired but deadly weapon—is the symbol.

Equally deadly in the story is the gossip, who parallels the earlier raven and crow, except that this tattler is never punished because its identity is unkown. The informer seems more sinister and reprehensible because anonymous.

The whole tale is a sequence of ironies, the last of which is that Procris dies content, and of repetitions of earlier motifs, the last of which is that Cephalus remains her grieving love, a breathing Niobe. Of course, the parallel is inexact, for he possesses Procris in the ultimate fashion, through the honeying cells of memory, the mother of the Muses. But it is Ovid who has fixed her so that time touches her not, nor Cephalus, and both lovers transcend their foolishness.

This story is better than melodrama or soap opera, though it is a forerunner of both. It ends Book VII neatly by balancing the absorbing, self-centered immoral destructiveness of passionate Medea with the pathetic, less damnably destructive but too intense mutual love of an all-too-human prince and princess. The book allows for an abundance of moralizing, which any reader can do on his own. Perhaps it is enough to remember that the world does not match the wishes of Medea or Procris or anyone. There is no perfect joy.

But private life and public service need not match. Cephalus, at the very end of the book, successfully completes his mission for Athens. Apparently treaties can provide surer bonds than love can.

METAMORPHOSES VIII: Problems in Piety

The daystar, day, and a favoring wind allow Cephalus and his Aeginetan auxiliaries to waft safely to a war-threatened Athens only so that the narrative may move to neighboring war-torn Megara and siege. Appropriately, the little epic about this heroic action begins *in medias res* and on a low note. Coastal Megara has been devastated, but the five-month siege of its capital is a stalemate.

The action begins with a young princess much in love with her father's antagonist. The basic situation recalls that of Medea and almost compels comparison of the princesses. Both say, with Milton's Satan, "Evil be thou my Good." Aside from these similarities, they are very different young ladies. Medea towers over Scylla, who is limited, silly, and slightly crazy in that her grasp on reality is faulty and she lacks restraint. Medea can sustain a line of reasoning and foresee the possible consequences of a line of action; Scylla cannot. Medea makes a longish, noble effort to fight off her emotions; Scylla does not. Medea has super-natural powers that Scylla lacks. And initially she is not as deluded as Scylla is. Medea also has an occupation or profession to occupy her. Scylla's father has a little magic that guarantees his life and rule and the safety of his kingdom, namely, his lock of purple hair. Medea's father had a much larger inventory of magical items and a daughter proficient in the occult, to boot.

Medea falls in love with a man about her own age, one she has had a fairly close look at. Scylla becomes enamored of a man almost old enough to be her father. She has seen him only from a distance. Hence, Scylla is more lured by romantic aura and superficial sensation than Medea, by the gold and purple, the white horse, plumed helmet, handsome face, and white tents. She is moved by the enchantment that distance lends, for she has no firsthand knowledge of the object of her passion, whereas Medea does. At such a remove, Scylla does not think of first making a pact with her hero; Medea does. Medea is intelligent in other ways and offers some thoughtful resistance to love. She has some tender family feelings and knows her father and her culture. In contrast, Scylla sees her father only as an impediment to fulfilling her desire; he is a man with a purple lock of hair and the keys to the city gates. To her, he is neither barbaric or affectionate, but distant. He is more of an obstacle than a person. In contrast, Medea has a brother and sister to think of and is aware of the men of her nation as possible love objects. Scylla has no siblings or close friends. She is not even aware of the men of Megara. Ovid presents her as an isolated romantic in her lonely tower. As a child she went to the tower, elevated above the common scene and secluded, and dropped pebbles on the city walls to call forth the music haunting them. A solitary pastime: the drop of the pebble and then the lovely rising sound. Then the next small stone. The desire and the satisfaction all within her grasp. Almost no effort required, no other person involved. The child controlled the music of the god. And now from this favorite eyrie, her psychic space, Scylla has for five months viewed the inexorable struggles of war as glamorous. Her romanticism and subjectivity have remained with her, but they have a new and more exciting subject: war, its panoply, its strange leaders to identify, its hazards, its blood and hard duels, and all the excitement of danger and men. It is all her own private gladiatorial display, more exciting because of the high stakes of the spectators. But Scylla's attention is turned away from her own kind, and she concentrates on and identifies with the invaders.

And so she participates as best she can. She falls in love with her vision of Minos and longs to make her his. For her, happiness is being Minos' possession, is being handled by him. And when she sees him riding his white horse, she almost goes out of her mind because of sexual excitement and resembles Shakespeare's Cleopatra yearning to be Antony's horse. Then Scylla dreams of being a peaceful solution to the war by becoming his hostage. But her vision of being a hostage comes to include a dramatic sudden appearance before Minos, a confession of her love, and Minos' wanting a marriage portion from her. Thus in visualizing the situation, she shifts her relationship from that of hostage to that of bride and bridal bed. She is, however, able to see that she may be asked to betray her city. (Is this possible after she has left it?) Here she draws the line. Two minutes later she withdraws it and all other restrictions. Filial piety goes out on the grounds that everything is within the power of the person willing to act, or, as Scylla says, aphoristically, " 'But surely everyone is his own god.' " In other words, prayers, wishing, and willing are inadequate; people make their hearts' desires happen.

Scylla does, at any rate. Having committed in thought the religious impiety of hubris, of rejecting the gods and their wills, she moves on to filial impiety. That night while others sleep, she in effect stealthily kills her father by removing his talismanic lock and thus his safety and well-being and the protection of the city. She takes the hair to Minos. He is terrified. After all, he is suddenly confronted by a keyed-up Megarian woman with a lock of purple hair in her hand, and he probably knows, via military intelligence and common report, who his foes are and what the lady and the lock signify. Either that, or he is relatively easily spooked.

Scylla is short and direct: Love impelled the act; she, Scylla, royal offshoot of Nisus, gives him her country and family; she wants no reward except him (a modest proposal); as proof of her love, he is to take the purple lock and to think of it not as her father's hair, but his head. Well, this is one way to make love, but it is one-sided and a bit crazy. This approach might appeal to a criminal or to a warped personality, but it gets nowhere with an international politician and power figure who is having problems with an unfaithful wife of peculiar sexual preferences. Who would want to marry a confessed Lizzie Borden? Besides, Minos, later judge of the dead for their misdeeds, shows his firm grasp of what is right and denies the validity of love as the excuse for crime and crime as the basis for reward. His sentence of Scylla makes perfect sense: she should be forbidden place on land or sea. He asks the gods to effect this prohibition, but he does, too, by refusing to take her across the sea to Crete.

Though Minos rejects the magic lock and the impiety that brought it to him, he does not fail to take over the city made indefensible by the loss of this amulet and to that degree put into his hands by the patricidal daughter. His action is realistic, but reality has put Minos in an awkward position with regard to piety. It is not only niggardly of a hero to gain a victory by such means; it sullies his hands. Even though he did not directly instigate Scylla's impiety, he accepts the resulting benefits, and his own piety becomes ambiguous. About victory won in this manner, there is no doubt. It puts Minos in the same class as Jason, that of hero-dependent-upon-woman, and lowers him in one's esteem. Minos is thus doubly betrayed by reality.

Scylla, as mentioned, does not have Medea's magic to support her in her need, and thus she lacks one important ability that made Medea interesting and effective. There is not much to be said for a silly little criminal whose claims on the readers' sympathies are solitariness, romantic delusions, and an inability to see any viewpoint save her own. When Minos prepares to sail, Scylla raves. As she does, she ironically indicates that she no longer has a fatherland and stresses the criminal nature of her behavior. She also reveals that she had suppressed her knowledge that Minos' wife was guilty of infidelity with a beast, for she brings it out now to shame and wound Minos. This merely means that she knew the fact before, and it was equally to Minos' discredit when Scylla loved him so distractedly. She also denigrates Minos' paternity and his character. There is more nastiness to Scylla: she knew all along that there was a wife that she would have to supplant. Nevertheless, some power watches her family: Nisus is changed into a fish hawk; Scylla's prayer that he punish her is almost granted; and she herself is changed into a bird, which seems more than she deserves, even though the gods have answered Minos' prayer concerning her punishment.

The next thirty-one lines effect a transition to the famous story of Daedalus and Icarus by sketching further the careers of Minos and Theseus. Minos is successful in his war against Megara and pious in keeping his vows to Jove. He proudly displays his trophies. But his domestic shame is displayed by his wife's monstrous bull-child, whom he tries to hide away in a maze. And another domestic blow, the loss of his own son, makes him cruel. For he sacrifices Athenians in a cannibalistic fashion to his wife's bestial son. As if this were not enough, his own daughter betrays him to Theseus, who kills the Minotaur and ravishes the princess. Minos is the victim of the disloyalty of two of his women and is thwarted by the bull lover of one and the Athenian lover of the other. Though Minos has fought a just war to avenge his son's death and given just laws to the conquered Megarians, he has been inflicted with horrors that he could not avoid and with some that he has created himself. Minos is great, but not enviable.

Nor is Theseus, the young hero who saves the Athenians from further sacrifice to the Cretan monster. He is successful, like Jason and Minos, because of the aid of a maiden. Yet it is sad that Ariadne should become for her father what Scylla was for hers, for Theseus, having used Ariadne, carries her off and then abandons her. The skeletal coverage of this part of Theseus' career makes him contemptible. Ariadne, however, receives divine attention.

The Cretan princess is embraced by the ancient Italian fertility god Liber and aided by him. To these honors Liber adds an everlasting memorial to Ariadne; he sends her crown off into the heavens to become a constellation. Also to her credit, she is instrumental (by means of her thread) in ending her father's savagery. That she was the means of revealing something disgraceful about Theseus may be to her discredit as well as his, for he abandoned her. That he ravished her was dishonorable of him, an injury to her because he did not love her. In this matter Ariadne is pitiable. But Theseus' carrying her off was probably her reward for aiding him, which she could not do without being disloyal to her father. She is certainly not all bad, but her position is not entirely that of a disinterested, unselfish humanitarian, nor is it without taint of filial impiety. It is, like much else in this book, ambiguous.

What stands out thus far in Book VIII is that kings, queens, heroes, and heroines are neither all good nor all bad. But they are interesting.

Having introduced Daedalus earlier as the designer and building of the monster's hiding place, Ovid has no trouble at all in returning to him, though he could have pursued the fortunes of Theseus and developed his next episode from that material. Daedalus is an unhappy man on three counts: he is in exile, presumably for murdering his nephew, an incident covered later; he longs for home; and he does not like Crete, but Minos will not let him leave. Although Ovid does not mention the fact, two young people have recently solved his best puzzle and thwarted his ingenuity, another reason for discontent. He says with heavy sarcasm: Minos may control everything (you and I know that is not true); he does not control the air. Then Daedalus makes wings so that man may become bird, and to do so, he turns his mind to unknown skills. *Arts* sounds more grand, but Daedalus is the backyard craftsman and inventor or, if you will, the precursor of Leonardo da Vinci. He is unusual in the corpus of myth, and he is in his own way more exciting than some of the heroes, deities, and heroines that we have been reading about.

Ovid now stops to pay homage to male inventiveness and painstaking work by describing the building of a wing and young Icarus' playing about the shop and hindering the work. Icarus is not the stuff of which inventors or craftsmen are made. The realism is not too detailed, but it is sufficient. Ovid builds it up by including flight and navigational instructions and by having Daedalus test his apparatus. While outfitting Icarus, Daedalus is overcome with concern for his son; he cries, his hands tremble, he kisses the boy. Then he mothers his fledgling into flight and fearfully gives him instruction and encouragement. Daedalus has done everything right, and the two wing softly off. Simple country men of lesser skills see the two and think that they must be gods.

All would have gone well if Icarus were not as unthinking as he had been back in the shop. He simply forgets the orders about altitude and following father, and carried away by the joy of flying, he soars too high and loses his wings. The drowning of the thoughtless boy leaves old Daedalus childless and grieving. Unfortunately, the son was not of his parent's caliber. The articifer is faced with building a tomb and burying his beloved son.

At this point Ovid brings in the reason for Daedalus' exile and the significance of his misfortunes: he has betrayed his family and his craft. This is the import of the joy of the partridge over the burial of Icarus and the sorrow of Daedalus. For this bird was not long ago Daedalus' inventive nephew. He devised the saw and compass, for which Daedalus envied him so much that he threw the twelve-year-old genius off the Acropolis. Minerva showed what she thought of the murderous intent and whom she supported by changing the lad into a bird that avoids heights. The addition of this aetiological myth shows Daedalus in a new light. He is not just the exploited and oppressed genius and loving father. He is also the envious craftsman so jealous of his own gifts and so doting upon his natural son that he denies both the kinship of the youth most like himself and their mutual devotion to their goddess. As a result, he kills his intellectual son and mourns a foolish child. He should have properly honored kinship through both blood and brains, but not doing so, he fails both where he hates and where he loves. He is also guilty of familial impiety in trying to kill his nephew, and by offending a patron deity of craftsmen, he is guilty of impiety toward that goddess.

Despite his remarkable achievements, Daedalus is as flawed a personality as Scylla, Minos, Jason, or Theseus. He ends his career, as far as Ovid is willing to trace it, being protected by a minor king, Cocalus of Aetna. Cocalus used military force to prevent Minos from repossessing Daedalus and, says Ovid, therefore is considered most kind. But the implication seems to be that Daedalus has become the valuable property of another monarch. His homeland is as far away as before.

Now Ovid does continue with Theseus, who is getting full credit for freeing the Athenians from sending human sacrifices to the Minotaur. There is much rejoicing in Athens with appropriate sacrifices. Indeed, Theseus gets Pan-Hellenic recognition as a troubleshooter. Ariadne gets not a single kind word. But Ovid is about to give her compensation as he seduces his readers into thinking that Theseus will loom large in the next thrilling episode, that of the Calydonian boar hunt. After all, as Ovid has points out in Book VII, Theseus had killed the troublesome sow of Cromyon.

Impiety has brought the vengeance of Diana upon King Oeneus and his people because they did not sacrifice to the goddess of wild animals at harvest time. In return, Diana has fixed them up with a wild boar of epic dimensions and meanness. This brute has spent spring, summer, and early autumn knocking down the grain, the grapes, and the green olives and killing the cattle. Ordinary men and dogs cannot cope with it. But the boar has to be stopped. Although Calydon has the hero Meleager, Ovid notes, Calydon sent for Theseus' aid, as well as that of all other available heroes, apparently, for the epic catalog of the assembled hunters reads a bit like a peerage of the generation before the Trojan War. And last, but not least, comes, in Mr. Anderson's words, the "glory of Mt. Lycaeus," Arcadian Atalanta. Meleager falls for this tomboy immediately, saying somewhat dramatically, " 'O happy any man this lady will think good enough.' " That is as much as he can say and remain manly and get the epic effort on its way. The heroic and the amorous are incompatible pursuits and different languages.

The Calydonian boar himself is presented with borderline realism, for he is neither a brazen bull nor Cadmus' serpent. He is too big to be normal, with his elephant-length tusks, and his grass-withering breath is too hot, but these details may be the rhetoric of overexaggeration. The thunderbolt issuing from his mouth is surreal, the rhetoric of fear. His native habitat is described in realistic detail—only slightly overdone—so that one can understand the difficulty of hunting in this tangled marshy wildness in or opening out from the dense wood. The hunt itself is also realistic and, better, exciting and varied, for the beast is no mean adversary, killing an untold number of dogs, laying low five heroes, and making Nestor vault into a tree. Atalanta gives the boar a superficial wound, something none of the heroes is able to do. Then Meleager wounds it badly with one spear and gets in close for the death thrust with another.

By and large, as Mr. Anderson points out, the heroes do not do very well. Sometimes they are comic. Blustering, Diana-defying Ancaeus has his blood and guts spilled over the ground when he foolishly tries to stop the boar with an axe. He is not comic, but stupid, arrogant, and impious. Eupalamus and Pelagon, laid low on the far right, are too young, hence, pathetic. Enaesimus panics before being hamstrung and, presumably, killed. Still no comedy. But when Nestor pole vaults into a tree to escape, Telamon trips while running after the retreating boar and goes flat on his face, Echion slightly wounds a maple tree, Jason throws too hard and misses, the whole group throw at once and their spears jar each other off target, and Jason hits a dog—or, according to Mr. Anderson, his companion Celadon—instead of the horrible swine, the reader has the sense of watching a flock of heroic incompetents spoof the heroic.

Theseus, whom the reader is led to believe is the star of the group, throws a well-aimed spear that is deflected by an oak branch. (Could it, then, have been well aimed?) His other act, an act of love, is to warn Pirithoüs to be prudent and not to close in. His speech reveals his strong affection for his friend, but it qualifies his manly virtue; that is, it raises the question whether he or Pirithoüs is brave enough to kill the boar because each is so much concerned for their relationship and, therefore, with safety. Thus Ariadne's passive revenge is complete: Theseus is not much of a man, either as heterosexual lover or as hero. Fame may have puffed his deeds in the Isthmus and in Crete, but when we actually see him in action and are not given a kind of *res gestae* coverage of his deeds, he is a background figure.

He is one of a crowd who were, in effect, not needed. Meleager was enough to do the job. Calydon had repeated the initial error of ignoring Diana by ignoring its local hero, and thus it created the situation containing the seeds of his destruction. For had there been no call on the heroes of Greece, there would have been no female hero Atlanta on the scene, no unsuitable love at first sight for Meleager, no jealousy over the division of the spoils, and no fatal brawl. Such are the ironies of the situation, one of which is that Atalanta, who bears no heavy weapon, has more manliness than most of the men.

Though the other heroes are delighted with Meleager's kill and congratulate him, they are still slightly afraid of the huge dead animal, a bit comic on their part. Yet they dip their spears in the boar's blood, an act which seems to mark or validate their part in the hunt and perhaps confers honor upon them. They do not, however, share Meleager's admiration of Atalanta's bravery. For when he gives her the trophies of the hunt, the boar's head and hide that he claims as rightfully his, they protest. His maternal uncles say that he is smitten by love and take away his gift, which was, indeed, making Atalanta look upon him favorably. Meleager, enraged, impiously kills his uncles at once.

At this point Ovid leaves the hunt scene for significant continuation of the action elsewhere, namely, Calydon, where Meleager's mother was taking the gods thank offerings for his victory. She sees the corpses of her brothers, learns who slew them, and craves revenge. The action now becomes a conflict between Althaea's commitment to her son and loyalty to her brothers, whom her son has slain. Meleager's act was impious ("*nefandus*") pure and simple, but it has plumped his mother into a set of ambivalences in which any behavior on her part is both right and wrong at once. Even if she did nothing, she would be doing wrong by not avenging her brothers and right by not murdering her son. But she is as passionate and impulsive as her offspring and is caught in an agony of opposing pulls. Long before *Catch 22*, poets were aware of the fact that societies can build antithetical imperatives into their systems and into their members' psyches. Finally she sacrifices her son to the shades of her brothers, "pious in [her] impiety," and then herself to her son's. Such are the ambiguities and dilemmas confronting Althaea. Her dignified and tragic debate with herself over the proper course of action shows the awful consequences of revenge justice, the hold a wife's siblings and parents had on her, and the ambiguities of piety, according to which all is perfectly clear here and nothing is clear. There is no right.

107

Somewhere Meleager dies ignorant of the cause of his death. Without glory, he is wasted away by magic fires caused by a hidden hand. He knows his end is unworthy of him, because unheroic, and when he dies, although he calls out to his father, brothers, sisters, and wife, it is a toss-up whether he called upon his mother. Is she, like Theseus' Ariadne, unimportant to him? Or does he suspect that his mother has a hand in his death? The reader knows that he dies because of his infatuation with Atalanta and because of his impulsive murders. Not as wise as Achilles when his dear prize was taken from him by Agamemnon, Meleager rashly shed blood. And when he envies Ancaeus for his death in the hunt, we know that he accepts the position of a braggart and a fool. Thus he identifies with a heroic tradition that Ovid has carefully undercut and suavely ridiculed. He is another example, further, of the hero whose life is not in his own power, like Jason or, on occasion, Theseus and Minos. And alongside these has emerged the woman who, whether good or evil, suffers deeply.

A backward glance over the catalog of Calydonian heroes shows that, including Meleager, Mr. Anderson's Celadon, and at least two sent by Hippocoön, there must have been at least forty noteworthies on the hunt. Of these, a few stand out in myth: Castor and Pollux, Theseus, Jason, Nestor. Fairly close behind come Acastus, Phoenix, Telamon, Pirithoüs, Admetus, Peleus, Laertes, Amphiaraüs, and Meleager. Atalanta and Iolaüs are minor. The remainder are figures important chiefly in their native communities. So much for the composition of bands of heroes: mostly second rate or lower. Of such is glory.

Nevertheless, Meleager's fading away as the ember turns to ash is an arresting image of his life's ending. Impressive in another fashion is Ovid's account of the resulting lamentation in Calydon. It is total. Meleager's father is prostrate with grief. His mother plunges a knife into her bowels. His sisters beat their breasts until they are discolored with bruises. They cannot stop touching his body and kissing it and its bier. After the cremation, they rub his ashes on their bosoms and cling to his tomb, wetting it with tears. Diana is finally satisfied that the family has suffered enough and turns all the sisters but two into guinea-hens. Meleager's sisters are not only long and intensely emotional in their grief; they are also pious. Diana by inflicting the family has certainly encouraged piety toward her. But her discriminatory treatment of the sisters puts the encouragement of piety on a percentage basis. Something similar happened in the hunt. Only one throw at the boar was frustrated by Diana. The other failures resulted from natural causes. Ancaeus openly defied Diana, and her boar killed him. Here piety was upheld. But the other hunters, though they did not voice their defiance of Diana, were also impious in attacking the boar. Only a few of them died. It would seem, then, that piety is unevenly upheld because impiety is unevenly punished. There is also the remarkable situation of Althaea. Through no fault of her own, she became a sacrifice to the conflicting claims of piety. It is further uncertain that Diana herself was responsible for bringing low the ruling house of Calydon. Had her boar killed Meleager, then most of the suffering would have followed. Had Atalanta been identified as her nymph operating on her behalf, then Diana's involvement in Meleager's demise would have been considerable. But as things stand, Meleager died because he was challenged by his uncles—he might have been challenged by any other hero—and because of his own quick and uncontrollable temper. Neither the uncle's repsonse nor Meleager's temper can be attributed to the goddess. In short, it is completely unclear that Diana herself punished Oeneus as extensively as he was afflicted and thus upheld piety.

Such are the ambiguities of piety.

While lofty Calydon is being laid low and suffering, Theseus, having done his bit part in the boar hunt, is trudging homeward with the other heroes. Perhaps Ovid will make him the hero of some great deed, for Diodorus Siculus speaks of Theseus as emulating the Labors of Hercules. At the moment, however, Theseus is engaged in none of these. He is merely going home when a flooding river bars his way. On the advice of the hospitable river himself, Theseus does not try to swim across, but stodgily takes refuge in the river's rough dwelling. At this point, Theseus is behaving conspicuously unlike Hercules. For Hercules, in Book IX, finds another raging river in his way. He swims across. The difference between these reactions to raging rivers reveals Ovid's evaluation of the two heroes. In this part of Book VIII Theseus does nothing more remarkable than listen to stories. Despite the deference given Theseus by Greeks, Ovid makes him and keeps him a background figure.

Acheloüs, the river and its god, invites selected heroes to the hospitality of his abode of soft inferior stone, damp mossy floor, and ceiling of sea shell paneling. Barefoot nymphs serve food and wine to reclining heroes, and the gemmed wine cups give a touch of elegance to the appropriately simple, freshwater rusticity of this minor deity. Acheloüs is not without his pride, however, for his knowing what Diana has done to Calydon gives him reason to point out what he had done to five nymphs who impiously failed to invite him to a party: he washed them away so that they became five islands in the sea. Acheloüs' point is that all gods resent and punish impiety. He has made it, but he goes on to render it ambiguous by telling the story of Perimele, beloved of Achelous, who was also turned into an offshore island. Her father, enraged because she had been Acheloüs' paramour, threw her from a rock into the sea. Acheloüs received her, buoyed her as she swam, and prayed Neptune to give her place in the sea, whereupon she became an island. Piety is ambiguous if those who offend a god and one who loves the same god end up the same. Perimele is in an even more perplexing situation, for she cannot love the god without offending her father or obey her father without offending the god; either way she is simultaneously pious and impious.

Now Ovid brings matters to a head. Piety and impiety come face to face. All of the listeners save one are moved by the marvelous events recounted by Acheloüs, river-god. The scoffer is Pirithoüs, son of impious Ixion. What Ovid has created here is a most curious exercise in pagan piety. A group of hunters who impiously hunted the beast sent by the goddess listen approvingly to pagan miracle tales told by or in the presence of a minor deity. Pirithoüs is the exception. It is inconceivable that a mortal should express his doubt of the power of the gods before a god and not be punished almost immediately, as Oeneus had been. Though Pirithoüs is the object of general disapproval and is silenced and refuted by the pious tales told next by Lelex and Acheloüs, his impiety is not punished. Nor is the refutation especially convincing. Ovid leaves the whole question up in the air, that is, whether the gods punish the impious and reward the pious and whether there is equity in these matters. He does provide a solution, but it comes from a rather unexpected quarter.

Ovid puts the question of piety in an unusual form, using the mouth of Pirithoüs. Pirithoüs calls the gods into question by saying, in effect, that the myths are fictions and that the gods do not have the power to produce metamorphoses. For when he confronts Acheloüs with such shocking statements, he attacks much of the corpus of mythology and certainly many of the tales that Ovid has already told. So those at hand do well to be disturbed. Something must be done or said to bring the debate to a close.

Ovid does this neatly. He has an artistically workable situation: a male dinner party that turns into an after-the-fact pre-Platonic symposium. Its topic is not love, but piety, one that Socrates dealt with, incidentally, in the *Euthyphro* and the *Apology*. Ovid does not use argument, but story, here, of necessity, myth.

Once again Ovid has constructed an elaborate spoof. After all, one does not discuss the reality of the gods, their attributes, and their powers with a god. For when one does, one is arguing against the evidence staring him in the face. Furthermore, as soon as one does, one makes a human being out of him and diminishes his being, so that he is not really a god anymore. This is what has happened to Acheloüs. His being has been called into question, and his stature has been reduced. As river and its force he can punish the nymphs and work with Neptune, but as anthropomorphic figure, he is a gracious troglodyte and primitive country gentleman. This is precisely the problem with myth and myth figures: they constitute a double vision, and because they do so, they are inexact and unevenly or only partially applicable to the phenomena they represent and, hence, only partly convincing. Therefore, Pirithoüs has grounds for scoffing, and Ovid has presented them in the myths he has told.

To answer Pirithoüs and present the other side, Ovid has Lelex, whom he describes as "ripe both in mind and years," epitomize the majority viewpoint by telling the story of Baucis and Philemon. This poor and rustic couple are pious toward each other, to the seeker of hospitality, and toward the gods. They are the salt of the earth in their decency, compatibility, friendliness, and acceptance of their poverty. Of all the couples that Ovid has presented thus far, they most resemble Deucalion and Pyrrha. In their mode of life, they most resemble the peaceable people of the Golden Age, though they have land and must work, and their simple diet is much more complicated to prepare and more tasty. Because of the realistic treatment that Ovid gives their cottage life, they seem to resemble the solid humble folk he might have known in the country around his native Sulmo. The passage is Ovid's tribute to such people and to their ability to enjoy life in an honest fashion.

The realism is not only effective as a tour de force and as change of tone; it captures something that everyone knows is true: reality is fascinating if one looks at it closely, human beings and their ways of doing things especially. And so in a tale of one hundred and eight lines, Ovid proves the point by devoting at least fifty-one lines to realistic detail about life in a poor cottage and making a good deal of the enjoyment of the story come from just this part of it. The punishment of the impious locals and the gorgeous Hollywood temple that replaces their cottage seem banal and tawdry in comparison.

When the gods reward Baucis and Philemon for being hospitable, the aged couple piously ask that they become the caretakers of the new temple, and they display their familial piety by asking that they die at the same time. Granting the first request is no problem, but the second is, for piety requires that the dead be buried, and Baucis and Philemon are alone. The gods solve this problem at the proper time by making Baucis and Philemon trees and also extending their lives. Hence, the gods do perform metamorphoses.

Lelex has said in effect, I'll tell you about the power of the gods. I was outback in Phrygia once and saw this oak tree with a linden beside it. The old natives told me that the trees were once a pious elderly couple whom the gods had helped by thus changing them. These men had no reason to deceive me. The natives venerated the trees, putting wreaths on them. I was convinced, and so I added one to the collection.

Lelex's story and conviction are testimonies to his own piety and to the facts that a given tradition existed in a certain place. It in no way proves that the tradition and the miracles it celebrates are based on fact, except that there were trees in that place and that they were worshiped. The circumstantial details about the stay of the gods with Baucis and Philemon are a tribute to Lelex's artistic ability and to Ovid, who provided Lelex with them. Further, sophisticated readers would be well aware that Lelex is a fiction telling a fiction.

At the end of his tale, Lelex produces a sententia that is pious and most apropos: " ' "Those the gods take care of are gods, and the worshipful company of worshipers should be worshiped." ' " In short, there is a community of the pious, and it participates in godhood and should, therefore, be revered. This maxim honors the gods for the good things that they bestow upon favored individuals, but it does more honor to the

111

recipients. In context, Lelex is paying an extravagant compliment to the group of heroes being cared for by the river-god Achelous. He is not, however, violating tradition, for ancient heroes sometimes were worshiped after their deaths, for example, Theseus. Nevertheless, both the fictional nature of Lelex's tale and the advantages that its lesson confers upon aristocrats render it suspect as fact and deucedly effective as propaganda.

All present are impressed by Lelex's tale. Pirithoüs does not open his mouth and presumably is silenced. Theseus, naturally, wants to hear more. And so Acheloüs complies, addressing Theseus as " 'o bravest one,' " a salutation that sounds unintentionally ironic to a reader aware of Theseus' performance at the recent boar hunt. Acheloüs carefully alludes to the fact that Pirithoüs' objection has not been answered completely. Lelex's story showed simply that the gods can change existing forms into new ones. Acheloüs completes the refutation by telling a story in which the god gives a new form to a mortal and repeats the process several times. Now this kind of change was given Erysichthon's daughter, as Acheloüs' story shows. It is also a tale about impiety and piety, and, being a whopping good one, restores one's faith in rivers and in Ovid.

One of the virtuoso dimensions of this tale is its skillful manipulation of tones. They range from the matter-of-fact initial background information, the horror at the stubborn sacrilege of the tree felling, the gruesomeness of Famine, the comic horror of Erysichthon's gluttony, the politeness of the exchange between his metamorphosed daughter and her owner, and the relatively rapid conclusion in which the villain feeds himself by eating himself—the logically impossible but emotionally appropriate end for one in his condition and of his character. Such a list cannot, of course, do justice to the various tones and the momentary shifts within them. Another bit of virtuosity is that the story's length and its meanderings (for example, the powers of changing shape that are given to Erysichthon's daughter are mentioned initially, but are not really given attention until about one hundred and sixteen lines later) fit the volume and course of a river, which does move on, but not always directly.

Mr. Galinsky is of the opinion that this story is essentially an "imaginative and tonal" virtuoso piece and a fantasia that is an "escape from morality and religion." He may be right. I find it moral from start to finish, regardless of tone. Famine is still an evil even though one enjoys her grotesque details. Erysichthon is cruel and inhuman whether the oak's leaves and acorns turn pale or not. His daughter, another of the unnamed female protagonists of the *Metamorphoses*, is a decent person, even though degraded by her father into a temporary slave and a cheat. She is admirable—and pious—though he is not. Acheloüs, from what he has said about Perimele, would approve of the daughter's yielding to Neptune and of Neptune's helping her. All these are moral judgments.

Yet Mr. Galinsky touches on something crucial about the story. How pious is it? Theseus wanted more miracles, and Acheloüs, who is naturally biased, has obliged with a complicated whopper. The story is a whopper precisely because it is a fantasy and because its tones are not always serious ones. It also involves at least one major illogicality, again that of contradictory premises. Acheloüs admits that this illogicality is present, for he says, "the fates do not permit Ceres and Famine to come together." And, of course, he is right in his premise: ordinarily food is consumed to eliminate the hunger, and the hunger is dispelled by the food; the one cancels the other. But here it is assumed that they can come together and that one does not cancel the other. In addition, it is also beyond the logic of circumstances for one to nourish one's self by eating one's self. In short, because of the illogicalities, the fantasy, and the sometimes comic exaggeration, this story is not only about piety and the power of the gods to change shapes; it is an intelligence test and a test of piety. The story is literally impossible. But if one is truly pious, he can believe the impossible. Would not that be Tertullian's definition of piety, belief in the impossible? Hence, Ovid's exercise in pagan piety shows that faith was as essential for the pagan as it was for the Christian. And so the episode ends with most of the listeners believing. But piety still remains fraught with ambiguities.

The theme of Book VIII is piety. From Book I on, tale after tale has been told that deals with piety or its opposite. But nowhere is the theme stronger than in Book VIII, where it appears prominently in every episode, and nowhere has it been handled more ingeniously. Arachne's contest with Minerva may call into question the justice of the gods, but the myth of Erysichthon challenges one's belief in them. Hence, it calls into question all the values that belief in the gods sustains. To adapt what Ovid wrote elsewhere, if it is expedient to believe in the gods, it is hardly expedient to tell Greek myths about them. But even so, Ovid has presented a solution to the problems caused by the ambiguities of piety. His open-ended test is effective, for it allows the listener to react according to his nature. Thus the sceptic reveals himself by his reaction, and the believer, by his. Pirithoüs has been silenced, but not refuted, for faith is something apart from rational argument. The test, then, results in self-knowledge, a possible aim of literature. It is realistic and unbiased. And as part of Ovid's gamesmanship, it obscures his position on the gods (for the moment) by the ingenious device of making the reader look at his.

Surveying the problems in piety in this book reveals that piety is more than just an empty ideal. Like Meleager's, Scylla's impiety reveals how ugly and damaging it can be. Furthermore, the survey shows that the problems become more complex as the book progresses, and their treatment becomes more ingenious. For Scylla, love easily overcomes piety. For Pasiphaë bestial love confounds it. Romantic love subverts Ariadne's filial piety, but her father's cruelty to the young Athenians is an extenuating circumstance. Forgetfulness was responsible for Oeneus' impiety to Diana, but Diana's uneven punishment of piety calls into doubt the justice of divine action in that area. Meleager's impious slaying of his uncles is complicated by the justness of his title to the trophies of the hunt, by his quick temper, and by his nascent love of Atalanta. His

113

mother's situation is even more complex. Althaea's piety places her in a desperate dilemma. Similarly Perimele cannot be a pious daughter and remain chaste because she will then impiously frustrate the river-god. Piety is then brought into question because it and impiety can bring the same results. What was a punishment for the nymphs who failed to invite Acheloüs to a party is Perimele's reward: all are changed into islands. Finally, in the most complicated and ingenious passage of all, piety is presented as a matter of faith, and belief in it is tested at the end of the book.

METAMORPHOSES IX: The Problems of Women

There are lovely, arresting things in Book IX: Alcmena's thumb, the boy in the doorway, Acheloüs' horn, and his quirky character. This last was built up in the preceding book as that of a country gentleman rustic in his ways, hospitable, locally important and powerful, and tied to the land. He is self-important, proud of his wooing and keeping the local nymphs in line, a bit lonely, a bit obsequious, and sly. His person and his vanity have been wounded by maiming and consequent diminution of power. Though Acheloüs is bluff and hearty, his loss of his horn was a traumatic experience and still troubles him so much that he first crudely conceals the loss with a rough wreath of reeds and last, when the heroes have departed, hides beneath his waves. His vanity, however, has better supports than his cosmetic arrangements. Though he can be dull when retailing local history about islands, he can hold his listeners when he tells the string of folktales about Erysichthon and his daughter. His native shrewdness sustains him, too.

The first story of Book IX, prompted by Theseus, picks up the end of Book VIII, where crafty Acheloüs has been arranging matters so that he will be asked to tell another story, one about him. He does this by groaning over his missing horn. And the "Neptunian hero," Theseus, falls into the little trap. He asks about the "mutilated" horn. The river-god, whose vanity is set on edge momentarily, engages in a bit of inelegant elegance by putting on the crown of coarse reeds. He is not deterred, however, by being irritated. Instead, he begins by appealing to pity, saying that Theseus' request recalls sadness. Yet no matter about the pain, continues Acheloüs, his vanity peeping through; the reputation of the conquered is enhanced by the fame of his conqueror. So he tells the story of the bride combat. Its object was Deianira. Acheloüs egotistically doubts whether anyone has heard of her. Thus he salves his wound by putting the lost bride in the status of nonentity. Anyone who knew about Hercules would probably know about Deianira, as Ovid demonstrates in his next two tales, so that Acheloüs' writing Deianira off as a nobody is not effective and makes the local god somewhat fatuous. But his remarks about Deianira and about being bested by someone famous show just how vigorously his mental agility works to promote his reputation and sustain his pride.

Words preceded the wrestling for the bride. Acheloüs summarizes Hercules' claims to Deianira: parentage (only Jove named) and fame for deeds (the famous twelve labors of Hercules), which were performed at his mother's command. (*Command* implies that Hercules did great deeds not of his own volition or perception of their worth. *Stepmother* sarcastically suggests that Hercules is not a legitimate child. Acheloüs retorted that he is a god, not the decendant of one; that it brings dishonor upon deity for a god to yield to an inferior being; and that as river-god he is already part of the kingdom of Deianira's father; in fact, he is rather committed to it. With quick-witted sarcasm, he noted that he has the advantage of not being hated by Juno and that he is not subservient to her, implying that Hercules' tasks are a shame that the hero has to bear and that, in contrast, he, Acheloüs, can stay at home and pay proper attention to business.

Then Acheloüs did something rather clever. He used the rhetorical device of offering two equally unacceptable alternatives to his opponent, thus: either you, Hercules, are a liar (i.e., Jove is not your sire), or your mother is a whore.

Unfortunately, this trick is not effective, rhetorically or practically. For one thing, Acheloüs is no one to talk; according to his own words, he either seduced or ravished Perimele, so that his preaching sexual morality is hypocritical. His line of reasoning would also reduce a number of heroes to the status of sons of shame, because conceived out of wedlock. It also makes consorting with Jove a sin, rather than an honor and a benefit. And it, therefore, involves Jove in something shameful. Acheloüs' retorts, then, are clever superficially, but upon close inspection are sometimes inconsistent, sometimes illogical, sometimes badly chosen. In contrast, Hercules' achievements are both real and his own, regardless of their instigation. Secondly, the real point at issue is relative merit, which here means power. Third, the insults are in bad taste, revealing Acheloüs as an ungentlemanly blusterer. Worse, they are ineffectual, for they do not avert the match, and they serve to make Hercules angry and increase his flow of adrenalin. Hercules properly resents them and asserts that physical force is more effective than words. Events prove him correct.

The fight is well handled: it has variety and surprises; the contestants are not too unevenly matched; Acheloüs is betrayed by his crafty metamorphoses, but Pirithoüs' objection to the idea that the gods have the power to change shapes is answered again; the confident wrestler throws grit over himself and his opponent, a realistic detail; and so forth. At first neither contestant can budge the other, and so the situation prompts Acheloüs to produce an epic simile. Unfortunately, the comparison is not too complimentary to either Hercules, Acheloüs, or Deianira, though the river-god thinks it good. He presents himself and Hercules as two bulls fighting for a glossy heifer. It is true that Ovid is writing an epic of sorts, that the situation at hand is heroic, or semi so, and that in the distant poetic past Homer had used similar imagery from untamed nature or from the farm, but it is unlikely that a metropolis-loving, cultivated Roman like Ovid would not have his tongue in his cheek here. That he does, is revealed by his having Acheloüs indulge in the comic hyperbole of calling the heifer "such a great kingdom." Acheloüs may be sincere in his imagery, but Ovid is not.

The stalemate is broken by Hercules' expertise. The hero manages to get on the back of his opponent, where, Acheloüs says wittily that he who had taken the place of the mountain and held up the heavens feels like a mountain. Acheloüs breaks this grip only to find himself breathless in a neck hold and forced to the ground. He changes himself into a snake, whereupon Hercules, who has wind to spare, reminds him that he had strangled snakes in his crib and later killed and torn open the extraordinary hydra—a horrible threat. Acheloüs then takes the appropriate form of a powerful bull, but Hercules turns out to be a more than competent bulldozer, for he not only brings Acheloüs low, but symbolically partially emasculates him by tearing off one of his horns. The story ends.

What this partial emasculation later turns out to mean is that Acheloüs has given part of his virility, in the form of his fertilizing water, to the agricultural productivity of the countryside. That is why it is his horn from which the harvest plenty spills when the goddess of abundances, Bona Copia, is depicted. Thus Acheloüs' defeat redounds to his credit. Such are the results of being tamed by the hero, according to the river-god.

Casually, now, but most timely, there enters a nymph girt like Diana. Ironically, because of the Calydonian boar hunt, she suggests the goddess in her role of helper of farmers because she restrains wild beasts. This nymph carries a Horn of Plenty, emblem of Bona Copia and Acheloüs, from which she distributes autumn fruits and apples, the desert course of the country meal, to Theseus and the assembled company. At this point it becomes clear that the tale of Acheloüs' defeat has been an elaborate ploy, begun with his reference to his missing horn at the end of Book VIII and carefully developed in Book IX so that his meal would end with a clever surprise, a dramatic compliment to himself. We have sat down to dinner with Petronius' Trimalchio and endured one of his laughable contrivances before he was conceived.

The next day the heroes cross the subsiding river, and disfigured Acheloüs conceals himself beneath his stream so that Ovid may melodramatically commiserate with Acheloüs, damaged because of Deianira, and move on to sympathize with Nessus, destroyed by passion for the same lady.

Nessus met her at a swollen river when Hercules was taking his bride home. By trickery, centaur Nessus (half man, half beast, as deceivers because of their duplicity should be) tried to run off with, or rape, Deianira while Hercules was on the other side of the torrent. There is a nice touch here. Hercules devotes six lines of dactyllic hexameter to warning Nessus not to trust in his fleetness of foot, quite a bit of breath to spend while, according to the passage, the culprit is speeding off as fast as he can. The effect, of course, is the lengthening of Hercules' bow shot; hence, he makes a more difficult one, as well as displaying his confidence that he can do so.

Master archer Hercules did shoot down Nessus. The arrow was poisoned, and Nessus felt the poison. His trickery did not desert him as he died, for he pulled off his blood-stained shirt and gave it to the unsuspecting Deianira as a love charm. Nessus apparently relied on several bits of general knowledge: that centaurs are notoriously hot-blooded and full of lust, so that anything with their blood on it might revive desire; that husbands' interests sometimes flag and do wander; that wives like having the psychological support of love charms and potions; and that women like souvenirs of men who have shown marked interest in their attractions. Such knowledge must lie behind his last recorded words, " 'I shall not die unavenged.' " He has his revenge, and he does not.

The apparent revenge of Nessus, which Ovid moves to next, comes years after the attempted rape. The Amphitrionian—Ovid manages to get in a sesquipedalian word for *Hercules*—is world famous. Juno no longer hates him. He is coming home from sacking a city and is bringing with him a young princess, of whom he is enamored, according to tattling Rumor, who mixes falsehood with truth and exaggerates. Obviously it is time to use Nessus' bloody shirt. Deianira sends it to Hercules, who puts it on and is stricken with the fires of revenge, not love.

The physical agony of Hercules is sufficiently detailed to stimulate the horror that Romans seemed to like. During it, the hero reproaches Juno for feeding on his pain, in itself a horrible image if one visualizes it, and in a series of rhetorical questions worthy of Cicero, he asks whether his strange misery and awful death are his reward for his spectacular twelve labors, many of which benefited mankind. Apparently he feels that good deeds and service merit good treatment. And he ironically verges on impiety because, being aware that his persecutor and inferior King Eurystheus lives and prospers, he says, " 'And there are men who can believe that gods exist.' "

His protest calls forth a complex of reader reactions. It is serious and tragic, and one feels that and feels that it is just. But one also knows that it is wrong. Neither Juno nor any god is responsible for the unbearable pain; Deianira and Nessus are. If not mad again, Hercules is unfortunately raving because he does not know. One might also feel anxiety that he might be punished for impiety. But any knowledge of the hero's story would dispel this uneasiness, for one would know that Hercules, unknowingly, is becoming a god. Thus dramatic irony here converts anguish into a sense of relief, a strange kind of exaltation and hilarity.

Before Ovid presents Hercules himself as experiencing this new and incongruous mood, he cleverly deals with its opposite, the fear of being sentient, exemplified by Lichas' fear of being hurt and the sailors' fear of hurting the metamorphosed Lichas. Both Lichas and the sailors contrast with Hercules, who suffers enormously and loudly, that is to say, heroically. His raging is a form of fighting back. Thus the Lichas episode, as far as feeling goes, contrasts the apprehensive with the noble, the one who shrinks back with the one who acts. Hercules, enraged because Lichas has brought him all his pain, slings the petrified messenger into cold upper air, whence he falls a flinty rock that now protrudes above the sea and is become the epitome of insensitivity. Hercules, in contrast, then builds his pyre and is sufficiently purged of suffering by suffering that he can fight fire with fire. He gives Philoctetes his bow and arrows in return for igniting what should be his torment, lies down in the conflagration with his club for a pillow, and is comfortable.

The Lichas episode not only modulates to the serentiy of Hercules on his pyre, the two episodes form a parable that preaches, first, that one should not be afraid to feel, to assert, and to react, for these are heroic, and, second, that through emotional expression one purges emotion. The two episodes also form a bit of Stoic instruction, and one should remember that Hercules was a model for the Stoics, because his example demonstrates that the hero who endures and acts will end immortal. Further, the pyre episode instructs about a mystery, the passage of the soul through pain to serenity just before death and thence exaltation to the level of the gods and immortality.

So, though the flames lick upward, they do not reduce Hercules to ashes in an urn or to a helpless shade. The fire eats away only his participation in mortality. The rest, coming from Jove, is divine. And Jove makes a god of his son, the rest of the gods, even Juno, assenting. Thus the agony of Hercules is metamorphosed into his "ecstasy at being ever," to use the words of Sir Thomas Browne. His true identity is established and he learns that there are gods, indeed. Here is another surprise ending. There is not only the paradox of the fortunate fall, but piety is shown to operate not only from men towards the gods, but from the gods towards men. Piety is thus validated.

(On the subject of piety that flows from a divine father to his offspring, Hermann Fränkel says of the hero's apotheosis, "The passage is notable because it prefigures the dogma of the two natures of Christ," the divine and the human, enunciated by Tertullian. One might note, too, that there is something oddly antedating Christian expression in Jove's saying that he will receive Hercules on the " 'caelestibus oris' " / " 'heavenly shores' " and in the paradoxes that the hero's weight is greater after his death than before and that dead to earth, he is alive with regard to heaven.)

It is not inappropriate, but certainly unexpected, that, since Hercules has just been splendidly reborn as an immortal, the next section should deal with the earthy problems of his birth. However, Ovid sets this tale and the next, both of which deal with anger because of an affront or injury and retaliation therefor, in a frame that also deals with anger and retaliation. Because of his wrath, Eurystheus hates even the descendants of Hercules and persecutes them after the hero's death. This situation, the first part of the frame, leads into the cares of Alcmena. After her story and that of her grandson's wife comes the second part of the frame, the saving of Alcmena, Iole, and the other Heraclids by the combined efforts of Hercules, Hebe, and Iolaüs, who retaliate against Eurystheus. The frame is meaningful, as we shall see, but its significance is implicit, rather than explicit, and the frame itself is so slight that it is likely to seem meaningless.   That it is not, is part of Ovid's playing with his audience.

The labor of Alcmena in giving birth to Hercules was an effort worthy of Hercules himself.   Juno was angry and vengeful because Jove had loved Alcmena and had Lucina, the goddess of childbirth, prevent the birth.   Thus Alcmena should have died horribly.   The birth did occur, however, thanks to Alcmena's loyal servant Galanthis.   She tricked Lucina into relaxing so that Alcmena could drop the child.

Looked at from one viewpoint, Galanthis is the warm-hearted, quick-witted servant of Greek New Comedy put into myth.   She is cheerful, spontaneous, suspicious, confident, and unawed by the great. Looked at in another way, she is Ovid's tribute to the perky, compassionate, faithful servant and to peasant stock that asserts practical humaneness in opposition to the higher powers.

Considered from the viewpoint of piety, Galanthis is punished as much for laughing at Lucina as for deceiving her.   Thus much for her impiety.   But, since she is working in the interests of Jove, for her mistress, and for fairness, she is to that degree pious.   On the other hand, Lucina, by violating her role of giving aid in childbirth, was not acting piously toward the innocent Alcmena.   The goddess is deficient in downward piety, as well as integrity.   As a result, Juno and Lucina are here less admirable than Jove was in his treatment of Hercules.   The ladies come off badly.   Galanthis was punished, of course, being metamorphosed into a weasel.   But Alcmena is loyal, giving her a place in her home.   And Alcmena still sorrows for her.

Alcmena also feels uneasy because of the warning that Galanthis' fate suggests: vengeful powers haunt the earth.   Her uneasiness stands as an omen qualifying the next tale, that of Iole's half sister, Dryope.   More innocent than Galanthis, for she did not intend to deceive or to offend any deity—Dryope protested her innocence at the time of her misfortune—she was punished for simply plucking the flowers of the lotus tree, partly to please her son, but ironically, partly for pious purposes: she was going to weave garlands for the nymphs.   For damaging the lotus tree, she was turned into one herself.   The events are all very pathetic: the young mother, her infant son at her breast; her terrified sister, who tried to prevent the change; the grieving husband and father; the parting of the tree-turning woman. It is also all very strange.

Seen as dealing with identity, the story tells of a drastic change in a personality: the madness occurring in a young mother after the birth of her child (he is not yet a year old).   This sort of thing, I understand, actually occurs, the result of ovarian atrophy and hormone imbalance. Humanly and statistically it is possible that such things happened in antiquity and the results were observed, though, as Mr. Fränkel noted with his customary astuteness, the ancients would have no medical explanation and no technical language for the explanation.   Ovid does his best, which is excellent; he depicts the onset of the condition by having the mother withdraw from her child, her sister, her father, and her husband and become a vegetable.

The story is open to at least two other interpretations. Either it deals with a person so traumatized by early loss of her mother and by being raped that the bleeding branches of the lotus shatter her damaged psyche, or it deals with nymphophilia, for want of a better word. According to the second interpretation, the details given about Dryope's life suggest a case history. She had been an only child. Her mother had died. Her father had taken another wife, who bore Iole. Dryope was extremely beautiful. Then Apollo raped her. The Latin of the passage indicates that Apollo used force and conveys the idea that Dryope suffered or endured sexual assault rather than yielded willingly to it. The Latin also suggests that Dryope experienced a definite sense of loss and that she missed her maidenhood. The implication is that her sexual experience was traumatic and, further, that the loss of virginity was a blow to her self-esteem. She received no special consideration from the god, and her reputation may have suffered somewhat. This is indicated by the fact that Andraemon married her even thus deflowered and was thought happy, presumably because of her beauty. As far as Ovid's Iole is concerned, Andraemon is a genealogical nobody; hence, though the alliance may have been convenient for Dryope, marrying him seems to have been another degradation for her. And now she has a child. Life and beauty have not always been kind to her. Hence, she might well wish to withdraw. Yet life has some holds upon her.

Andraemon and Dryope's father are devoted to her. Indeed, they come looking for her as though they were worried about her. Dryope's major concerns during her change are not for them, but for her reputation, her child, and the nymphs. For as the bark closes about her, she protests her innocence and guiltlessness, gives instructions about the child, and warns against harming the nymphs. Then she bids a loving farewell to husband, sister, and father.

As Dryope is being encased, she is concerned about her person. She knows that the bark will perform the rite of closing her eyes. As a tree, she does not want to be nibbled by sheep or pruned. More striking, during the transformation, she refers with vanity to her own white neck. Thus she was not only aware of contemporary criteria for feminine loveliness, she was also conscious of her own attractiveness. With marriage and child-bearing, she is moving away from these and from the freshness and freedom that the unmarried state allowed. Such qualities belong to the nymphs. And it is important to note that Dryope has a keen appreciation of feminine beauty in plant form.

Hence, her coming to worship the nymphs by bringing them garlands is very significant. It reveals what she adores, or worships, most, the nymph condition of human life, when the maid is intact, young, unburdened, lovely, and free. In short, though Dryope was a loving mother and affectionate spouse, she was unalterably attached to the nymph state, which means that she was unwilling or unable to break away from her earlier maidenly condition. In her heart and mind, she was still a nymph, hence her change into a tree.

Dryope's crisis occurred when she came to a pool, an emblem of femininity, since pools are the dwelling places of water nymphs. The pool was surrounded by myrtles, emblems of Venus. The two emblems are spatially separated, according to Ovid, indicating a separation in nature; that is, taken together, the two elements form an emblem of contrast between physical love (Venus' myrtles) and naiadness, or female independence (the pool of the nymphs). That the lotus grows close to the pool and is called aquatic indicates its closeness to the state of nubile maiden and arrest there. Indeed, the plant was once a nymph named Lotis, who, Iole says, fled from the repulsive sexual parts of Priapus. The ancient Italians commonly portrayed this garden god with enormous ugly genitalia, so that Lotis represents aesthetic horror caused by the physically grotesque aspects of male sexual construction. In this respect she represents the free maiden state and would naturally have been attractive to Dryope, an attraction that Dryope responded to by reaching out and plucking the lotus blossoms. The irony of the situation is that one can think of honoring the nymphs by violating them, that is, by gathering their leaves and flowers to make garlands for them, as Dryope did.

Even as lotus, Lotis resented being deflowered, for as nymph, she had striven to avoid defloration. As a result of Dryope's picking her blooms, the lotus tree dripped blood and shuddered with horror. Dryope reacted somewhat similarly: she became terrified and desensitized, immobilized like the plant. Her calling upon the nymphs for aid and her frantic attempts to resist metamorphosis were natural enough. Iole, who witnessed all of this, notes that the rising bark covered Dryope's private parts, that her breasts grew hard, and that Iole wished to be covered by the bark herself. At the moment she has had her uterus filled with the noble seed of Hyllus, so that she is gravid and distended and most unnymphlike. But earlier she had almost plucked the lotus herself and had wanted to become a tree nymph like her half sister, so that Iole was once sympathetic to and empathized with her sister's condition and like her wished to escape from sexuality and from sensitivity.

As Dryope's grievous change progressed, she became languid and resigned to the living death of being a woman in tree form. She asked for protection as a plant and wanted her son to play beneath her branches, but she warned him against the pool and picking flowers. In other words, Dryope would make her son a respecter of the nymphs. And so, concludes Iole, Dryope ceased to be. The tree, of course, did not. Thus Dryope truly worshipped the nymphs by becoming one. Either way, accepting sexuality or rejecting it, a woman's lot is hard.

It is possible that Dryope's tale is, as Ovid in his poetic person says, a wonder, simply and purely that, a miracle to propagate piety. He has made it seem very real by having a realistic pregnant woman tell it to her equally realistic, though mythic, grandmother-in-law. But it is the two women who are realistic, especially in the account of the pregnancy, though having one tale of anguish follow another is realistic enough. The telling realistic detail, however, is Alcmena's thumb *(pollex)*. Telling about Dryope renews Iole's grief, so that at the end of the story, she is crying. At this point Alcmena dries her tears, not with a handkerchief or an edge of her garment and not with the tips of her fingers, but with her thumb, a gesture so real and so down-to-earth and homey that it sheds its aura not only over the whole situation but also contributes to the feeling that Iole's experience actually occurred. The details that Iole gives are so numerous that they contribute to that feeling, of course, but the natural, everyday motion that a woman might make to comfort a child is a stroke of genius.

And Ovid has done all this to cap it with a different and still greater wonder, the boy in the doorway. The apparition of this youth in Alcmena's doorway sweeps away the sadness of the two women. Iolaüs is a transition figure, appropriately, because that is what being in a doorway suggests and because he has moved the women from grief to joy, but mostly because Ovid uses him to move into the topic of miraculous changes of age. Iolaüs, however, is an arresting figure because both he and his effect on Alcmena and Iole are unexplained. He is a bit of Ovidian shorthand and the second part of the frame referred to earlier. To fill in what Ovid merely hints at, Iolaüs was restored to youth by Hebe at the request of her husband, Hercules. The rejuvenation enabled Iolaüs to kill Eurystheus in battle and thus free Alcmena, Iole, and the Heraclids generally from his attacks. As a result, Hercules is avenged, and Alcmena and Iole have some of their cares removed. Iolaus' appearance in the doorway announces these reasons for joy. But his being an enigma jolts the reader and makes him aware that Ovid has informed him, but also eluded him.

An emblem of the past renewed and the present joyous because the future is secure, Iolaüs also stands for one type of change, rejuvenation. Having seen Iolaüs restored to youth by Hebe, the gods want to obtain the same treatment for their loves, but Themis indicates that love is insufficient reason; few will have any change of age, and those few will receive it to avenge a father (a pious act).

The gods noisily protest this decision, each arguing for his or her antique amour or favorite. Jove stops this jangle in the most surprising way. He asserts (1) that all such occurrences of change of age are the work of Fate and (2) that the Fates rule all the gods, including Jove. The clearest general effect of these declarations is to remove Jove from the position of supreme deity and to place him in an inferior one somewhat like that of lord chancellor. The other Olympians have already presented themselves in the roles of wrangling, self-centered courtiers.

Ovid elsewhere repeats the idea that the gods are subordinate to the Fates. In Book V, the narrating Muse asserts that Jove merely delivers the Fates' decision about Proserpina's annual return to earth and that the Fates' decree is superior to Ceres' resolve to have her daughter back. In Book XV Ovid declares that the gods cannot break the iron decrees of the Fates, and Jove tells Venus that the decrees of the Fates are adamantine.

One hundred and some years later Lucian wrote a dialogue in which it is argued that if the Fates rule Jove, Jove is impotent, and being powerless, he is useless; being useless, he is worthy neither of respect nor worship. Neither are the other gods, because the Fates control them, too. Ovid does not go so far, though one might extrapolate Lucian's position from the one Ovid gives Jove. Ovid does, however, take a step in the direction of Lucian's argument. If nothing else, he demotes all the gods by taking away some of their power and independence.

Ovid also reduces the gods in stature by having them engage in noisy quarreling and Jove appeal to their respect for him. Themis' prophecy, stuffed with irrelevancies, long-winded and obscure, seems like a small satire on oracles. And the whole group, Jove included, does not seem either impressive or worthy of reverence. The whole passage, therefore, is not a very elevated treatment of the gods. But there are powers at work. Some are rivers like Acheloüs; some are plants like Lotis-lotus; some have to do with childbirth and are goddesses, spells, or charms; some are the Destinies, or Fates.

Minos' career ends in Book IX. Jove names him as an aged son whom he would like to restore to youth and as a king ineffectual because of his years. Ovid picks this lead out of all the possible ones presented in the rejuvenation passage and mentions potential conflict between the suspicious failing ruler and the vigorous younger luminary, Cretan prince Miletus. Apparently to avoid any disastrous consequences inherent in the situation, Miletus fled from Crete, an act of piety in a way, and founded Miletus in Asia Minor. HIs true importance for Ovid is that he sired the twins Caunis and Byblis. And to the latter's story Ovid now turns.

It is a straightforward tangle of hormones, imagination, and law. One must read it, of course, in order to participate in Byblis' experience, which is naughty and intense. It is so bad that Ovid explicitly tells the reader at the start that Byblis' tale is a warning against unlawful, that is, incestuous, love. One thing to notice is that Byblis uses the language of self-seduction. She is extremely sensual and passionate, and she is not very innocent in that, although she apparently has not had sexual intercourse, she knows perfectly well what it involves and can imagine it. Her desire for her brother is not a sudden thing, but develops out of sisterly affection, which is pious enough, and for a long time she is not aware of what is happening. Ovid seems to be describing a naturally affectionate young girl who moves toward puberty and beyond it and in the process allows her libidinous imagination to possess her. Since the earliest object of her affection was her twin brother, the results of her fixation can only be unfortunate.

Ovid treats Byblis somewhat sympathetically, tempering what he said of her in the *Art of Love*. There, to belittle women, he asserts that if the man did not ask the woman, she would ask the man; men are more temperate than women; manly desire "knows a lawful bound"; the incestuous ones were the women, witness Byblis and Myrrha; in short, women are the lust ridden of the species. In Book IX Ovid finds Byblis both fascinating and damned, but his position on the sexual proclivities of women in general is not outrageous. Nor does he support Byblis' rationalizations when the girl mounts a scandalous attack on conventional sexual morality.

This attack does come from a female, it is true. Byblis lusts and is aggressive, sending her brother a proposal. But she is young, and her reasoning is inconsistent and weak. It is she who enunciates a wild oats principle, a silly theory of laws for the elderly only, and the idea that there is a generation gap. Young, she sets aside the wisdom of her elders, for she knows only what she feels. In her mind, there are only two restraints: shame and law, or custom. Her theorizing dismisses these. She is also confused about the difference between love and lust, a distinction that still baffles many, especially the young. When she writes her proposal to her brother, she claims that three restraints do not exist for them: paternal restrictions, a concern for reputation, and timidity. Like Scylla's, her romance occurs in her own mind, and her passion sweeps away all constraints. Her twin, however, lives by the book. None of her attempts to seduce him move him to anything but disgust. Finally he runs away from the repugnant situation. It is then that Byblis runs mad and declares her unlawful love to the general public. Nymphs offer her remedies for love, but she is too far gone to heed now what she had not thought of or sought before.

As Byblis approaches distraction, Ovid revamps a line that he had used of the contending brother winds in Book I, namely, "so great is the discord of brothers." Of Byblis, he writes, "so great is the discord of an irresolute mind." The fighting winds had been about to tear the world apart, and that situation carries over here as echo: Byblis is about to be torn apart within by her struggling passions. A few lines later, rejected by her brother, she goes mad. The important matters to realize are that Ovid once again attacks disharmony, and he implicitly advocates a Stoic serenity. His monstrous Byblis is the forerunner of the frenetic Medea and Atreus of Seneca's tragedies.

Byblis wanders far to no purpose and finally collapses weeping, ever weeping until she becomes a fountain beneath an oak.

Her change into a spring would have been the talk of Crete, Ovid says, if the island had not had its own wonder to preoccupy it, the change of Iphis from female to male. He calls the change of Byblis *monstrum*, which fits, and the second, *miraculum*, as, indeed, it is, for it is a miracle brought about by the goddess Isis. The whole story, in fact, is a testimonial to Isis, and it ends Book IX as Book VIII did with a bit of piety. Isis represents humaneness and thus gives the quality divine status. Through her the gods are shown to uphold natural and familial love and normal heterosexual relationships. In addition, as Mr. Otis points out, the tale is a document of social protest against the ancient practice of infanticide. The protest is made gently and indirectly by appeals to piety and human feeling—the father's asking Piety to forgive his decision to expose a baby daughter, the parents' tears, the mother's insistence that the child be allowed to live—as well as the goddess' intervention.

Isis stands out in marked contrast to the preceding Graeco-Roman deities. To a modern, she seems like a religious figure, not a personification of some force or abstraction; she is mysterious; she is compassionate and helpful; she is not primarily self-interested and self-indulgent; and in the *Metamorphoses* she is not presented as the center of a heavenly court or divine family. In short, she is humane, but not completely or fully humanized. It is no wonder that Iphis and his mother record their grateful testimony in a votive tablet that caused a sensation. Also noteworthy is the fact that this story involves common people, not nobles, princes, and kings. And it might be well to remember that Iphis' mother is a pious worshipper of Isis, to whom she has turned for aid. She and Iphis thus contrast with Byblis, who turned to no deity.

Unlike Book VIII, Book IX ends with an affirmation of religious piety, not a test of it. The reason is simple. No one had seen a person literally turn into a plant or animal or constellation, but sex changes of the sort Iphis went through were reported as fact in antiquity.

The theme of piety, prominent in Book VIII, is continued in Book IX. Ovid inserts a bit when he blesses the nuptials of Iphis and Ianthe with the presence of the customary Roman deities Juno and Venus. Thus he ends the book with a touch of patriotic piety.

Piety receives intermittent treatment in this book, but it emerges constantly. It is a subject that can scarcely be avoided in Latin poetry because it involves the relationship of men and gods, or the numinous; the relationships between the members of a family, an extensive category because even the gods and some nymphs belong to families; and also obligation to the community or native land. Acheloüs alludes to the matter of piety when he objects that it is dishonorable for a god to give way to a mortal. He also notes the ambiguity that can accompany piety, for he adds that, when the bride combat occurred, Hercules was not yet a god. Hercules had the potential for godhead, but it had not been made apparent.

Dryope makes the theme of piety explicit. She uses the word in asking her family to protect her branches. She also swears by the " ' "numina" ' " and protests that she has not done anything wrong; that is, in her piety, she has not offended or injured or been unjust to any power. Nevertheless, she is punished, a consequence that both she and Iole feel is unjust. Dryope is caught in a fairly common dilemma in connection with

126

piety. She wants to honor the nymphs with garlands, but to do so, she must injure them by breaking their boughs and plucking their flowers.

With Jove the theme of piety is covered over, but present, for he is profoundly impious towards members of his family and the community of gods when he belittles their importance by saying that they are all subordinate to the Fates. Byblis' monstrous affection begins as filial piety, but as it turns incestuous, it becomes impiety because it disrupts the life of her family and goes against the laws of the community. It can hardly be pious of her to use the incestuous marriages of Saturn, Oceanus, and Jove as precedent for her own or to hail Venus and Cupid when she revels in the recall of her erotic dreams. Ovid seems careful to keep Venus and Cupid free of any responsibility for Byblis' behavior.

Piety is not stressed in the episode of Nessus, Hercules, and Deianira, but it seems impious of Nessus to break the agreement that he volunteered, namely, to swim Deianira across the swollen river, and to violate the family relationship just established by Deianira and Hercules. Hercules piously submits to the toils imposed upon him by Juno, and his being made a god is evidence that, as well as his sharing the divine nature, he has not behaved unjustly toward the gods or angered them. Piety receives marked support in the story of Iphis and Ianthe in the mother's pious devotion to her child and her devotion to Isis. If Ovid seems impious because the tale is incredible, what challenges belief lies in the realistic possibility of keeping a child's sex concealed for seventeen or so years. The miracle itself was not incredible because it was possible.

Looking at Ovid's piety, which is our present concern, we find that he presents the Greek gods as the muddle the Greeks made of them. He neither completely accepts nor rejects them. Instead, he transposes them, so that they become agents in meaningful stories. It is more likely that he believed in *numina*, rather than the Olympians.

Another theme that stands out is that of love. The *Metamorphoses* presents an extensive coverage of the varieties of love, beginning with the marital devotion of Deucalion and Pyrrha in Book I. Book VIII gave readers the unrequitted romantic love of Scylla, Daedalus' paternal love, Meleager's incipient love inspired by Atalanta's appearance, Althaea's divided familial love, Acheloüs' liaison with Perimele, the rape of Erysichthon's daughter, the bestiality of Pasiphaë, and the marital compatibility of Baucis and Philemon. Book IX presents Acheloüs' self-love; the effects of love, such as pregnancy for Iole and Alcmena, hatred and revenge for Juno; Nessus' lust; and socially unacceptable love, such as Byblis'. The book begins with bride combat (Acheloüs versus Hercules for Deianira), proceeds to the bridegroom's kill in order to keep his bride (Hercule's shooting Nessus), moves to married love later in life (rumor of Hercules' love for Iole, Deianira's effort to retain Hercules' love), and then deals with the two pregnancies and the loyalty of a servant and a relative (Galanthis and Iolaüs). Iole tells the story of Dryope's nympho-philia and affection in a young family; it includes Iole's love for her half sister. There follows a section on the inability of love to reverse the effects of time. Last come two tales dealing with love at its freshest and most erratic, teenage love, one dealing with incestuous love (Byblis); the other, with homosexual love miraculously straightened out (Iphis and Ianthe). Hence, the theme of love is another unifying element running throughout the book.

Though one would not expect it, in a book that opens with heroes and is bound together by the themes of love and piety, the overall unifying theme is the problems of women. The heroes, Acheloüs and Hercules, receive attention only in the first two hundred and seventy-five lines. The remainder, except for the Iolaüs episode, is not boy-talk, but girl-talk. Even the Iolaüs passage is concerned with one of women's problems, defenselessness. And though the theme may seem unlikely at the beginning of the book because the feminine figure is in the background and is merely named, she is essential, for she is the reason for the wrestling match between the heroes. Deianira receives more attention in the incident with Nessus, naturally, since he attempts to rape her, and even more in connection with the death of Hercules, which she causes. After this event, women receive major attention. The overall effect is that of a progressive stress on the importance of women. Once one realizes this growing concern, one sees that one of Deianira's, or women's, problems is men: she is the object for whom men contend, but she does not participate in the decision about her. Furthermore, much depends upon the man who wins her, for her future depends primarily upon his character and ability.

Another problem for Deianira is inequality in love. Whether Deianira loves Acheloüs or Hercules or anyone else does not matter in the least. What is important is that some man desires her for some reason. In addition, one has the impression that Hercules may love promiscuously, but Deianira may not. And as far as physical love is concerned, Nessus attempts rape, but it is inconceivable that Deianira should.

Other kinds of women's problems emerge with Alcmena. The first is childbirth and its fearful pains and uncertainties; next, the jealousy of other females—Juno did excruciating things to her rival. Then there are the aesthetics of love and the matter of personal preference. Lotis rejected the advances of Priapus because his private parts were repulsive. Another aesthetic operates with Dryope. She loves the nymphs, the foliage and flowers, the serenity and loveliness of plants more than she loves the married state. And then there is age, which wastes away attractiveness and renders lovers impotent. Or a girl may find that morals forbid her sexual union, as Byblis did. A mother may be ordered, quite in accordance with custom but in violation of her feelings, to kill her infant, as Telethusa was. A girl may have the desire to mate with another girl, as did Iphis.

Reviewing the stories from this approach, one concludes that life for women is hard. Only they endure childbirth. They are comparatively defenseless. They have fewer freedoms than their male counterparts and less power. They are likely to be less gratified emotionally than men. They are certainly not unimportant. Their mental and emotional processes are just as interesting as those of men, perhaps more interesting thus far because women are more repressed than men. But their problems throw into relief what Ovid has shown over and over again with both sexes, namely, the the their emotional lives, their thinking, and their psychological dimensions are as fascinating and fantastic as any global catastrophe, any hunt, or any fight in a hall.

Reviewing Book IX, one is forced to conclude that Ovid has played his game well. At the outset it would be impossible for one to guess that Ovid could begin with stories about Hercules and end with one about Iphis and Ianthe. The ingenuity and steps taken to get from one to the other are beyond calculation. Yet Ovid makes the moves and even contrives to have thematic unity, which is even more remarkable.

METAMORPHOSES X: Orpheus' Complaint

In Book X itself, balance is lost. The theme of piety tends to disappear in the glare of love that is extreme, disturbed, hectic, or bizarre or is at odds with itself. In fact, as far as the *Metamorphoses* as a whole is concerned, Book X is the torchy apex. Yet ingeniously Book X balances Boox IX by focusing on the problems of a male figure, instead of on those of women. Roughly, Orpheus' problems are that he loved too intensely, that he was thwarted in his heterosexual love, and that, as a result, he turned to homosexual love. In addition, though gifted like his sire, his abilities, like Apollo's, fail to bring him the marital happiness, or sexual happiness, that he desires. Another of his problems is blindness. Like the Minyeïdes, he reacts to a situation by rejecting it and finding a substitute for it. The Minyeïdes reject the Dionysian experience and turn to story-telling; Orpheus turns from the love of women to that of boys. But his sterile program, like theirs, allows him to see only so far, to seek only his own temporary gratification. Like Narcissus, Orpheus is destructively self-centered. Therefore, he experiences and responds, but he does not understand much, for he does not perceive how disruptive his attitude is. Women are just about to tear him apart, literally. He does not perceive that the intensity of his love for Eurydice was harmful because excessive, overwhelming, and one-sided. This is another aspect of his blindness, and it is the artistic reason that Eurydice, contrary to our expectations, is kept such an undeveloped character: she is not to detract attention from Orpheus; his egocentric personality is indicated by Ovid's relating everything to Orpheus and his desires.

Since the whole of Book X is devoted to Orpheus, either as protagonist or as storyteller, the reader has to remember his limitations. Elsewhere in literature and other classical remains, Orpheus is musician, bard, magician, religious innovator, civilizer, companion of heroes, and oracle, as well as husband of Eurydice, effective pleader before the gods of Hades, and enterprising journeyer to and from their abode. Ovid drastically reduces Orpheus to magical singer with erotic problems. In the first quarter of the book, Ovid sketches Orpheus' problems. In the remaining three quarters, which Orpheus sings, the reader needs to remember that Orpheus' character qualifies his compositions. Because Ovid focuses on Orpheus thus and because the songs all deal with erotic relationships, almost the entire book is devoted to the topic of love as Orpheus experiences it or views it.

The whole of Book X is also Ovid's, and Ovid, though he is not unsympathetic to Orpheus, seems to find him strange. For Ovid makes Orpheus' songs, as well as Ovid's own about the Orpheus-Eurydice relationship and about Cyparissus, deal with varieties of love that deviate from the normal or the pious in various ways; and these songs imply, from Ovid's overview, that disturbed, distorted, or perverted love is unhappy or that a love that thwarts Venus in some way is bound to be unfortunate. Orpheus' songs, from his position, boost homosexual relationships almost exclusively. In the stories of Ganymede and Hyacinthus, Orpheus has gods set the pattern for them. In other stories he disparages women: it took a miracle by Venus on her own island of Cyprus to produce one honest woman; Myrrha is a sexual abomination; and Venus, in her amour with Adonis, is rather a featherhead.

Taken as a whole, then, Book X is devoted to two views of an extremely gifted mortal, an unusual variety of unhappy hero. Either he is written about, or he presents himself through his songs. And the hero's career is largely caught up in the battle between the sexes. The topic is handled at times with finesse and discernment.

Consider the outset of the book. Here Ovid presents the reader with a puzzle: what is wrong with the marriage of Orpheus and Eurydice? He makes it abundantly clear that it contrasts with the union of Iphis and Ianthe. There it took a miracle to produce a happy marriage between two mismatched lovers. Here the mates are suitably heterosexual from the start, but the marital miracle fails to occur. Why? Ovid does not even ask the question explicitly, but his details cry for explanation. Once again there is a joyless ceremony, one of tears and without passion. And the indications are that Eurydice is emotionally, psychologically, and physically still separate from her husband after the wedding night, for the new wife does not linger abed with him, but goes walking with her companion water-nymphs. She is still virginal enough to prefer the company of young women. Further, the cause of her remoteness is also implied: Orpheus is not only too self-centered, he has been too aggressive. Ovid later indicates this characteristic in two ways. First, the marriage of Orpheus and Eurydice is destroyed by a phallic form, the snake that attacked her. Second, when Orpheus turns to homosexuality later, his partners are boys, a preference that suggests his being sexually aggressive, perhaps overly or hectically so.

The fact that his marriage has not joined Orpheus with Eurydice in mutual flames in no way weakens his strong, enduring, and agonizing love for her. He goes through hell for her. At this point Ovid gives one the feeling that Orpheus overdoes his mourning. Not only does Orpheus bewail his loss "sufficiently" (the word seems a bit sarcastic) to the upper airs (they seem empty and unresponsive), he "dares" to try out the empty forms of the dead. *Dares* sounds like bravery, boldness, and excessive effrontery. And Ovid's phrase for *try out* suggests that Orpheus is being a calculating nuisance in testing the shades of the dead and causing a disturbance. He appears pesky and conceited, and Ovid, sarcastic. In general the wording of Orpheus' grief and great venture suggests a rather pushy poet who emotes and wants everyone to hear him. Thus the characterization is not without its reservations.

In Hades Orpheus presents his case to music. Unfortunately, the music is lost, for the pleading itself uses the obvious arguments, and the pleader is annoyingly aware of himself, his feelings, and his needs. It is not admirable of him to say that he *wished* to have the strength to bear his grief, nor is it considerate of him to ask for the "use" of Eurydice, even though the word may be a metaphor for "loan." Nor is it tactful to remind Pluto and Proserpina of the rape that brought them together. Orpheus' next remark (" 'Love joined you, too' ") makes the point while avoiding the suggestion of painful memories to Proserpina. It also suggests that the two couples have something in common, the love that brought them together. And that hint reveals that Orpheus loved Eurydice and took her by force as Hades had Prosperina. Next, when Orpheus asks the rulers of the Underworld to reverse the Fates, he is either asking the impossible or is out of tune with the realities. We know that this is so because of Jove's statement about the Fates in Boox IX.

And there is the excellent point that Mr. Anderson notes in connection with Orpheus' plea. Orpheus says that he has not come to Hades as a sightseer, something of a slight to Aeneas and his visit to Hell, nor as a conqueror, like Hercules. In other words, Orpheus denies heroic curiosity and heroic achievement. Thus he piques interest, but when he states his reason for coming, he is, by comparison with these heroes, uxorious and bathetic: he has come for his wife.

The entire speech is dignified, and wives are not to be sniffed at. But Orpheus' love is lamentably and ridiculously egocentric. And his speech is astonishingly mediocre.

Nevertheless, it is surprisingly effective. All Hell is moved. One might expect sympathy from the dead and bloodless, and the damned, not at all surprisingly, take time off from their torments. Those sentimentalists the Furies weep copiously. All these details are comic. Proserpina is moved to grant Orpheus' request. Perhaps she is unable to stand the emotional strain and Orpheus' threat to remain in Hell if he cannot take Eurydice back to the light. And so a limping (good pathetic-bathetic touch) Eurydice is returned to her spouse, provided he does not look back at her until she is above ground. If he does, the gift is void.

Apparently the grim lords of Hades know their man. Wanting Eurydice very much and afraid that she is not following him, he looks back. Once again he is overly emotional. And he is insecure, trusting neither the infernal deities nor Eurydice. She, whom he has never really had, fades from him into the depths. Significantly, she registers no grievance. For, says Ovid, what could she complain of, except that she was loved? A question worthy of question. Once again Orpheus has been too hasty, too self-centered, too intense, and too agressive in his love.

Stupefied by this reversal, Orpheus fails in an attempt to re-enter Hades. He returns to the upper world maladjusted. For three years he shuns venery with women, though many find him attractive and grieve at being rejected. Instead, he introduces to Thrace the practice of loving young boys in their first flower. The alternative causes of Orpheus' homosexuality, according to Ovid, are that sexual relations with woman had turned out badly for him or that he was keeping faith with Eurydice.

133

But the fact that Orpheus does not give up sexual pleasure and has a series of boy mistresses—young adolescents, presumably—fills in Ovid's portrait of him: he is strongly sexed, aggressive, curious, and insecure. And he does not wish to have his ego wounded again. His choosing boys suggests that he desires the more pliant, innocent, inexperienced, and yet girlish male, someone dependent and capable of infatuation and someone who will not be the object of a lasting commitment.

Thus far in the *Metamorphoses* Ovid has shown Venus and Cupid operating in connection with heterosexual love, but the implication of his phrase *"femineam Venerum"* (literally, "womanly Venus," or "sexual relations with women") is that there is a manly Venus. In other words, Venus and Cupid are also behind homosexual love. Ovid uses this shocking suggestion to indicate what a muddle the Greek myths have made of love. Examples occur later.

Having urbanely exposed the power of Orpheus and his lyre in Hades, Ovid now, with humorous irony, shows the pair charming other shades, not those of the dead, but those of living trees. Orpheus requires them for his comfort. The trees that crowd into a shade for Orpheus include twenty-two distinct varieties to show the extensive range of his appeal and to provide a humorous—because idyllic, not epic—catalog of the trees. Leading the list, doubtless as a courtly compliment, is one of Jove's oracular oaks from Dodona in Epirus. This oak has traveled a far piece to get from Dodona to Thrace; hence, the compliment extends to the magnitude of Orpheus' potent magic. Mentioned next, to continue the spoofing and to make it more obvious, are the Heliades, who had even farther to travel, for they had become poplars by their brother's tomb on the banks of the Italian Po. Then come ordinary trees interspersed with Daphne's laurel from Thessaly, Lotis' lotus tree from Euboea, Attis' pine from Asia Minor, and Cyparissus' cypress from Ceos. All in all, a fine piece of deadpan humor.

Umbrella pine Attis unsexed himself for the goddess Cybele and, therefore, makes an appropriate shade for the similarly sterile Orpheus, also done in by devotion to a female. But, since Attis emasculated himself because of religious frenzy, he is hardly a figure to dwell on in a book dealing with sexual love. Ovid merely mentions him as a most inappropriate figure in a most appropriate place, giving shade.

The last tree in the list, this time, is the one Ovid is going to tell about, the cypress, once the boy Cyparissus. Cyparissus is a beautiful nobody, a mortal whose parentage Ovid does not even bother with, nor does anyone else, apparently. Apollo's love for him is his only claim to fame. This affection is inadequately returned, for all the indications are that the boy loves to distraction a tame stag, all men's pet and sacred to the local nymphs. The stag is huge and is more decked out than Cleopatra. It has gold-plated antlers, jewelled collars, a silver forehead amulet, gold and jewel berries on its temples, and purple reins. Cyparissus takes it to fresh pastures and clear waters and rides it and loves it dearly. And one suspiciously hot, sunshiny day when the tired stag is resting in the shade, Cyparissus, who should not have been hunting at noon, perhaps not at all, kills his darling by mistake. The fatal weapon was a javelin, which had to be thrown. Even so, the size and gleam of the ornamented animal and the limited range of a weapon thrown by a boy in a forest make one wonder about the way in which the story is told. Is it realistic enough to be convincing? Has the blazing sun-god scrambled the boy's wits? Or is the point of the story not divine jealousy, but something else? Is it about lack of judgment? So it seems.

Overwhelmed by grief, Cyparissus decides to die himself. Apollo tries to comfort him and advises him to grieve moderately and appropriately with regard to the cause of his sorrow, but the silly child begs that heaven will let him grieve forever. He cries and cries and becomes so exhausted that his legs and arms begin to turn green—a good touch of humorous pathos to frighten inconsolable children with. He becomes, oddly enough, not a spring or a pool, but a tree. Apollo, left to mourn for him, says that Cyparissus-cypress will always be a symbol of grief.

It is clear that the tale embodies the ideas that love may be largely an emotion, like the boy's for the stag, and have no sexual dimension and that loving out of one's own level of being may bring great grief. A moralizing parent might use the story to teach a child to restrain his grief over the death of a pet, to illustrate the point that not even a god can make a body stop being foolish, and so forth.

More important, however, is the way that Ovid's tale fits into Book X. It is Ovid's story of a homosexual love, and the love is a failure because there is lack of emotion on the side of the junior partner. Had Cyparissus loved Apollo, he would have been consolable about the death of the stag. But being a boy, the homosexual relationship was not meaningful to him. Urbane and tender as Apollo is, Ovid represents such love as a failure. Such is Ovid's evaluation, and it contrasts with Orpheus', for in Orpheus' tales, the homosexual relationship is a gratifying one, though it may end in tragic accident.

Cyparissus' being dealt with immediately after mention of Attis calls attention to the boy's sterility, as does their both becoming ever green, that is, arrested in an unripe condition. Early in the story of Cyparissus, Ovid calls attention to the similarity of the cypress to the cone-shaped turning posts of the Roman circus, the *metae*. By doing so, he calls attention to the phallic nature of the tree. What the cypress represents, then, is mourning for lost sexuality. Since neither Attis nor Cyparissus nor Orpheus fecundate, they belong to the same pattern. But since both Cyparissus and Orpheus are, or were, capable of doing so, not having castrated themselves out of religious frenzy like Attis, they seem culpable.

This blame is indicated in another way. When Cyparissus killed the stag, he was killing the male principle with a male symbol, the javelin.

The stag is not only male; it is a fertility emblem "noted for its sexual fury," according to A. de Vries in the *Dictionary of Symbols and Imagery* (Amsterdam and London, 1974). More than a pet is involved here. The boy has killed something essential.

Having lightly ridiculed Orpheus' ability to move trees, Ovid now provides him with an audience: wild animals and flying things. This is a tribute to the power of the bard's music; Ovid says so at the start of the next book. But since Orpheus proceeds to tell the owl and the wild pussy-cat about Ganymede, Hyacinthus, Pygmalion, Myrrha, and Adonis, there is something comic about the situation, just as there would be about singing true romances to a tortoise. In addition, Ovid is once again engaging in self-adulation by composing songs for a famous and most moving poet. Incidentally, some of these songs are superior to the one Orpheus sings to the rulers of Hades. Ovid has thus introduced criticism of Orpheus by having the song most intimately connected with his life be inferior to those he sings about others.

At this point Ovid uses one of his comic devices, later imitated by Chaucer. Instead of saying that Orpheus tuned up, Ovid takes two and a half lines to make the point. His elaborate and periphrastic statement of the trivial or obvious is this: "And when he had tried the chords by touching them with his thumb, and his ears told him that the notes were in harmony although they were of different pitch, . . . " So that his reader will not miss the device, Ovid later repeats it twice in this book. The compression of expression that Latin allows and that Ovid has made use of earlier and the fact that he has omitted elsewhere more important details or ones that one feels the need for, throws this device into relief. One must add, however, that this detail, though unnecessary, is meaningful: it shows Orpheus as self-conscious and pedantic about his artistry, as striving for impression by making much of minor technical matters.

Now Ovid allows Orpheus to begin his songs, and he does so in the best tradition of the Homeric hymns, calling on his Muse-mother Calliope to inspire him to begin with Jove and paying his respects to Jove, whose power all obey. Then, sounding very much like a first-century-B.C. Roman poet, Orpheus says that he is giving up heavy themes such as Jove's war with the giants for lighter ones: boys loved by gods and girls smitten by forbidden flames and justly punished for giving in to them. Orpheus' biases are showing, and there is an acid, vindictive quality to his expression of them.

His first story, an eight-liner, pays homage to Jove by recording his successful homosexual rape of Ganymede and his snubbing of Juno. The episode is not much as openers, but it does reveal that Orpheus is more interested in self-justification than praise of Jove and that the genre of the Homeric hymn is being adjusted to Ovid's poetic needs. As for the rationalization of homosexuality by implying that Jove is authority for it, one should note that Orpheus has Myrrha do precisely the same thing with myth later on, that is, use it for validating her sexual preference, incest.

Next Orpheus sings of a homosexual affair that his father Apollo had with Hyacinthus. This love propelled the god out of his oracular seat and sedentary activities into hunting and athletics. And one day about noon, when the lovers were competing at discus throwing, a rebound smashed Hyacinthus' face and broke his neck. Apollo vainly tried to heal the youth and suffered suitably. He blamed himself for the accident, but added, how can loving be a fault? (Orpheus seems to have his own excessive love for Eurydice in mind.) Apollo could neither redeem Hyacinthus' life with his own nor die with the lad, so he proposed memorials in song and flower. The flower was marked with the syllables of woe, which, the god rather pedantically remarked, would later be associated with Ajax. Orpheus concludes, Spartans are proud of Hyacinthus and still celebrate his anniversary.

(In passing, it should be noticed that this narrative contains another of Ovid's easy deaths, here a hideous and shocking one glossed over by flower imagery. See Evelyn Waugh's *The Loved One* for a similar cosmetic impulse in American mortuary practices. The death of Eurydice is another example. The bride simply slips from the earth into Hades. Both of Ovid's passages tend to make death an artistic event, rather than a human catastrophe, and to avoid the gruesome truth. Emma's death in Flaubert's *Madame Bovary* is a much less aesthetic, but a much more moral treatment because it is realistic.)

Next Orpheus turns comtemptuously to Amathus in Cyprus, that venereal soil. Unlike the home of Hyacinthus, Amathus has little to be proud of, according to Orpheus. Neither, for that matter, does Cyprus, as Orpheus deals with it. Venus, however, is not faulted—not yet. She appears as a discerning, humane, and just deity, for she punishes the Cerastae, a horned people of Amathus who impiously and defiantly sacrifice human guests, strangers, on the altar of Jove Protector of Guests. At first Venus considers abandoning Cyprus because of this lot, but she sees that all Cypriots are not guilty. She then has to decide what punishment to inflict, and her choice is interesting because it sheds light on Ovid's title: Venus chooses metamorphosis because it is halfway between exile and death. Further, like Gilbert and Sullivan's Mikado, she makes the punishment fit the crime and the criminals. She changes these horned people into fierce bulls, who might themselves be sacrificed. Thus the reader can feel sure that many of the metamorphoses, if the circumstances warrant, have a punitive element and that some are as close to a death penalty as one can get.

Another group of impious Amathians are the repulsive (Orpheus uses " *'obscenae'* ") Propoetides, who deny that Venus is divine. The goddess punishes them by making them prostitutes, mechanical sexual performers lacking any of the finer aspects of love. One of these finer feelings connected with physical love is shame or modesty, and this the Propoetides lose. They become hard, and it is not much of a change to turn them into rocks. Venus here is presented as the goddess of heterosexual activity conducted with decorum and discrimination, or selectivity. Modesty and an awareness that something transcending copulation is involved in love are required by the goddess of her true devotees.

The foulness of these women is noted by their fellow Cypriot Pygmalion, who, like Orpheus, decided to avoid the company of women because—and here Orpheus generalizes for himself and for Pygmalion—of "'the faults which in such full measure nature had given the female mind.' " That such unqualified generalizing is wrong of itself, Orpheus should be well aware, for a few lines earlier, he himself pointed out that Venus had almost committed the same error. She had been about to abandon all the people of Cyprus because of the abominations of one group, the Cerastae. In other words, she had been about to generalize about a whole population on the basis of the behavior of a fraction of it. Certainly Venus has avoided one mental error, or fault of mind, that Orpheus and Pygmalion do not. Furthermore, as singer and reteller of myths, Orpheus should have known that the corpus of myth contained Pyrrha and Baucis as well as Myrrha and Byblis. But it is part of Orpheus' blindness that he is unaware of his own inconsistencies and limitations.

His vignette of the Propoetides suggests one more thing. Orpheus labels their crime as that of denying that Venus is a goddess, that is, that she has power over human beings. The nature of that power is not defined, but if the punishment of the Propoetides fits their crime—and we have reason from Lycaon on to believe that punishment does—then we have grounds for assuming that Venus' power normally causes one to fall in love with a particular individual and that it also produces sexual gratification, even ecstasy. If such are Venus' normal effects, we may again infer that Eurydice, whatever her emotional attachment to Orpheus, was not completely given over to Venus' power, namely, that she was frigid and did not reciprocate Orpheus' physical love for her.

As mentioned above, Orpheus' homosexuality and misogyny qualify the point of his narrative about Pygmalion, making it in this context a fable against the innate integrity of women because it takes an artist plus a tender, devoted lover plus a pious male and a miracle to produce one pure and loving wife, whom Orpheus does not bother to name, another slur. It may also be significant that Pygmalion's creation has never been exposed to the society of other women. Whatever the case in that area, the event is singular, and it seems unlikely that the proper components will recur often, if ever.

Up to the Pygmalion myth, the erotic in Book X has been comparatively generalized and colorless. With Pygmalion's love story, Orpheus begins to exercise his imaginative powers and reveals himself further. He sees the ideal woman from the man's point of view; indeed, she is a man's creation, the projection of his mental image, or fantasy, and the careful product of his shaping hands. She is inert, unfeeling, passive, and unaware until the proper venereal moment arrives. Until that time she is the model that male society desires: she is beautiful, and she looks as though she would like to be aroused, sexually as well as physically, if it were not immodest to be so. She is somewhat like Sleeping Beauty. In Orpheus' fantasy of the realization of the male's dream, the relationship takes because the innocent, ignorant, just-aroused maiden lifts her newly opened eyes and sees the heavens framing her lover, the only man she knows, and the sky blue rubs off on him. The whole scene is a delicious example of masculine naivete and romantic idealizing. And one is likely to feel that, whether inert or alive, the lady will always be a doll.

The story shows that Orpheus does like feminine beauty; that he expects perfection, innocence, dependency, passivity, and compliance, as well as adoration, from his woman. He is aware of the processes of emotional involvement: projection, idealization, physical contact, endearments, tenderness, gift giving, adornment, and the like. He has, in fact, produced a sketchy manual of courtship and at the same time given an account of the success of one who properly worshiped Venus. One remembers that it was Hymen who was called to Orpheus' wedding, but it is Venus who is singled out here as attending the " 'marriage she had made.' " The implication is that something Venus would have provided, was missing from the marriage of Orpheus.

There is another thing that comes out about Orpheus. He knows how much detail to give to stimulate the imagination so that the erotic is delicately rendered and is not gross. Yet there is something odd and uneasy making about a man who makes a statue and treats it as though it were human. His eroticism does not seem quite normal, nor does the man who tells his story so intensely.

Since Pygmalion has exteriorized his own vision of Venus in the chaste, but love-inviting statue, since Pygmalion and his ivory maid wed with Venus' blessing, and since their union is fertile, Orpheus continues his presentation of Venus as a respectable and beneficent deity. At this point, however, he turns to the second of his announced themes: girls stricken with unlawful passion and " 'paying the penalty of their lust.' " He thus brings up the question, is lust sent by Venus, or is it not? Are there a divine love and a base one? Apparently there are, for the Propoetides exemplify one kind of damnable love, that of the prostitute. But then how different is their love from Orpheus' homosexual relationships? Are both not mechanical? Apparently not. Apparently his are selective and involve both the emotion of love and aesthetic appreciation of the youths involved, as well as sexual gratification. At the moment, however, Orpheus devotes his attention to incestuous passion. This he finds too horrible to associate with divinity, for he takes pains to have Cupid clear himself of any responsibility for it. But later Orpheus says of Myrrha's son, Adonis, and his amour with Venus that Adonis, by exciting love in Venus, " 'avenges his mother's passion,' " as though Venus has been responsible for it and was, therefore, the culpable one. Orpheus cannot have it both ways without making Cupid more discriminating and more moral than Venus and thus damning the goddess. But Orpheus seems willing to condemn Venus for some things, perhaps because of his marital experience, and to praise her for others. We should notice, however, that Orpheus does not put homosexual love on a par with heterosexual, but uses it as a substitute, placing it lower than ideal heterosexual love. In addition, it is clear that he regards some types of amorous and erotic attachments as better than others and some as intolerable.

At the outset of his narration about Myrrha, Orpheus makes it clear that she is vile, and through her he makes his strongest condemnation of women because of the depths to which they can sink. Before he can tell about her, he feels impelled to warn fathers and daughters not to listen, or if they do, to separate pleasure in listening to her tale from belief in it. The warning is very interesting. First, it implies that such pleasure combined with the belief that the behavior can occur, because it is presented as happening, incites the reader or listener to imitate it. Hence, a reader must be warned specifically against believing that a bad model of behavior or an immoral protagonist could exist. In the present situation, the warning is both ineffective and disingenuous. The really important matter is not whether Myrrha's incestuous passion is a fiction, but whether it and its fulfillment are humanly possible and whether a warning is an effective preventive. Orpheus ignores these important considerations and pours out a tale that some moralists would prefer not to be told, even though Myrrha is finally punished.

The warning is interesting for another reason. It is long, about sixteen lines long. It moves from saying that Cinyras was unfortunate and that the tale is horrible to telling fathers and daughters not to read it—or if they do, not to believe it happened—to indicating that a crime is involved and punished and, in fact, is probably in defiance of nature, to congratulating Thrace that it occurred far away, to saying that the crime was too high a price to pay for a new perfume and that Cupid had no part in the crime—it was caused by a Fury—to finally indicating the nature of the crime. Somewhere in this drawn out and repetitious but vague warning, perhaps the bathetic bit about the high price or the falsely pious command to fathers and daughters not to read farther, one realizes that Orpheus is not only warning and slanting one's attitude, he is luring the reader on.

As for revealing more about Orpheus, the passage shows him to be histrionic, hectic, and prurient. And Ovid is using him so that Ovid can disavow responsibility for the story.

Turning to Myrrha's complaint, Orpheus has her pray to the gods, the power of parents, and piety to keep her free from sin. Then she rationalizes. She is not sure that incestuous love is impious. Nature, she observes, allows incest among animals. Happy are they to whom such things are allowed! she exclaims. At this point Myrrha relies on nature, freedom of impulse, and pleasure as the bases for ethics, for she adds that human pains or effort have produced malicious laws, grudgingly forbidding what nature concedes. Then Myrrha turns to cultural relativism as the basis for ethics: it is reported, she says, that there are peoples whose offspring have sexual intercourse with their parents. She sees that this practice can be accommodated to the morality of her own people, saying that in such a relationship family piety increases with a doubled love. Her wretchedness, she concludes, is merely an accident of place, implying that local conditions are not and need not be acceptable. (In all this she sounds curiously like the social rebels of the 1960's and 1970's.) In the next breath, however, she accepts local morals by commanding her prohibited desires to be gone. Later she indicates that she would be breaking nature's law if she violated her father's bed.

In desperation, because she is being pulled apart by conflicting impulses, Myrrha decides to hang herself. Circumstances conspire against her. Her devoted nurse stops her and offers aid. None of her remedies, however, can dispel passion. At this point a fertility festival, ironically, takes Myrrha's mother from her father's bed for nine days, so that it is most helpful of Nurse to offer Cinyras a loving maiden his own daughter's age. To increase the irony, when Cinyras and Myrrha copulate in the dark, they refer to one another as " ' "father" ' " and " ' "daughter." ' " And thus their words suggest a latent desire for incest on the part of Cinyras. It is even more repellent that Orpheus plays on the word " 'viscera' " in connection with the first assignation: " 'into the obscene bed the begetter received his child/viscera.' "

Dramatic ironies abound. But after a number of nights together, Cinyras discovers the girl's identity, goes into shock, and tries to kill Myrrha. She flees westward all across Arabia, falling exhausted in the spice-producing kingdom of Sabaea. Now nine months gone with Cinyras' child, afraid, as well as worn out, she makes a pious end, praying that in her deserved punishment she not offend the living or the dead. Her prayer is granted; she is changed into an incense tree, and so she is neither a living human being nor a shade. Unlike the changing Dryope, Myrrha shows no interest in her child, but she does go into hopeless and painful labor as a tree. The goddess of childbirth hears, pities, and effects the delivery of Adonis.

By exile, wandering, and suffering, Myrrha has purged passion and expiated sin and returned to piety. She is obviously a penitent sinner and redeemed, and her metamorphosis is an ostracism that is both a condemnation of self and a blessed release. Myrrha can now offer a pleasant odor. *In extremis* she receives kindly treatment from Orpheus, but only then. Thus in the total scheme of things there is the unexpected possibility that even vile passion can produce something of value.

Once again, however, Orpheus attacks womankind in order to justify himself.

It so happens that Myrrha's child, Adonis, is the spitting image of Cupid, and so he grows up. This fact saves Venus from an incestuous love, for when one of Cupid's arrows scratches Venus as her son is kissing her, she falls in love, not with Cupid, but with his semblable. At this point

141

Orpheus remarks that Adonis avenges his mother's passion, implying that Venus caused it and Myrrha's consequent disaster. Thus Orpheus, who earlier had exonerated male Cupid as the cause of Myrrha's incestuous desires, now identifies the Fury that stimulated them as Venus. And in the tale that follows, Orpheus punishes Venus by having her love a mortal (a penalty inflicted on her in one of the Homeric hymns), by having her lover ungrateful, and by having her lose him. Orpheus also portrays the goddess as not very bright and as long-winded.

Venus does not feel déclassé as she deserts Olympus to hunt up hill, over rocks, through thorn and thicket with Adonis, exposing her boudoir physique to the ardors of the chase as well as those of his arms and going after bunnies and deer, nothing nasty or risky. She is slightly comic because definitely out of place, but she persists. Naturally, since she does not want to lose her beautiful lover, whose parts she praises, she advises Adonis to play safe and avoid dangerous animals. She fears and hates them. The implication is clear that she fears them because they are dangerous. But why Venus should tell Adonis a story about the origin of her hatred for tamed lions is not clear. One would expect her to tell a fable whose moral is, do not hunt fierce beasts. Does she? Not at all. Venus hates lions because she associated them with ungrateful lovers. But it is silly of her to expect Adonis to make any such connection between Venus' warning and her tale. The latter would not keep a novice swimmer away from a hungry shark. If it is cautionary, it would seem to warn against fast women with bad horoscopes, against taking favors from Venus and then not thanking her, and against profaning sacred places by having sexual intercourse therein, even though the participants are properly wed. None of these admonitions directly applies to the dangers of the hunt. Thus the fact that Venus tells Adonis an apparently irrelevant story at a crucial point in their relationship makes her appear foolish.

The fact that the tale is long makes her appear long-winded. And the fact that it is about courtship and sexual intercourse and Venus' feelings makes it in character. It also damns Venus' character; for, in essence, the situation of Hippomenes and Atalanta is that of Orpheus and Eurydice: love brought them together to their undoing. But Orpheus more clearly implicates Venus as the responsible personage in Atalanta's mating and misfortune than Ovid does in Orpheus'. Without her valuable aid, Hippomenes would never have won the maid. And both he and Atalanta are Venus' worshipers in that they fall in love. Hippomenes early acknowledges the power of the goddess by invoking her. Thus far in the story, goddess and mortals function in harmony. But when, after all the excitement of falling in love, being responded to favorably by the one loved, receiving the goddess' advice, and winning the race, Hippomenes is leading his bride home and happens to forget to thank Venus, she suddenly becomes very angry, like a moody wench, and allowing no time for the couple to regain their wits, Venus selfishly, hastily, and spitefully ruins them. They were already doomed, according to a prophecy, but Venus does not have to mar the match that she had made, nor does she have to do it in such an underhanded fashion, by having them offend another deity

142

who then punishes them. As Orpheus presents the story, one can feel only that he puts Venus in a very bad light.

He presents Atalanta similarly. She is competitive, bloodthirsty, and wanton. After she receives the oracle, fearing marriage and shunning suitors is no doubt wise on her part. But setting up the race is unnecessary, except to show off her athletic ability. The death penalty for the male losers is cruel and vindictive. Furthermore, the race conflicts with her desire to avoid the prophecy, for the contest exposes her to the hazard of losing and, hence, of marrying. And worse, the oracle tells her that she cannot escape her doom, so that Atalanta impiously tries to prove the oracle and the god wrong and also wastes human lives. In effect, the race assures Atalanta of only three things: the possibility of being beaten, a husband in excellent physical condition, and disaster. Indeed, like other Ovidan heroines, she is ambivalent, but her struggle takes an unusual form, much to Ovid's credit.

The tale has some fine comic touches. Racing to avoid matrimony, which Atalanta was originally interested in or she would not have consulted the oracle, is not a foolproof device. It did not insure Atalanta against breaking a leg, being outwitted, or falling in love. The last two happen to her and undo her, because Hippomenes makes her go all soft. Before the fatal race occurs, she and Hippomenes produce a neat parody of the boastful interchange characteristic of epic heroes before they contend. Hippomenes vaunts his pedigree, while Atalanta, who likes very much what she is looking at, deplores the impending destruction of such male beauty, precious life, youth, manly courage, and high birth. Then she notes, last and best, the fact that he wants to die if he cannot have her. Since it is Atalanta, not Hippomenes, who makes this statement, she is deceiving herself about Hippomenes' death wish and is flattering herself into pity. Then she does the wobble of the Ovidian ambivalents, here between love and pitilessness. Love wins, of course, for in the race Atalanta is diverted by Venus' love apples. In other words, Atlanta is thwarted by her own desire.

Had Venus' deceit and golden persuasion not prevailed, Hippomenes certainly would have lost the race and died, and the *virtus*, or manliness, that he boasted of would have put him into the hands of the executioner. It is the same *virtus* that a bit later sets hunter Adonis in the path of the boar, and Orpheus may be hinting that there would be fewer beautiful young male corpses if there were less of the cult of the male.

Moody, spiteful Love, we have seen, can be destructive. Now that her cautionary story is over, we learn that Venus can also be destructive merely by being thoughtless and withdrawing her support. This is what she does to Adonis. She brings about his death by going off on a trip for no reason at all. As long as she was his companion in the hunt, she forced him to go after small game and thus restrained his manly drive to go after the really challenging beasts. With Venus gone, Adonis immediately becomes heedless and daring. A boar guts him. Venus returns at once to express her violent grief and memorialize it, not Adonis. Orpheus ends his song and the book with a nice ironic blast at Venus and womankind: the memorial of her grief does not last long.

Various themes appear in Book X. That of piety, not conspicuous at the beginning of the book, reappears with the Cerastae, who violate Jove's laws of hospitality, and the Propoetides, who deny Venus' divinity. Pygmalion is clearly pious, and Myrrha gives explicit attention to piety. Atalanta and Hippomenes are impious when they couple in the grotto before the archaic idols. Hippomenes is pious when he calls upon Venus for aid, but impious when he neglects to thank the goddess. Sometimes matters of piety are clear-cut; sometimes, not. Sometimes they are forgotten or are complicated. Other emotions may obscure what is pious.

There are, in addition, many echoes of earlier types and situations: the ambivalent personality, the intelligent young woman overcome by passion (Medea, Byblis, Myrrha), the tomboy (Callisto, the Calydonian huntress, Atalanta), the unfortunate love. The love chase of Book I (Daphne-Apollo, Pan-Syrinx) appears in a new form, the race, an athletic contest. Each motif is varied in some meaningful or entertaining way. The result overall is that one perceives such metamorphoses functioning significantly, for nothing is ever the same, though life constantly repeats itself, and the changes give storytelling and life their enduring interest and charm.

Reviewing Book X itself, we see that its focus is almost exclusively on love as Orpheus lived it or sang about it. It has its hopes and expectations and its delights and rewards, but it is not a many splendored thing, for it is flawed, grotesque, cruel, disastrous, or agonizing. And it is a jumble. It includes the mechanical performance of a physical act and in this form it is subhuman and contemptible. So the Propoetides demonstrate, for with them physical love is on the level of a twitch occurring under anesthetic. Love can be unqualified lust, the sort of thing driving men to the Propoetides for gratification. This, too, is base. It may take the form of Hippomenes' lust for his bride and his impulsive union with her in the grotto. This is modified by his affection for her and admiration of her beauty. But it is impious and brings disaster. Myrrha is also driven by lust, but there is nothing unfeeling or hasty about her, for she is long and agonizingly conscious of it and its abominable nature. Far more satisfactory than such loves is that of Venus and Adonis, a companionable infatuation. But it is an unequal love, for Adonis is more interested in hunting than in Venus, and Venus is flighty and her commitment is not lasting. Among mortals, Pygmalion comes out best, but he goes through his love agony first. And when he is gratified, he is rewarded by receiving the girl of his shallow dreams. Even with the gods, love exposes Apollo to the pangs of bereavement. Only Olympian Jove is relatively successful in love, but he has a resentful Juno to face daily. Orpheus himself knows only too well the suffering caused by a poorly returned love and by his loss of Eurydice. Because of it, he turns to a temporary substitute. There is not a completely happy love in the bunch.

144

And as for the goddess of love, she is a jumble. She is logical when she reasons that not all of the Cyprians are like the Cerastae, but illogical when she tries to warn Adonis by telling him an inappropriate story. She is moral when she punishes the Cerastae and the Propoetides, but she ignores the latter's clients, whom she impels toward them. She is responsible for the incestuous love of Myrrha, which is about as bad as one can get. She is in character when she helps Hippomenes win his love, but when she is vindictive in bringing about the catastrophe in their lives, she is no longer a goddess of love. She is selfish, hasty, and devious, like a spoiled, pampered woman, for she gives the newlyweds almost no time to express their gratitude, and she nastily arranges things so that they commit impiety and so that Cybele punishes the lovers, though it was Venus who caused their misconduct. Her immorality in affairs of the heart appears in her helping Hippomenes to win the race unfairly. In the area of morals, Venus is rather a handful. So are her effects: happiness, agony, torment, grief, punishment, penitence, frustration, confusion, honor, shame, immortality, and immorality.

As Orpheus considers the goddess and her effects in his songs, he is not only engaged in a justification of his homosexual behavior, he is expressing his grievances about love. Its manifestations are so varied and its effects are so often injurious or painful that they lead him to expose the confusion it causes and the harm it does. He strikes back. Yet who can or would avoid this precious bane, golden Aphrodite, and not suffer winning its delights? Not Orpheus, who surveys them and sings his complaint against love.

METAMORPHOSES XI: The Art of Sinking

Though the gods provide some exceptions, all of the prominent characters in Book XI display a distinct talent for plunging from positions of eminence to inferior conditions. This common tendency gives the book its theme, and, indeed, the book amounts to a small manual on the art of sinking. It places most of the blame for such descents on one characteristic, namely, being excessive. The manual shows that excess may take various forms. Orpheus has been immoderate in his peculiar sexual loyalty to Eurydice and in the practice of his art, so that he dies while singing to non-human audiences. The maenads who destroy him are inordinate in their revenge and, as a result, become less than human. The snake that would attack a dead and mutilated bard is rendered powerless. Midas is brought to the verge of starvation and dehydration by his limitless greed and excessive stupidity. The latter also causes his majesty to become something of an ass and an object of ridicule. Laomedon twice loses his city because of blinding greed. The hero Peleus and the sea-goddess Thetis become involved in an unheroic and unladylike (*ungodly* has the wrong connotations) wrestling match and sink far below the dignity due their status. Peleus later falls from grace and felicity, becoming an exile because he acted excessively and murdered his half brother, and he descends from heroic magnanimity by lying to his host, King Ceyx, thus showing that he is overly concerned about his reception by the king. The wolf that carries out Psamathe's vengeance is uncontrollable and loses life as a result. Daedalion is ruined by his extravagant attachment to his daughter, as she was by her immoderate pride in her own beauty. Ceyx and Alcyone love one another beyond reason, and they suffer also from extreme nervousness and excitability. Aesacus suffers because of too much aggressiveness in the pursuit of his love and from too much guilt when his pursuit causes her death.

As for the gods, Somnus represents the nadir of deity, for he is limited to one characteristic, drowsiness, and his inactivity is a negative variety of excess, close to death. Like him in being excessively limited is tipsy Silenus, the eternal companion of Bacchus. Apollo, when he appears as a posturing and overly ornate musician, falls in one's esteem.

Book XI even has an emblem of excess and the depths to which it can plunge things, namely, the storm that overwhelms Ceyx and his ship.

Sinking as the result of excess of some sort, then, is the theme of Book XI, but not the complete theme, for excess causes those who sink to rise to some degree. Were it not for their excesses, the Thracian maenads, Silenus, Midas, Laomedon, the wolf, and Chione would not be memorable. To that degree, the excesses that bring about their falls also raise them above the commonality and thus make them impressive. Peleus is the exception, for he redeems himself and will be further elevated by his remarkable son. The remaining mortals of Book XI are elevated above their falls by their unusual love. And it is this emotion that Ovid pays homage to in Book XI. For it is love that makes Orpheus, Thetis, Daedalion, Ceyx, Alcyone, and Aesacus rise above being merely memorable to being estimable as well.

In sum, the golden mean may be a civic virtue, but it will never make the headlines the way that excess does. The memorable persons or events are the egregious fools and Scrooges, the ludicrously inappropriate wrestling match between goddess and hero, the uxorious spouses, the uncontrolled forces of nature, murder or savage slaughter, the hysterically anxious. And to this list one must add the great lovers. These are of various sorts, but the greatest in this book are husband and wife, Orpheus and Eurydice and Ceyx and Alcyone. In this respect Book XI, in which Ovid tells the tales, not Orpheus, balances Book X, in which Orpheus' tales mostly support homosexual relationships.

Part of the art of sinking, then, consists of falling from high estate. The fall may result in death, as with Orpheus, or in becoming an inferior form of life, as with Daedalion, and may elicit varying degrees of sympathy. It may involve participation in a belittling situation, such as Peleus' wrestling with the nude sea-goddess. Ridiculousness may take other forms, such as Midas' begging to give up the golden touch that he had so wanted or his having ass's ears, or Aesacus' becoming a scrawny, long-necked, long-legged bird and diving, diving, diving. Part of the art is native to the tales themselves, and part consists of Ovid's throwing in bits that are incongrous and that, in effect, sink the material or tone that he has created. For example, it is Ovid's imagined narrator who describes Aesacus as being of illustrious descent and heroic worth and one of love's notables and who also suggests that Aesacus' neck was long enough to resemble that of the scrawny bird into which he was changed. Another example occurs when the mountain Tmolus prepares to judge the contest between Pan and Apollo: Tmolus has to unclog his ears by removing the trees from them. And when, after listening to Pan, he turns to Apollo, his forest turns as he just did. This detail is comic because it implies that trees have faces and that they can turn around as though they were not rooted. In the Ceyx myth two examples are masked because they occur in situations of grief or despair. In the first Alcyone was standing on the shore after the dream announcing her husband's shipwreck and saw a body floating toward her; "and now it had come close to land, now she could see clearly what it was. It was her husband! ' 'Tis he!' she shrieked. . . ." The juxtaposition of the two identifications effects a redundancy of the obvious, a simple-minded repetition that spoils, indeed, reverses the intensity of Alcyone's shocked reaction. The result is bathos. It is bad writing that condemns overanxiety by presenting it as melodramatic. Similarly the realistic account of the storm is impressive until Ovid produces redundancies: twice the waves seem to reach the sky, and twice the darkness of the night is doubled by the storm clouds. The result is that the reader is wrenched out of the storm and into resentment because repetition has been presented as though it were intensification. Bathetic repetition of another sort occurs in the device of retelling a basic story and making it inferior to the earlier one. Ovid had done this effectively in Book I by following the tale of Apollo a bit later with the parallel one of Pan and Syrinx. The unmistakable inferiority of the second story of frustrated pursuit is bathetic, but the bathos is justified because the dull story is used to put a watchman to sleep. In Book XI the Aesacus-Hesperie myth is presented as an inferior variety of the Orpheus-Eurydice pattern; it, too, has redeeming functions, one of which is that it includes a second and emphatic, because it ends Book XI, emblem of sinking. To conclude, Ovid uses bathos intentionally for an urbanely comic effect, but he extends the art of sinking to stimulate more sober perceptions.

As well as developing a complicated theme and presenting lessons in a particular art, Book XI finishes the Orpheus story and explains part of it. The conclusion, Orpheus' death and his reunion with Eurydice, is given at the beginning of Book XI, which thus carries on the action ending Book X. Orpheus' death is a brutal catastrophe that is reversed by his post-humous compatibility with Eurydice. Furthermore, at the end of Book XI, there is elucidation of what went wrong with Orpheus' marriage; it is given in a tale so like that of Eurydice's death that it startles one into looking for further similarities between the two. In this episode a young Trojan prince chases a nymph; during his attempt to possess her, she is bitten by a snake and dies. His aggressive sexual behavior and her retiring nature lead to her accidental death. By introducing these parallels to the events of Orpheus' marriage, Ovid explains what went wrong with it: Eurydice was similarly withdrawn and unresponsive and Orpheus was equally aggressive.

Book XI functions in a number of other ways. It brings Trojan (Laomedon) and Greek (Hercules) into conflict and thus moves toward the confrontation central to the next book. It moves chronologically to the generation before the Trojan War by introducing Peleus, the father of Achilles, and Aesacus, son of Priam and half brother of Hector. Thus it prepares for what is to come. There is also a deceitful Greek, Peleus, who is also a murderer; he is neither the first nor the last of Ovid's unethical Achaeans. Worse will follow. Laomedon represents what is base in the ruling house of Troy, and his punishment typifies those of men who try to cheat the gods.

The pathos of much of Book XI is considerably different from that of Book X. But it pervades only the tales of Orpheus and Eurydice and Ceyx and Alcyone. As usual, Ovid is careful to craze his patterns, and he interrupts the sweet sorrow so dear to human hearts with two stories about an asinine king, a marvelously appropriate description of Sleep and his cave, some inappropriate long-windedness on the part of Peleus' herdsman, an occasional upbeat at the end of a tragedy—for example, the saving of Daedalion and the posthumous happiness of Orpheus and Eurydice—and a comic grace note here and there.

The first of such grace notes is Ovid's reminding the reader in line 1 that "with such songs"--namely, the preceding tales of homosexual love, prostitution, idealized love, incestuous love, love that profanes, and love

149

between a goddess and a mortal—Orpheus enchanted beasts, trees and stones, entities not likely to be interested in such topics. Only one of Orpheus' tales deals with a tree, the myrrh, and that one is not in his audience. For the rest, flint and granite, boar, lion and bull might find their kind important in the stories, but they are not spoken well of. "Such songs" creates the feeling that Ovid is doing more than having Orpheus play his traditional roles of soothing the savage beast and of casting spells on things. Ovid is also satirizing the kind of audience that will listen to anything, whether it understands what it hears or not and whether it is being spoken ill of or not.

In Book X Ovid belittled Orpheus by showing the futility of man's attempts to circumvent death, no matter how beloved the dead, for song cannot restore the dead to life, except as momentary phantoms following the song. Ovid also criticized Orpheus obliquely for excessive grief and for rejecting sexual relationships with women, a practice that led him to homosexuality and to teaching it to the men of Thrace. Now, in Book XI, this homosexuality causes his death at the hands of the Thracian women whom he had treated with contempt. During a Bacchic mountain revel, they come upon Orpheus in concert and begin their clumsy, brutal revenge. For a time his harmonies render their missiles harmless, but finally the maenads make such a discord with shrill flutes, blatting horns, drum thumps, clapping, and ululating that they drown out Orpheus' magic music. The women drive away what Ovid refers to as a theater audience —surely the earliest one in myth—of birds, snakes, and wild beasts, tearing some of them apart and then dismembering Orpheus. His soul departs.

There follows a brief passage of sweet sorrow in the form of pastoral elegy, in which birds, beasts, rocks, and trees (appropriately, since these had been the bard's audience), rivers, naiads, and dryads mourn the dead singer, whose members lie here and there. The respect being paid is somewhat exaggerated, softening the effect of there being bloody limbs on the scene of the mourning. However, unless the reader visualizes as he reads, he may pass over these details. They are likely to be ignored because a marvelous thing occurs. The head and the lyre, thrown into the river Hebrus, both make piteous moan, to which the river banks mournfully respond. More marvels follow. The head and lyre are seaborne to the Lesbian shore near Methymna. There a barbarous snake is about to bite the head, but Apollo turns this adversary to stone.

The arrangement of lyre and Orpheus' sea-wet head on an alien sandy shore and an attacking snake is arresting, almost surrealistic. The silent image, suspended in the poetic context, not clearly leading to anything beyond, not clearly needed to round off the unfortunate marital career of Orpheus and Eurydice, is as teasing as the Grecian urn was for Keats. But it should not tease us out of thought. For it is another emblem like the lady on the bull, Pelops' ivory shoulder, and the marble beast and hound. It is more complicated than these, because so many significances cluster associatively around head and serpent as symbols—see J. C. Cooper's *An Illustrated Encyclopaedia of Traditional Symbols* (Thames and Hudson, 1978) for data. We should consider the image, however, in the context that Ovid has given it. But we may begin by taking a cue from Cooper and regard the lyre as a symbol of harmony. In context, we add that the lyre represents Orpheus' bond with Apollo. In the context of Ovid's rendition of the Orpheus myth, moreover, the snake stands for the masculine sexuality that caused the alienation of his love, Eurydice. It also stands for death, since it was the instrument of Eurydice's death, and for the realm of the dead, as well as for their souls, Cooper tells us. Further, the maenads who slew Orpheus would have had snakes about their persons. The snake that attacks Orpheus' beached head is obviously hostile and may represent the maenads; it might also be an incarnation of a frustrated and hostile Eurydice or symbolize natural or chthonic forces hostile to Orpheus. In brief, a snake is what kept Orpheus and Eurydice apart immediately after their marriage, and a snake is attacking him now. In light of the preceding data, the head-and-snake image poses a question, namely, will sexuality or anything else continue to part Orpheus and Eurydice in Hades? The lyre suggests the answer, for Apollo's turning the snake to stone indicates that neither Orpheus' sexuality nor the creatures of the Underworld nor anything else can thwart their being together. The god of harmony deprives hostility of its force.

This metamorphosis is followed immediately by a scene in which Ovid shows the two lovers happy together in the world after death.

If the arresting image is a surprise, so is the happy ending to Orpheus' career. There is yet another. Now that Orpheus is to spirit gone, his body and its sexual dimensions left behind, he and Eurydice can love mutually and be on an equal footing, for there is no longer aggressive behavior, withdrawal from it, or insecurity on either side. This is what their mode of walking together indicates. Further, because of their loyalty and mutual affection, they perambulate the fields of the pious. And so for Ovid, Orpheus' story is primarily a love story about a man and a woman.

But it is not all love story. For after bright Phoebus stopped the "savage serpent," Bacchus punishes the maenads for murdering his bard. These two passages thus represent Orpheus as a religious poet serving both gods and, therefore, as himself Apollonian and Dionysian; that is, he harmonizes these opposites. Such reconciliation implies a softening and amelioration of the mountain riots of the maenads, which included hallucinating and bloody rituals. In short, Orpheus is one sort of civilizer.

It is important to note that Bacchus upholds Orpheus, for the Thracian bacchants holding the god's orgy on the mountains follow the ritual partly, for example, in tearing the oxen apart and even, perhaps, in gobbeting Orpheus, but their motive is damnable. They are not communicating with the god of frenzied liberation, but using his worship to accomplish revenge and to mask bloody murder. Bacchus punishes them for their hardheartedness by turning them into very tough wood and completely rejects them and their country. At this point Ovid explicitly calls attention to Orpheus as a religious figure by asserting that he "taught the rites of Bacchus" to Midas and to the Athenian king Eumolpus.

Now that love has triumphed after death and crime has been punished, Ovid changes the mood of his narrative by turning to that immortal ancient alcoholic Silenus and to his genial drinking companion and benefactor Midas, whom Bacchus rewards for aiding and entertaining Silenus. Midas has been drinking for ten days with Silenus and is happy when he returns Silenus to his foster son for safekeeping, so that when Bacchus gratefully gives Midas one wish, the king is probably more muddled than usual. The results stress Midas' witlessness, for he is soon dying of hunger and thirst because he is unable to eat or drink gold. Nature does not allow such greed, and so Midas confesses his fault, repents, and prays for mercy—this sounds oddly Christian—to Bacchus as god of the wine-press and, hence, of natural wealth or abundance. Bacchus kindly allows Midas to wash away the gift, transferring it to a nearby river.

The tale, however, tests one's discernment. Was Midas so witless? He ended up with one golden oak twig, one golden stone, a gold clod, golden wheat-heads and an apple of gold, uncounted pillars of the same substance, some golden water, some very precious golden food and wine, and as many aureate miracles as conversation pieces. It is true that Phrygian Midas has to confer his golden touch to the Lydian river Pactolus, making it gold-bearing and its neighboring fields rigid with gold. But this loss reflects some glory upon him. And even with this loss, though Ovid's Midas may seem slow, he remains considerably richer. Though Ovid says that Midas is stupid, the facts that he gives do not completely support his evaluation. Once again Ovid has been playing games with his reader.

In the next episode, Midas is indeed witless. He now hates wealth and turns to country life and associating with Pan, who is playing his musical reeds to rural girls. Pan unwittingly provokes a musical contest with Apollo. The whole affair is good-natured comedy. As mentioned above, a mountain judges the music, first getting the trees out of his ears; and the trees turn their faces with that of their local deity. Apollo is described as an overdressed, posturing performer with a bejewelled instrument. He wins, of course, but he seems painful. Only Midas is fool enough to question the mountain's verdict, and Apollo gives him ass's ears to show what he thinks of Midas' musical judgment. To conceal his shame, Midas wears a royal purple turban, which must have been enormous. But Midas' barber knows about the disfiguring ears and tells a hole in the ground, and then whispering reeds ironically, because they are associated with Pan and his music, betray Midas' secret. It is as though Pan had reaffirmed the mountain's judgment.

Leaving the dull-witted Midas, Apollo visits another Asian king, one who, like Midas, does not learn from experience. Laomedon, who is abuilding Troy, twice has his land ravaged because he is fraudulent and

152

impious. The fact that he is erecting his city where there is an altar to Jove Panomphaeus, or " 'author of all oracles,' " suggests that the current destructions of the area by Neptune and Hercules and the reasons for them (impiety, violation of contract, greed) are prophetic of the fall of Priam's Troy, punished by the Greeks under Agamemnon for similar reasons. Because he aided Hercules in subduing faithless Troy, Telamon was given Hesione, Laomedon's daughter. Peleus—Ovid expects the readers to remember this fact—was also a partner in the campaign; he received no princess as war prize, for he was famous for having a goddess as his wife. This transition allows Ovid to flash back to Peleus' winning Thetis, an event important in connection with the coming Trojan War.

Because of a prophecy that Thetis' son would excel his sire, Jove, though ardently desiring the goddess, properly restrains his love, remembers how important his position is to him, and avoids union with Thetis. In all this he behaves properly with regard to prophecy and much as a proper old-time Roman aristocrat and politician might. His prudence goes further, for he orders a mortal grandson of his to marry Thetis. Thus not only will that branch of Jove's descendants be strengthened and given more prestige, but Jove also forestalls a possible rival, for example, a son of Neptune whose augmented powers might be hard for Jove to cope with.

The realistic setting of the union of Peleus and Thetis is idyllic: a sickle-shaped Thessalian harbor with clean, hard sandy bottom, too shallow for shipping, hence unfrequented by sailors. Close by the shore is a wood of myrtle, a plant sacred to Venus and, therefore, love. And in the grove is a grotto made by nature or art. Ovid decides for art and thus indicates that man has fashioned the grotto for the worhsip of Venus, or, if you will, as a venereal retreat. Into this harbor Thetis often rides her bridled dolphin. She is naked. She comes to the grotto and naps. So far, so idyllic. But the winning of Thetis is no easy task, even though Peleus knows all about the place and about Thetis' habits. He steals upon her, clasps her, and, when she awakens, implores her to be his, that is, to lie with him then and there. Virgin Thetis refuses. Peleus attempts rape. But she is slippery and crafty: she changes shapes. He holds her fast. But when she becomes a tigress, he lets her go.

Peleus then prays and offers to the sea-gods, whereupon Proteus gives him encouragement and a *modus operandi*. It works, for after changing shape to no avail this time, Thetis knows that some god is aiding Peleus and yields to superior force and to him, technically freeing Peleus of the charge of rape. However, the equally aggressive pair are happy. Hence, a marriage resulting from force can work out, especially if commanded by Jove and especially if both partners accept force as determining the outcome. Since Thetis is yielding not to Peleus, but to a divine power, she can give up without losing face and without harboring resentment for Peleus. From the spectator's viewpoint, there is something very earthy, indeed, infra dig, about a hero's grappling with a naked goddess, and the whole situation seems somewhat comically erotic, a quality modulated by the heroine's changing shapes and finally yielding to penetration and impregnation. It is at this time, Ovid is careful to note, that Achilles is conceived.

Peleus is fortunate in many ways, including his marriage, but unfortunately Peleus has murdered his half brother Phocus and is forced into exile to expiate the crime. He goes to Trachis for aid, taking comrades and herds with him. Ceyx welcomes Peleus. But Peleus lies to his host about his reason for fleeing and does not tell him the crime he committed. Thus he is unfair, deceitful, and devious. Since he is Greek, he tends to represent his people and their faults. Furthermore, he is adding to the perplexities of his host, and the anxiety resulting from them will soon send his host on a disastrous journey. At the moment, however, Peleus simply asks the opportunity to support himself in Ceyx's kingdom. Ceyx presents himself as the kindly, well-disposed ruler of a land of opportunity for all classes. He immediately offers Peleus what he wishes, especially because of Peleus' fame and his descent from Jove. Indeed, Ceyx offers Peleus as much of a share in the realm as he wishes, an amazing offer. Ceyx also indicates that the kingdom is in a sorry state, and he begins crying, thus revealing that it is not the kingdom, but his own state of mind that is depressed. Thus far Ceyx is a generous practical politician and a peaceable person. His very countenance usually radiates gladness and serenity. The explanatory narrative he tells deals not with the nation, but with his own family. Ceyx is upset because he has lost his brother, a violent, courageous, fierce, and war-loving man, just the opposite of Ceyx, for he was a conqueror of kings and peoples. As Ceyx elaborates on the character of his brother, now a predatory bird, one realizes that Ceyx is unbalanced because he has lost the necessary compensating figure of his kingdom, his warlord, and that warlike Peleus is a most welcome replacement for that brother. Still, Ceyx seems over-wrought. He relieves his emotions by telling of the distressing marvels that have happened to his family and ending with a lesson about the emotions, namely, that because a person suffers, he makes others suffer.

Ceyx tells of Daedalion's excessive grief for Chione ("snowqueen"), his beautiful and proud daughter. At the marriageable age of fourteen, she had thousands of suitors. However, she had the honor of being anes-thetized and raped by Mercury; and, on the same night, she was seduced by Apollo, who gained entrance to her in the guise of an old woman. Gods are nothing if not potent; hence, in due course Chione bears two sons. They are not twins, but close to it. Hermes' son is Autolycus, famous for craftiness and deceit—and in other sources for being a thief and the grandfather of Odysseus—and thus he is another representative of the undesirable qualities of the Greeks. Apollo's offspring is, appropriately, a singer and lyre player. Divine descent, sexual intercourse with gods, and divinely begotten children, alas, are not sufficient for Chione, whose beauty is her own claim to merit and applause, and she belittles the beauty of Diana, who shoots her dead. Daedalion, mad with grief, tries to destroy himself, but pitying Apollo turns him into a savage bird. It is at this point that Ceyx remarks—with a psychological insight that, unfortunately, he does not apply to himself—Daedalion makes others suffer because he suffers.

This observation partly applies to Peleus, a sufferer who is on the verge of causing Ceyx and Alcyone a great deal of suffering, for no sooner is Ceyx's last astute observation uttered than Peleus' herdsman rushes in with a speech like that of the messenger in a Greek tragedy. The messenger in tragedy usually tells of events over and done with, but here the action is in progress, and countermeasures are needed at once. The herdsman, however, is exasperatingly long-winded. As G. M. H. Murphy points out, it takes the servant twenty-three lines to get to a call for action and to say that there is not a moment to lose. Before that he describes the seashore and the cattle resting there, the nearby temple, the marsh, the horrifying wolf, and its slaughter.

Ceyx listens with great trepidation, but acts forcefully, calling his troops to arms. His wife rushes in, distraught. She cannot bear the thought of his exposing himself to danger, for she loves him so much that she will die if he does. The reader is again in the presence of excessive love, like Daedalion's for his daughter, and with another overwrought personality. Alcyone, however, has reason to be disturbed, for the facts are that Ceyx is not the man for fighting and that Trachis has lost its military leader.

Peleus now does the right thing and shows that the Greeks are not all bad. He politely declines Ceyx's offer of personal aid and says that he must pray to a sea-goddess. He remembers, though he does not reveal the fact, that he has murdered her son and reasons that he is being punished for it. Thus Ceyx is revealed as a man who acts in a way that seems to fit the situation, but does not because his comprehension of it is faulty. That is, in this instance he does not have all the facts. Peleus, having the facts, takes the action that is needed. He prays to the goddess, and his prayer is effective, not of itself, but because his wife, powerful in sea circles, seconds it. The wolf is called off from its killing, but it is carried away and will not comply. In order to stop it, the sea-goddess changes the wolf into marble while it is fastened to the neck of mangled heifer. Ovid's language is clear: the wolf is changed to stone, not the heifer. The marble wolf is completely realistic except for color, but there is another bit of realism, for it holds the bleeding cow, a creature of flesh, in its stone jaws. What Ovid has achieved for the moment is an unusual combination of the marvelous, the real, the grotesque, the bloody, and the savage—a tribute to the Roman fondness for all five. The bloody Orpheus-as-stag-in-the-arena, an image of lines 25-27, has been reproduced with variation as art with life in its jaws.

Once the slaughter of Peleus' cattle and men is over, Peleus, driven by the Fates, leaves Trachis for his ultimate purification in Magnesia. All is well for him, but he leaves behind him a kingdom without a general and a ruler in confusion, a mental confusion to which Peleus has contributed.

One might think that generous, gentle, benevolent King Ceyx, whose face used to beam, would now regain his happiness. But he does not. Recent events are not completely comprehensible, and they make him apprehensive about the future. He is overreacting to the misfortunes of others. He has done nothing wrong. Nothing evil has happened to him. But Chione's death, his brother's lamentable madness and metamorphosis, the monstrous wolf, its killings and its petrifaction—all seem ominous. Alcyone's recent outburst is unsettling. The daughter of Aeolus, king of the winds, she gets the wind up very readily. To a Homeric Greek, her spontaneous reaction would seem like an omen, and it would be likely to contribute to Ceyx's fears. So for a number of emotional, not rational, reasons, Ceyx prepares to visit Apollo's oracle, not at relatively nearby Delphi, but at far away Claros, reachable only after a long voyage across open sea. He makes this decision because fierce battle-leaders, like Daedalion in character, bar the land route from Trachis to Delphi. On the other hand, as son-in-law of the god of the winds, Ceyx must have known something of their force; and as witness of the wolf's ravages, caused by a sea-nymph, he might have recognized them as indicative of the savagery lurking in the sea. Were he not conscious of these, Alcyone brings them forcefully to his attention; for when she implores him not to leave, she presents in a reasonable way the real dangers of the sea and adds that her father, Aeolus, cannot help Ceyx once the winds are loose. Again her fears are omens. Yet they and even her love for him and his for her are powerless to change his mind. He is clearly doomed. He gives no rebuttals or refutations to her arguments; as a result he appears simply irrational, driven by apprehension and anxiety. Both he and Alcyone fail to propitiate the gods before he sails, an omission that is ominous because it gives the gods grounds for anger at the lovers' lack of piety. Concentrating on the pain of parting, they are aware only of what they mean to one another.

However, no vengeful deity sends the storm; it simply occurs. Others on the doomed ship call on gods for help, but not Ceyx. He thinks of Alcyone and home until the ship is smashed. Only then does he call on Aeolus, who his wife told him would be helpless, and on Lucifer, his starry father—not the best deities for saving storm-tossed sailors. The last we hear of him alive, he is calling, "Alcyone!" (Her name is ironic; it means "queen who wards off [storms].") There is no doubt about Ceyx's love for his wife, but his wisdom and piety are questionable.

But Ceyx has prayed, addressee unspecified, that the waves will bear his body to Alcyone and that she will inter him. The first part of his prayer comes true. As for the second, he receives more than he asked for. After Ceyx's death, a god does react: Lucifer masks his face in cloudy grief. Only thus does the supernatural intrude upon the action. The deadly storm itself is straight naturalism, savagely and impressionistically done. The vessel is battered until it is a leaking hulk, and finally it is plunged to the depths by a mountainous wave. With no comrades around to speak of, Ceyx clings to a bit of wreckage until, on the night of his departure, waves overwhelm him. He does not die; he is merely painlessly obliterated. Ovid has provided one more beautiful death.

Ceyx is clearly a decent person and benevolent royal administrator, but he is not a heroic figure. He is too amiable, uxorious, unaggressive, easily disturbed, and lacking in good judgment. Clinging to wreckage, he lasts a fraction of Odysseus' endurance record under similar circumstances. But because of his unflagging love, he belongs in Venus' Hall of Fame.

Alcyone, unaware of Ceyx's death, prays and sacrifices to Juno, goddess of marriage, for his protection. Juno finds these devotions on behalf of one dead, violations of ritual purity and, therefore, intolerable. To stop them, she arranges to have Alcyone informed of her loss. The means, a dream from the Cave of Sleep.

The Cave of Sleep is enjoyable for all its drowsy details and its primitive psychology, as well as for providing a respite from the tension of the storm, the sadness of the drowning, and Alcyone's anxieties. It is located in the perpetually dark land of the Cimmerians, near which Odysseus found the entrance to the Underworld, presumably because sleep is close to death. The detailed description of the place and its inhabitants is proof that the Disney stratum of the human mind that enjoys playing with personification and allegory and building elaborate fantasies is an enduring part of Western intellectual apparatus. And so ironically the reader is given relief from the turmoil of the storm and the pain of separation by having Iris and Sleep prepare a very sad dream for the queen.

The dream naturally precipitates Alcyone into agony. She does all the right things, such as tearing her hair and clothes, and says all the right things and is unusual only in her love, which, like Ceyx's, amounts to identification with the beloved. Like Heathcliff, of whom Cathy is a part in *Wuthering Heights*, Alcyone stresses her participation in and identification with Ceyx, and like Heathcliff, but roughly 1830 years earlier, Alcyone decides to join her love in death, thus outdoing Orpheus. She goes to the beach to relive their parting, sees Ceyx's body, rushes toward it, and is changed into a skimming bird. Flying to her mate, she embraces him with her new wings and tries vainly to kiss his cold lips with her hard beak. Then, *mirabile dictu,* like Pygmalion's ivory maiden, Ceyx responds to his wife's caress, and the pitying gods change him into a bird, so that they may live and love in their new forms. Thus love enlists the aid of the gods and conquers death. This is the first resurrection of the dead in the *Metamorphoses.* Because the conjugal love of Ceyx and Alcyone persists in their halcyon state, Aeolus arranges a winter calm to protect his hatching grandsons. The details about the gods are noteworthy because they reveal that the gods do not operate on an around-the-clock schedule, nor are they always consistent. Neither is human piety uniformly operative. But, as "some old man" watching the flying halcyons observes, such enduring love is worthy of praise, and when he says this, the human response and that of the gods coincide, for both men and gods are sensitive to love and watch for it.

It is very human to have one story evoke a similar one, and so the old man or someone near him tells the story of Trojan Aesacus, the secretly born son of Trojan king Priam and nymph Alexiroë. This prince but no prince is an unusual specimen in Ovid's typology in that he is antisocial, but not without finer feelings. He loves the naiad Hesperie, whom he chases through the woods. This expression of attachment seems more gauche and athletic than refined, especially since the nymph keeps running away. One day he sees her drying her hair on her father's bank. She sees him. She runs away in fright. He pursues. But this time a snake in the grass bites her. She dies. That she may be recompensed by his death, Aesacus, bitten by remorse, dives from a high cliff into the sea. Out of pity a sea-goddess changes him into a diving bird. He is not allowed to die, and the fact angers him, so that, like Orpheus, he reacts peculiarly. It is only as one of love's devotees that he is remarkable.

Brooks Otis calls attention to the length of the Ceyx-Alcyone story, noting that it is one of the longest in the poem. It should also be noted that episodes form unitary sequences, the first long one being the concentration on Cadmus and his house in Book III, returned to and concluded in Book IV. The second concentration of such length is that on Orpheus in Book X. His story is concluded, paralleled, and explained in Book XI. Somewhat similar but shorter sequences deal with the Minyeides and their tales in Book IV and the Muses' problems and narratives in Book V. These sequences constitute novel ways of constructing a narrative by interrupting it, another form of crazing a pattern and of surprising the reader.

Finally, one should keep in mind that Ovid is moving toward the Trojan War; that, in the stories of Orpheus and Ceyx, Eurydice and Alcyone, he is paying tribute to marital love and to devotion beyond death; that even those who sink may, like Phaëthon, somehow rise because of their falls; and that in various ways Ovid is still master of the games.

METAMORPHOSES XII: The Paths of Glory

The paths of glory, subject of Book XII, lead to the grave or to further conflict. The only good things that can be said about them are that they are exciting and that the glory lives on among the living.

At the beginning and end of Book XII occurs the frittering found in each book, but the bulk of the storytelling here is put in the form of an extended joke, Nestor's social outmaneuvering of Achilles and capturing a conversation. This sort of humor contrasts with the boisterous kind found in the *Iliad* and the *Odyssey*, for Ovidian laughter, as opposed to Homeric, is the product of a much lighter and much more subtle sense of humor. It occurs, for example, in Book XI when Ovid refers to silly King Midas as the "Berecyntian hero." Like Book XI, Book XII begins lightly with comic touches undercutting the serious narration. Aesacus is gone, and so Priam buries his missing person in an empty tomb. He does not know, says Ovid with parenthetical humor, that his son is living and has wings, that is, is a bird. The mourning of Priam and his sons is sad; the entombment of a missing body is respectful and honors the feelings of the bereaved, but it is somewhat futile; the winged Aesacus, however, now an ungainly bird, is comic. One realizes the fact in a moment if one makes the assumption that Priam knew what had become of this son and if one then imagines meeting Priam on the strand and asking how Aesacus is. "He is over there diving," replies the aging king, pointing to a long-legged, long-necked thing going repeatedly beak first into the sea. The situation would be pathetic and ridiculous at the same time. Thus by means of a minor comment, Ovid brings up the question whether 'tis nobler to be a dead prince or a live bird.

It is wry that Paris is not present at his half brother's unnecessary memorial services because he is, apparently, off stealing Helen. One Trojan, in short, was willing to die for love; the other is willing to sacrifice his people for love. Thus the living Paris is more to be bewailed than the apparently dead Aesacus.

Ovid now turns his attention to another set of grief-bringers, the Greek expeditionary force. It had a thousand ships. There is nothing exceptionable about this figure if it is pattered off as Homer does it. (Actually his catalog comes to about 1,175.) But Ovid's mentioning the number is sly, and Romans would have smiled at it. For the opposed fleets at Actium, two of the largest of antiquity, together totaled between 900 and 1,000 warships.

There is also an amusing inconsistency concerning the Greeks' revenge for the rape of Helen. In one place Ovid says that it would not have been delayed but for the adverse winds and seas at Aulis, but a few lines later the Greeks are told that it will take over nine years for them to conquer Troy. It is unlikely that Ovid is advertently nodding here. If he did nod, he probably did so, as he does elsewhere, in order to be caught in his discrepancy, for it makes him resemble Homer. But, more important, the discrepancy calls attention to the fact that peoples plunge into war certain of swift victory, only to learn that the cost will be much greater than they expected.

The length of the war is revealed to the shore-bound Greeks by an omen (a snake eats nine birds in a tree) and by their augur, who interprets it. The snake, of course, stands for the Greek heroes and their war; the birds, the city of Troy and its people, especially the young, as well as the winged years. Ovid calls the snake "greedy," implying that the Greeks have motives other than revenge, namely, mercenary ones. Having devoured the birds, the snake is, Ovid notes, petrified, this condition representing a divine judgment upon the snake and, of course, the Greeks. The petrification of Psamathe's wolf and the serpent attacking the head of Orpheus was a kind of restraining order, but here it is a warning of possible punishment or incapacitation. The seer, Calchas, does not comment on the change, but as Ovid uses it, it stands as a doom, or judgment.

The Greeks, even after the omen, cannot leave Aulis because of the winds and seas. Their seer knows that a virgin must be sacrificed to Diana. After her father goes through an inner struggle between father and king, Iphigenia is readied for sacrifice. The weeping of those present overcomes Diana, and she substitutes a deer for the maiden. This humaneness on her part is admirable, but unusual. One recalls Actaeon, Niobe, and Chione; and although they had sinned and Iphigenia had not, still the Greeks were about to; yet the angered goddess relents. She, therefore, seems a softer, more sympathetic deity than she had earlier. The substitute sacrifice is accepted, and the ships sail. Ovid explicitly passes over the adventures, trials, and ordeals experienced by the Greeks on their way to Troy; in other words, they do not fit his purposes or emphases. Instead of building up the heroism of the Greeks, he does something completely unexpected and interrupts the progress of the war for a fanciful account of the central intelligence, not of the Greek war machine, but of the world. This is a description of the House of Fame, or Rumor, but since the Latin is synonymous with "report" and "repute," as well as "fame" and "rumor," it is best to use the Latin *Fama*. The description gives Ovid's opinion of news in the ancient world: everything arrives at Fama's domain, is doubled and confused, falsehood being mixed with truth, and fictions being added as reports are passed along. The sounds are broadcast. Obviously what is disseminated is grossly inflated and inaccurate. And so the description functions to write off, or discountenance, glory, which is a variety of Fama. It thus colors the way one reacts to all the reputed glory that follows.

Yet a certain amount of rumor is true, for the Trojans know that the Greeks are coming and stand ready to defend their land. Hector kills Protesilaüs, the first Greek ashore. Ovid then clumps the early battles together: Greeks and Trojans slaughter one another plentifully, thus proving the stuff of which they are made. Cygnus has killed his thousand. Achilles levels armies and goes off looking for an opponent worthy of his talents, either Cygnus or Hector. Hector's death has been postponed for nine years; consequently, Achilles chances upon Cygnus, and the ensuing encounter frustrates the expectations of a god, as well as those of men.

Achilles' approach to Cygnus is a mixture of the comic and the straight. It is straight enough that Achilles urges his horses on, for drivers do talk to horses; that he directs them toward Cygnus; and that he goes at full speed. But he has no charioteer. It is, therefore, remarkable that as he approaches his enemy, he is shaking his shaking spears with his arms. One notices that shaking one spear with one arm is not enough for Achilles. Furthermore, the spears that he shakes must also be shaking themselves with an additional quivering. This doubling has the effect of comic exaggeration, as it does with Tartarin de Tarascon, who has double muscles.

There is even something comic about the boast that Achilles hurls at Cygnus, whom he is approaching at a dash: " 'Whoever you are, o young man, have as consolation for your death that you had your throat cut by Achilles of Haemonia.' " Boasts before individual combat are traditional epic elements. But for one young man to call another young man " 'young man' " makes the speaker seem fatuous, as though he thought he were burdened with years of experience. Besides, it is gross of Achilles to use " 'iugulatus,' " even as synecdoche for kill, for the built-in idea of throat- or neck-cutting makes Achilles seem like a butcher or a brigand. The connotations of the word stress the brutal and bloody aspects of killing and undercut the gentlemanly and the heroic. There is, in addition, something amusing about having a hero unintentionally reveal by his own word choice exactly how low an act his fame is based upon. Finally, though being slain by a mighty warrior might have brought the consolation of limited fame to a Glaucus or Sarpedon in the context of the Iliad, the idea is not especially convincing in the context of the Metamorphoses, in which pity for the dying is stressed, dying is often glossed over, and usually every effort is made to keep unfortunate mortals alive in some form, even though an inglorious one. And when, as in the fight in Cepheus' hall, the killing has been detailed, it has been done to amaze and please by stressing the novelty coloring the sensational events.

After Achilles' spear bounces off Cygnus, the young Trojan hero replies to the Greek with his own form of boasting, which begins with a question. He asks why the goddess-born (i.e., Achilles), whom Fama had earlier made known to him, was astonished—a rather simple-minded question under the circumstances, for Fama obviously has not made Cygnus' charmed life known to Achilles. Then Ovid adds with equal simple-mindedness, "for he [Achilles] was astonished," to explain what does not need explanation. Though Ovid's mock ingenuousness remains what it is, Cygnus' question obliquely calls attention to a fact not alluded to elsewhere in Book XII, though it is implied later in Cygnus' speech where he boasts in connection with his invulnerability that his father, Neptune, is better than Achilles' mother, Thetis. The matter referred to indirectly is Achilles' almost complete invulnerability, which Thetis has provided by holding her son by his heel and immersing him in the river Styx, as well as to the blanket invulnerability conferred upon Cygnus by Neptune. In short, one bit of Achilles' reputation is referred to in such an oblique fashion that it is almost obscured, the fame of being invulnerable. And everyone else in Book XII ignores this piece of glory, so that Achilles is robbed of some of his prestige.

Cygnus' retort courteous is overly long, overly polite and overly instructive. It begins with the formulary phrase " 'nate dea' " (" 'goddess-born' "), a polite and proper acknowledgement of Achilles' parentage. But since the phrase had been notably and frequently applied to Aeneas in Virgil's earlier *Aeneid*, its use here ends to belittle both Achilles and the progenitor of the Romans by making both a bit less unusual: more than one hero was goddess-born. And, if one recalls Midas, born of goddess Cybele, some were less than heroic.

In this speech, Cygnus also gives away vital combat information: he is invulnerable. Silly, windy, overconfident, Cygnus makes himself the victim of one of the oldest traps known to man, the guarantee with loophole. For being invulnerable does not mean being indestructible. It remains to be seen whether Achilles will discern the difference. Cygnus then boasts about his own parentage: his father, Neptune, is superior to Achilles' mother, Thetis. The comment is, of course, true, but irrelevant. Neptune and Thetis are not engaged in combat, their children are. Furthermore, what counts in battle is ability. And at this moment Cygnus shows that he is Achilles' inferior; for after bragging, his spear throw, though good, does not go completely through his opponent's shield.

At this point there is a stalemate. Ovid is using his earlier device of contradictory premises in a new guise: since Achilles can be wounded only in the heel, we have for all practical purposes, one invulnerable hero facing another. And there is a new variation, for in addition, an invincible hero faces an invulnerable foe.

The stalemate infuriates Achilles, who fires away at his enemy, but cannot penetrate him, even when Cygnus exposes his body to Achilles' spear. Achilles' frustration is laughable. He rages and then races after his last spear to take a look at it, but it does, indeed, have a point. Achilles refuses to accept the truth. He reviews his former triumphs in order to reassure himself and then kills an ordinary infantryman to prove that he has not lost his touch.

It is Achilles' rage that solves the problem his brain could not. He buffets Cygnus about, throws him down, and, abandoning weapons, throttles him. Thus he wins and has his trophy, but he is cheated of the kill, for Neptune changes his son into a swan. Achilles has not completely won, but he is not so frustrated as Cygnus and Neptune, whose gift of invulnerability is set to naught.

After all this effort, we are told, everyone needs a rest and a truce. Achilles' duel, then, stands for the whole battle: its braggadocio, silliness, madness, bloodshed, and exhaustion. Only the metamorphosis of Cygnus transcends this furor.

During the respite from battle, Achilles sacrifices a cow to Pallas (Minerva), goddess of war and, ironically, also of wisdom. Its entrails are burned on the altar, and, says Ovid with a straight face, their smell, loved by the gods, rises to them. Most of that animal becomes roast for Achilles and his noble dinner guests. These heroes drink wine and avoid light entertainment, such as music, for discourse about heroic things, namely, valor and battles and especially their own deeds, which they enjoy reviewing again and again. Ovid quietly ridicules the heroic mind by asking, what else should Achilles and the others talk about? Naturally the talk turns to the hero of the hour and giver of the feast, to his annihilating Cygnus, and to the marvel of that demigod's impenetrability. (Achilles' is ignored.)

At this point Nestor moves in and seizes the conversation by piquing the curiosity of all, even of Achilles. There are clearly heroic speakers as well as fighters. Nestor's storytelling occupies slightly more than half of Book XII. His status as fighter and as king of sandy Pylos, his age and wisdom contrast with his reputation as a windbag, incongruities that place him in the category of high comedy. So does his ingeniously putting the hero of the hour in the background. Achilles may have done away with Cygnus and may be the giver of the banquet, but Nestor takes the spotlight and holds on to it. Part of the reader's entertainment lies in appreciating Nestor's *modus operandi*. He begins with a bit of courteous belittling: his fellow heroes are easily amazed because they are young and have lived only long enough to know one invulnerable man. Older than they, Nestor has known two. The earlier one was the redoubtable Caeneus from Thessaly, like Achilles in bravery, Nestor implies, but, he adds craftily, more remarkable, for he was originally a girl. This addition may be a covert dig at Achilles, whose mother once disguised him as a girl to keep him out of the war, but it clearly presents for the assemblage a marvel greater than that which Achilles has just bested. Nestor has defeated Achilles in the arena of heroic experience, and Ovid now has his reader at the post-game party for the team, and the heroes have finally gotten around to sex, indeed, to a sexual marvel of the only sort that suits their present mood. Everyone on the scene is interested, even Achilles, who stresses his interest in Caeneus' deeds and in who, if anyone, killed him. As it turns out, Caeneus is not much of a hero, another amusing fact.

Nestor begins his tale with a verbose prologue aimed at establishing his credibility. It is another piece of epic boasting and includes the incredible fact that he is living in his third century. He, therefore, has about three times the experience of the ordinary person, and, despite his modesty about his memory, we find that with regard to Caeneus, it is extraordinarily good, just as he said it was.

Caeneus, originally Caenis, the daugther of a Lapith prince, lived in the youth of Achilles' father. She was so beautiful that she could have been Achilles' mother, if Peleus had not had other commitments. Many men wished to marry her, but she refused marriage and went walking alone on the beach. Rumor had it—we already know what Ovid thinks of Fama—that Neptune raped her there. He was delighted by their sexual congress and gave the young woman a wish, but Caenis felt injured. She did not want to go through that experience again, and her wish was to become a man. One concludes that being a woman is awful, especially the sexual part, and that maleness is the superior condition. Neptune graciously added something that every man wants, the equivalent of Caenis' desire not to be penetrated, namely, invulnerability.

Nestor merely mentions that Caeneus thenceforth engaged in manly pursuits throughout the whole of Thessaly, but does not name any noteworthy achievements on Caeneus' part. Instead, he immediately plunges into another Lapith story involving a brawl over the bride, a brief rustic parallel to the Trojan War that, like it, begins with a violation of hospitality. Only 249 lines later do the reader and Achilles learn that Caeneus was involved in this unfortunate mess and that he was killed during it. Thus Achilles finally learns what he wished to know, but he may well have fretted because gratification was so long deferred. There is humor here, too, in frustrating and confusing the reader and in the portrait of a garrulous old man who spins a good yarn, is irritating, gets what he wants, comes through as he promised, and yet is somewhat muddled.

One matter that is confused is the setting. Does it consist of a well-shaded grotto and a palace? or are grotto and palace one and the same? Are the centaurs restricted to the cave? If they are, how do they spy the bride and her attendants? Assuming that grot and palace are the same because the centaurs do behold the bride, one concludes that the palace is as much of a jumble as its description, for it has not only the proper atrium, inner rooms, a shrine, and a chandelier with numerous pendant lamps, but an altar ablaze, a nearby pine tree with deer horns hanging from it, a large movable threshold stone, and a bearskin rug with a wine-drugged guest reclining on it. The whole place is a rustic abode for which *palace* is a courtesy word.

The other inconsistency involves both Nestor and Achilles. For it is a fact that Nestor tells the tale as though Achilles were completely unfamiliar with it, but it is equally true that if anyone in the group besides Nestor ought to have been thoroughly versed in the story, it is the young hero, because it involved his father, rather prominiently, as a matter of fact. For if one counts kills, the score on the Lapith side is Theseus, 8; Pelates, 1; Phorbas, 1; Dryas, 1; Pirithoüs, 5; Peleus, 6; Anonymous, 1; Nestor, 3; Periphas, 1; Ampyx, 1; Mopsus, 1; Caeneus, 6. Vulnerable Peleus ties for second place with invulnerable Caeneus, the object of the story. Nestor also gives marked attention to the killing of Crantor, Peleus' dear armor-bearer, and Peleus' revenge. Further, Nestor refers to Peleus as "your father," taking pains to note Achilles' relationship to a personage prominent in the fracas. Earlier he had noted that Caenis, later Caeneus, was born in Achilles' country and was so beautiful that she might have been Achilles' mother, a humorous possibility. The tale, then, is about Achilles' family background, in part, and Nestor is careful to bring out this dimension.

Because it seems unlikely that Achilles would not have been told about the smashing brawl over and over until he knew it like a nursery rhyme, it is just possible that Achilles has himself been manipulating Nestor by encouraging him to tell the tale so that his father's fame will be remembered. For after Nestor finishes, Tlepolemus pouts because his father, Hercules, has not had his exploits recounted.

In the brawl, Theseus receives treatment appropriate to the ranking hero, but he does not dominate the scene. Focus moves from this personage to that, ending on Caeneus. In mythology, however, Caeneus is distinctly minor, more often a name (four times out of five) than anything else: he is listed as one of the heroes attending the Calydonian boar hunt; he is listed among the Argonauts; and he is twice named as an ancestor, once as father of Coronus, king of the Lapiths on Mt. Olympus, and once as forebear of Cypselus, tyrant of Corinth. In order to build Caeneus' stature, Nestor provides a storm worse than the one that raged around Ceyx, one of blood, guts, and brains—all spilled by unusual weapons in novel ways in the fury of semi-civilized beings—as the background for Caeneus' one detailed and, therefore, distinguishing exploit, the killing of six centaurs. Since Caeneus cannot be wounded, the really remarkable thing about him, as it is about Cygnus, is his death. The centaurs strip two mountains of trees in order to press Caeneus to death or to suffocate him, certainly an end more novel than that of Cygnus, as are the results, for Cygnus turns into a swan, whereas Caeneus becomes a unique creature, a bird with golden wings and without species. All details considered, Caeneus is a subject superior to Cygnus.

Within the free-for-all there are some light touches. Cyllarus is the height of masculine beauty and fashion among centaurs because of his black body, golden hair, white legs and tail, and his curly first beard. He is complemented by his love, Hylonome, a coaxing and winsome centauress who twines flowers in her hair, washes her face twice daily, and carefully selects the hides she wears as garments. And there is some coarse comedy in Latreus' epic taunting of Caeneus for being a woman who merely looks like a man and who should be weaving instead of warring —and who was given her new appearance in return for sexual favors.

But on the whole the fighting is disgusting and appalling. The point is made clear: in order to be even a minor hero one must perpetrate nauseating violence or be the victim of it. Not only does the Caeneus passage present this evaluation, namely, that the heroic is revoltingly brutal, but certain details about the melee stress the fact. The centaurs and the Lapiths are, according to myth, relatives, both begotten by

Ixion. This tie means nothing in the face of lust or retaliation. One character accidentally smashes a friend with a threshold stone too heavy for him to handle with discretion. A centaur who fell into a drunken sleep before the fight began is senselessly slain by Thessalian Phorbas out of blood lust and prejudice. Nestor himself points out that domestic utensils used for feasting, merriment, and sustaining life are now perverted into implements of war. The bride herself is dragged about by Eurytus, initially with intent to rape, and other centaurs seize Lapith women for the same purpose. The wedding has become like the sack of a town. One Lapith, struck on the crown with a huge log, oozes brains through all the apertures of his head like cheese curds going through a sieve. Though Nestor interrupts the slaughter with a twenty-four-line description of the centaur Cyllarus and his love and proves that even centaurs have refinement and tender feelings that a Greek opponent can admire, the sympathy and fondness for them are built up only to be butchered along with the lovers. Over and over the physical details of many slayings are described sensationally and gruesomely. Ovid omits only loss of bladder and bowel control.

Then because Caeneus, one man, is unfairly killed by a mass of enemies, the Lapiths become more incensed and kill until night falls. Here Nestor's story ends. And here is glory for you.

At this point Tlepolemus objects to Hercules' being slighted in the storytelling. This objection is irrelevant and petulant, for the conversation of the evening has moved reasonably enough from Cygnus to Caeneus and Caeneus' career. In view of the heroic ego and the revenge motif common in Homeric material and prominent in this book, Nestor's response is very illuminating. He recognizes the challenge; admits his hostility toward Hercules; mourns the loss of his twelve brothers, slain by Hercules; resents the undeserved destruction of Elis and Pylos and his own home, also done by Hercules; dwells on the cruel death that Hercules inflicted on one of his brothers; defines his own revenge, namely, a refusal to praise his enemy Hercules, having earlier admitted that the earth is filled with that hero's merited praise; and buries the hatchet, saying before all that he and Tlepolemus are friends.

As Ovid notes obliquely, there is a sweetness about Nestor. And his speech to Tlepolemus demonstrates that in his two hundred and more years of living and suffering, he has experienced the suffering that heroes can cause their victims. Thus he has learned something. But not much. Pathetically, fighting and a tempered heroism are still the only things that make life worthwhile. As an old man in command of his body and his faculties, his significance is his experience, but among his most vivid memories are the ones just recounted: the surprising death of a Protean brother, a kingdom wasted, and a bloody brawl, complete with an epic catalog of combatants, their novel weapons, and their unusually revolting wounds.

166

As for Achilles, he had asked about Caeneus' military service, his opponents, and his vanquisher. He receives, instead, a donnybrook replete with details. And he learns of Caneus' killers, a mob of tree-throwing demi-men who conquer ungallantly, using means somewhat like Achilles', and yet are more rational than Achilles in his overcoming Cygnus, because one of the centaurs rationally figured out how to kill Caeneus.

This, then, is the entertainment of heroes, the retailing of blood and guts. They learn nothing from it, receiving only the pleasures of sensationalism and a surrogate for the excitement of combat, which they have just been through on the battlefield and from which they wanted a respite. And Nestor, who has just recalled the destruction of his home and cities by an invader and who is one of the wisest of the Greeks, is on his way to sacking someone else's city.

After Nestor concludes with Tlepolemus, the Greeks have a final drink and sleep. In the next thirty-nine lines, Ovid completes the pattern. In the first thirty-six of them a vengeful Neptune, furious over the death of Cygnus, incites an equally hostile Apollo, who brings about Achilles' death with the cooperation of Paris, the Trojan archer. Achilles does not die fighting. He is snuffed out ignominiously by a cowardly sniper's arrow. Ovid makes the point explicitly: Achilles would have preferred to die fighting, even if cut down by a female warrior and with an axe, that is, in hand-to-hand combat with a weaker foe wielding a weapon easier to cope with than a stabbing one. And now the hero is reduced to a handful of dust in an urn. The paths of glory have led to the grave.

But then in the next three lines, Ovid reverses the above pattern by adding that the glory transcends the grave and is the true measure of the man. If this is true of Achilles, it is true of Cygnus and Caeneus as well. And so we understand that the invulnerability of the three heroes, the swan, and the bird with the golden wings are the same as their glory. But we also know that the glory is Rumor, Repute, Fama—a combination of lies, truth, exaggeration, confusion. And we also know the savagery upon which heroism is based.

As for Achilles, he, indeed, lives on through his glory, which is very much alive, for his arms still fight by causing conflict or dissension. And this matter Ovid will take up in his next book.

METAMORPHOSES XIII: The Modulation to Romance

Book XIII moves from quarrelling among the Greeks, past ruin'd Ilium, past Greece and Crete with Aeneas to Sicily, where—Ovid still provides surprises—epic matter is abandoned for romance. The first section, the contention between Ajax and Ulysses is, among other things, the Greek agony, presenting a catalog of numerous sufferings endured by the Greeks, many of them self-inflicted. Next comes the Trojan agony after the fall of Troy; it consists of the miseries endured by the Tojans because of the Greeks. The focus then follows Aeneas' saving remnant as it moves from Troy past hostile Greece to Crete and thence to Sicily and to a completely new mood resulting from a focus upon romance.

The overall movement, then, is from cunning, conniving, angry words, bloodshed, and deceit—in short, from baseness—to the brutality and heartlessness of war and conquest, and then, by means of a journey that leads to new horizons, to peaceful cities and finally to temporary rest on a beach. In this new place, epic adventurings are digressed from in favor of the doings of sea and shore girls and their suitors. The final setting is idyllic. The general progress is from the distressing events of war, which are markedly realistic, to the serenities of rural settings and the complications of love. These last stories are, in comparison, markedly unrealistic and patently fictitious, which is what one expects of romance, as opposed to the myth-legend of epics and of heroic exploits. The result is that by the end of this book one has been led into the serenities of art.

This ending mood is prepared for by minor modulations of a similar sort that occur throughout the book. The first comes after Ajax in angry pride plunges his sword into his heart: a flower is born. After the Trojans have been lacerated time and time again come the weird obsequies of Memnon, too fantastic to really disturb or to produce anything but wonder. And then, more pacifying, soothing, and cooling, Aurora's grief for her son becomes perpetual dew. Anius' daughters, abused by Agamemnon, become doves. Orion's daughters sacrifice themselves ineptly and painfully, but they are later reconstituted as two young men. Even in the myth of Galatea, her slain lover is retrieved as far as may be. As for Scylla and Glaucus, their story is interrrupted. Each flees the spot of their encounter, so that the reader is left with the implicit calm of a vacancy, an empty seascape.

Most turbulent, however, is the rhetoric at the beginning of Book XIII. Two pieces of deliberative oratory are presented to a public decision-making body, the Greek assembly. The matter for debate is, who should be given the arms of the dead Achilles? Ajax or Ulysses? None of the other Greek leaders has entered a claim, although the *Iliad* suggests that Diomedes might have because of his ability and Agamemnon might have because of his self-importance and greed. Thus the contest is reduced to two, and the debate is simplified to show off the oratorical abilities of Ajax and Ulysses, who might be labeled Brawn and Brains and might appear in a classroom rhetorical exercise, as well as in a gathering of peers. In any event the epic situation is probable enough. At the outset it is striking that no one seems to think that Achilles' arms might properly belong to his heir or family. Certainly Ajax does not; it remains for Ulysses to bring up the point. Because the arms are very beautiful and valuable and since they were carried by the foremost of the Greek fighters and were made by the god Vulcan, they represent incomparable prestige, as well as wealth; and the result is that the egotism and greed of those present prevails. No one questions the basic validity of these claims to the arms, which are regarded as awards of merit. No hero needs the arms for the war, Ajax and Ulysses, for example, having gotten along splendidly without them thus far.

Who will win? Many of Ovid's audience probably knew. By what appeals? This is what the ancients would have been eager to learn, for they would want to enjoy the argumentation that Ovid provided the great competitors and his cleverness. They probably knew, as Ovid indicates, that the fortified Greek camp was by the seashore, that the fleet was beached inside its walls, that Hector had led the Trojans in a breakthrough and almost burned the ships, and that the Greeks are presently assembled near them. The audience might realize, too, how important the ships are for supply, possible retreat, and transport home.

Ajax speaks first because he cannot control his angry annoyance. He thus puts himself in the weaker position, for he gives his opponent the opportunity to answer his arguments and other appeals and then go beyond them. The second speaker has the added advantages of being able to size up the mood of his listeners, play upon them longer, and, coming last, be the one whose impact is fresher. Also, Ajax's irritability may prejudice his audience against him if it makes them think him unwise.

Ajax's opening is effective. Having taken the floor, he pauses and looks at the nearby ships. Then he begins with characteristic openness, force, and manliness by calling upon Jupiter to witness or authenticate what he says and by adding present witnesses, an emotionally and tactically important part of the immediate surroundings, namely, the ships that everyone had fought to save. Thus he appeals to the piety, senses, memories, and emotions of his fellows. As for his opponent, he merely names the fellow as though the name itself indicates someone so contemptible that nothing more need be said.

Ajax develops this beginning by contrasting his heroism in saving the ships with Ulysses' yielding under the Trojan attack. He thus calls to mind his own past achievements, gives proof of his merits, and makes an emotional appeal to gratitude. He also poisons the well by calling Ulysses a coward, a device that might cause some resentment among his audience. Worse, he seems boastful by claiming that he alone saved the fleet, for such a claim might annoy other Greeks involved in the fray, no matter how willing they might be to acknowledge that Ajax had been the back-

170

bone of resistance. A *we*-approach might have been more effective than the *I*-approach used.

However, Ajax's opening has virtues. It is spontaneous. Ajax shows astuteness by knowing where he is (i.e., near the ships) and by using the situation to his advantage. The fleet suggests—and he takes the hint—the Trojan attack on it as a recent and important illustration of his virtues and Ulysses' defects. And this approach, because it occurs on the spur of the moment, seems quick-witted, inevitably right, dramatic, vivid, and incontestably true. Ajax also stirs up war memories (as did the conversation of the Greeks feasting with Achilles in the preceding book) and passions about an event in which he was a major figure, and these bind the audience to him in a unity of shared emotions.

As he speaks, Ajax engages in a peculiar bit of slanting. He seems to equate talking with lying, tries to turn a defect, lack of effectiveness in speaking, into a virtue, and implies that deeds generally are superior to speech or talk. He thus admits implicitly to intellectual limitation and, in the present oral context, then, to defeat. His statement suggests that war is all fighting, brawn without brains, and that ingenuity, persuasion, and quick wits are not especially useful. Ajax next acknowledges that Achilles' armor is a great reward, but he asserts that the honor of receiving it is halved by his having to compete with such a contender as Ulysses (the equivalent, apparently, of matching a hero with a bum). Then he comes forth with a good line: Nothing, no matter how great, that Ulysses aspires to, could confer honor upon Ajax. The statement is pointed, devasting, and counterproductive. For, no matter how magnificient it sounds, it begs the question. It also contradicts Ajax's preceding admission that the prize he seeks is a great one. Indeed, Ajax continues with the same grand inanity: Ulysses has had sufficient honor already, for when Ajax has won, Ulysses can boast that Ajax was his opponent.

Briefly, Ajax's following appeals run after this fashion. First, Ajax's family is better than Ulysses', for Ajax descends from Jove through Aeacus (now a judge in the most important of courts, that of Hades) via Telamon (conqueror of Troy with Hercules and also Argonaut). Achilles was Ajax's cousin. In contrast, Sisyphus, son of the wind–god and ancestor of tricky Ulysses, is condemned to doing eternal rock work in Hell for fraud and robbery. Second, Ulysses is merely a social climber, trying to link his name with that of the Aeacidae. Third, Ulysses does not need the armor, because he is not a fighter. Fourth, Ulysses tried to avoid coming to the war, even feigned madness. Fifth, he has actually harmed Greeks in vicious ways, for example, in his treatment of Palamedes and Philoctetes. The former he framed, charged with treason, and had executed. The latter he had marooned. Sixth, Ulysses was criminal in his desertion of Nestor on the battlefield. Seventh, despite Ulysses' behavior, Ajax recused Ulysses when he needed help on the field of valor. Eighth, Ajax stopped Hector when he almost burned the ships; hence, Ajax saved them. Ninth is a magniloquent rhetorical appeal: Indeed, Achilles' arms ask for greater glory than Ajax does; they seek Ajax, not Ajax them.

171

(This statement is not only untrue, it is the height of soaring self-inflation by means of hot air.) Tenth, if the arms were to go to Ulysses, they ought to be divided with his inseparable helper, Diomedes. Eleventh, the arms are useless to Ulysses because they are too heavy and are not suited to ambush, night fighting, picking pockets, or running away. Ajax ends his one hundred and seventeen lines with a proposal: Let there be a real contest for the arms: put them in the middle of the enemy forces, and let Ulysses and Ajax fight their way to them. The proposal is as great souled as it is impracticable.

Nevertheless, the Greeks applaud and by applauding show either their politeness or their stupidity.

Ulysses waits, letting the impact of Ajax's grandiloquence fade away. Finally he stands up, but he looks at the ground a bit, then at the chiefs, establishing eye contact. Then he begins his two-hundred-and-fifty-three-line speech by softening up his fellow Greeks. He shows comradely feeling by lamenting the loss of Achilles. He seems to wipe tears from his eyes. Then, without naming himself, he claims credit for bringing Achilles into the united Greek effort, and thus he establishes a close link with the former owner of the arms. Keeping a straight face, he asks that Ajax's dullness not be a point in Ajax's favor and that Ulysses' use of his own wits and eloquence on behalf of the Greeks not damage his cause.

Ulysses' major points are these. Merit, that is, one's own acts, not ancestors, should measure one's worth. However, Ulysses' family is as good as Ajax's, for Ulysses also is descended from Jove and, to boot, on his mother's side, from Mercury. Besides, Ulysses' father, unlike someone he might name, did not shed his brother's blood. Further, if relationship gives title to Achilles' arms, they should go to his father or his son. Ulysses' deeds include exposing the draft-dodging ruses of Achilles' mother; therefore, Ulysses deserves credit for all of Achilles' exploits during the war. (The argument is specious, of course, as many of Ulysses' are, for a man's acts are his own and may be bad as well as good. According to Ulysses' reasoning, Ulysses would be accountable also for Achilles' sulking in his tent.) Ulysses persuaded Agamemnon to sacrifice Iphigenia for the common good. Ulysses it was who tricked Clytemnestra into sending her daughter to be sacrificed. It was Ulysses who presented the Greek grievances and demands to the Trojan senate of heroes and who was almost mobbed, as Menelaus witnessed. In the long period of combat inactivity between the early battles and those of the tenth year, Ulysses was busy with strategems, missions, logistics, morale building. Ulysses prevented the Jove-instigated abandonment of the seige of Troy. Therefore, Ulysses deserves credit for all of Ajax's deeds because it was Ulysses who brought Ajax, among the others, back to the fight. True, Ulysses operated with Diomedes, a tribute to Ulysses' trustworthiness, but what Greek has wanted to praise Ajax or seek him out? Ulysses has killed a number of Trojans and has wounds to show for his combat, which Ajax has not. Ajax was not the only Greek to face the Trojans or to confront

Hector. As far as being able to sustain the weight of the arms of Achilles, Ulysses hoisted them and the dead weight of their owner on his shoulders, though grieving and surrounded by the enemy. Ulysses, not Ajax, is the one who understands the art decorating Achilles' shield. If Ulysses was reluctant to join the forces going to war, so was Achilles. Ajax, moreover, says shameful things about the Greeks. Item: was it base of Ulysses to accuse Palamedes falsely and not of the other Greeks to condemn him? Item: did Ulysses maroon Philoctetes without the consent of his fellows? Was the advice to leave Philoctetes on Lemnos harmful to him? did he not need rest? is he not still alive? And now that Philoctetes is needed at Troy, who will be able to dispel his hatred of his brother Greeks and coax him to Troy, Ajax or Ulysses? Who goes on night missions, Ajax or Ulysses? Who spirited away the Trojan Minerva?

At this point Ajax murmurs that Diomedes was Ulysses' partner on a number of missions; thus Ulysses has not given him due recognition, but has been taking all the credit. Ulysses meets these objections head on. He acknowledges what Diomedes has done and then turns Ajax's objection against Ajax by demonstrating that he is the one guilty of claiming that his deeds were performed without aid from his fellow Greeks.

Ulysses ends by maintaining that his mind is more useful to the Greeks than Ajax's muscle, and it is intelligence that will be needed to end the war. He suggests that if the arms are not given to him, they should be given to Minerva. (The goddess, one should note, is his patroness and divine counterpart.)

Ulysses' oratory carries the day, and he is awarded the glorious armor and weapons. But in the debate both Ajax and he, especially Ulysses, have painted a devastating portrait of the Greeks. They are unfair. They twist things and are themselves manipulated by false arguments. They are greedy, deceitful egomaniacs who indulge in human sacrifice for expediency and are faithless to one another. In short, they are the ignoble contrivers of their own agony, or at least much of it.

After the decision in favor of Ulysses, Ajax, mad with resentment and unable to stomach defeat, commits suicide, in his own words, " 'so that no one but Ajax may be able to conquer Ajax.' " What magnificence of language! Alas, it ignores the facts, for he has already met defeat from the tongue of Ulysses, and Ajax is not conquering Ajax, but getting rid of him in a fit of injured pride. And though Ajax makes good his assertion with his sword, his real message seems to be that certain kinds of men are self-destructive. (Indeed, Achilles had always been recognized as physically superior to Ajax, and Ajax should have known that he was, in this sense, defeated by this cousin.)

Despite the interest of the combat of words, if not of wits, the arguments used during it show that the Greeks are or can be crafty, brutal, unjust, and base. They are the Greeks of quasi-history. Ovid now transposes from the key of pseudo-realism, by means of a hyperbolic pump, Ajax's heart, to the domain of fancy, wherein Ajax becomes identified with Hyacinthus through the flower whose petals bear the letters appropriate to both the boy and the warrior. The reader is briefly in another world, one where shed blood becomes bloom; grief, a commemorative sigh; and a maddened hero, the equivalent of an unfortunate boy. So ends the Greek agony, in an aura of sentiment and loveliness. Art and imagination make the real bearable. The imaginary is here preferred to anything closely resembling the actual.

The next section of Book XIII presents the Trojan agony, mainly a sequence of horrors and brutalities that ends with the dehumanizing of Hecuba through atrocities and grief, so that she can no longer express herself like a woman, but barks like a dog. It begins with Ulysses' living up to his commitment and bringing back two requisites for winning the Trojan War: Philoctetes and the arrows of Hercules. The war is won with the sack and burning of Troy. Cassandra is dragged off by her hair. Priam is slain at the altar of Jove, his blood soaking into it. The Trojan women are taken off as loot. Hector's orphaned infant son is thrown off a tower. A wind favorable for sailing home arises, and the Trojan women are hustled aboard ship. They hardly have time to kiss their native earth goodbye; as for words, they get out three—the brevity indicates the speed of their embarkation: " 'Troy, farewell! We-are-raped.' " But Hecuba, the aged Trojan queen, is different, even though Ovid cannot resist playing upon a phrase used by Virgil and with verbal cleverness turning *mirabile dictu* ("wonderful to tell") into *"miserabile visu"* ("piteous to behold"). Last to board, Hecuba has been pried loose from her sons' tombs by Ulysses. She saves from the sack only Hector's ashes in her bosom. At a brief stop on the Thracian coast, she loses her daughter because the ghost of Achilles demands Polyxena as a sacrifice to his vanity. The girl dies nobly, regretting only that her mother will have yet another child to mourn and condemning human sacrifice. The Greeks weep, but butcher her. Thus is Achilles, the hero of heroes, avenged upon Paris and Priam. It is Hecuba, however, who lives to suffer; yet while she mourns her daughter, she recalls that her favorite child, Polydorus, is safe with the local Thracian king, and safe with him is some Trojan treasure. Then at the seashore, Hecuba discovers the body of her son, murdered by the greedy king in order to seize the gold. Seeing the corpse, Hecuba intuitively understands all this. With the aid of the other Trojan women, she takes revenge on the Thracian king, and by the time that his people stone her, she is so psychologically disturbed that she can only bark like a dog. Gods, Trojans, and Greeks are all moved by her fate. But not those barbarians the Thracians.

Just as Ovid modulated earlier from literary realism to myth, he now does so from relatively realistic mourning to the grief of a goddess, Aurora's for Memnon. Once again the effect of the marvelous is soothing.

Fighting for Troy, Memnon was killed in combat by Achilles. Aurora begs Jove to provide some form of honor for her dead son. The result is that, when Memnon's funeral pyre crumbles into ashes and emits tremendous smoke, the whirling ashes are turned into two flocks of battling birds that finally die in honor of their sire's funeral. They are an ironic honor, for they are provided by the substance of the dead hero himself, and thus he dies twice. They are also a most unusual form of savage funeral game. And beyond this, they are a most grim and paradoxical emblem of the results of heroism: death perpetuating itself. But even more marvelous, they repeat their performance each year. Ovid ends this tale of wonders by repeating his contrast of the real with the artful: Hecuba howls; in her grief, Aurora daily covers the world with dew.

Troy may be down, and the line of Priam, practically extinct, but some Trojans still live and have hope because of Aeneas. Ovid's Aeneas is as pious as Virgil's, but more shadowy and vaguer as a character. Ovid indicates his basic piety by having him perform the traditional feat, namely, rescue the sacred images and his sacred father. These and his son, Ascanius, are his wealth—not gold or gems, but gods and his family. With others escaped from Troy, Aeneas sails off, leaving the criminal homes of Thrace, which share the guilt of their greedy and murderous king, an evil variant of Midas. This saving remnant goes to the birthplace of Apollo. There Anius, priest-son of Apollo, receives Aeneas graciously and tells him how badly Agamemnon and the Greeks treated Anius' children, namely, a son favored by Apollo and four daughters gifted by Bacchus with the ability to turn all they touched to wine, grain, and olive oil. These agricultural magicians Agamemnon snatched so that his Greeks would not lack. When two escaped to their brother, Agamemnon forced Andros to violate brotherly peity and give them up, but Bacchus, on request, changed the girls into those notoriously fecund creatures, doves, sacred to Venus. Anius does not place a high value upon this sort of aid.

In context, Anius' story stresses the Greeks' lack of piety, their reliance on force, and the occasional odd behavior of the gods. Metamorphosis, seen as a boon by a deity, is not so regarded by a mortal; hence, we have a new evaluation of it. Existence is not easy in this passage, but the horrors are subsiding, and one has the sense that life is approaching normal peacefulness.

At departure, Aeneas and Anius exchange gifts, an act suggesting a pledge of friendship between emerging Rome and Apollo. Anius gives a scepter to Anchises, that is, kingship, which as a Trojan prince he had not had before. Ascanius receives gifts appropriate for a noble boy. Aeneas receives a wine-mixing bowl that, because it involves the presence of Bacchus, symbolizes release, fertility, and prosperity. According to J. C. Cooper, the gold acanthi carved around its top may indicate life or immortality, as well as respect for art. In short, the bowl is a prophecy of good fortune. Also symbolic are its scenes. They tell of the self-sacrifice of Orion's daughters to save their fellow Thebans from annihilation. In return, so that the daughters' line will not be obliterated, two pious youths, the Coroni, spring from their ashes. This story suggests the future of Aeneas, who will sacrifice himself for the good of his people and whose line will be preserved. In contrast, Aeneas' gifts to Anius (a chest for incense, a libation bowl, and a crown) are appropriate for a priest-king, but they are not prophetic, because Anius' destiny has been fulfilled

Following the instructions of the Delian oracle, Aeneas seeks the Trojan land of origin and tries Crete, but he and his Trojans are unable to bear the air there, probably because of the disease and lack of rainfall mentioned in the *Aeneid*. The Trojans now set out for Italy through rough seas and by hazardous places, such as the dangerous harbor of the Strophades with nasty harpy Aëllo, islands controlled by hostile Ulysses, and other Greek-controlled territory. In passing, Ovid includes Actium and pays homage to its Apollo. The emigrants land at Buthrotum, where Trojan prophet Helenus had built a replica of Troy on the Greek mainland, and learn good things about the future. Then they proceed to stop at Sicilian Zancle, near the navigational hazards Scylla and Charybdis.

The journey has had its risks, but it has had its haven within enemy territory, and on the whole it has required nerve and endurance, but it has been without active hostility or traumatic brutality. Things are improving for the refugees. But as narrative, the voyaging of Aeneas and his company is largely itinerary with bits and pieces thrown in. These parts have little development, and, although the whole passage has a theme (the ancient wanderings in quest of a new destiny) and a function (to show the gradual improvement of the Trojans' conditions), it also frustrates and annoys the reader because he waits for some weighty and significant tale to appear.

Such an episode now emerges with the mention of Scylla, for Ovid at this point ignores the Trojans, abandons his frittering with their travels, and turns to idyllic myth.

The Scylla who destroys mariners is a female monster with a girdle of dogs guarding her sexual organs, a proper change for a miss who rejected numerous suitors, remained virgin, and regularly told the sea-nymphs all the details. Once, before the change, while combing the hair of Nereid Galatea ("milk-white"), Scylla ("the female who tears") told of her adventures. As fitting in girl-talk, Galatea sighs because Scylla can fearlessly reject the importunities of men, gentle sorts of being. (Her description is ironic in view of the way the Greeks have just been treating women.) But Galatea is thinking of her sixteen-year-old prince, a refined human lover, and of that unruly beast Polyphemus, and she wafts the reader off into the pleasurable world of untrue romances, pleasurable because untrue and because sad.

Thus far the scene is a charming seaside idyll. One girl is kneeling behind an older one and combing her hair. They are exchanging confidences about the exciting things in their lives, namely, men. Each is about as well descended as the other, but Galatea has two things that Scylla lacks, metamorphic powers and experience. Naturally, then, it is Galatea who tells her Love Story to one whom she accurately and

176

spitelessly calls "o virgin," conveying wistfully and apparently unconsciously the superiority of the woman who has loved and been wounded.

Things can be difficult, even for a well-born Nereid with flocks of sisters, Galatea says plaintively, and then gets to the point: she was not allowed to flee from Polyphemus' love without grief. She weeps. Scylla dries her tears with white fingers and says in effect, "Darling, tell me everything. You can trust me." (Her speech in the text is more stately, courtly, and verbose.) Galatea seems never to have thought of not trusting Scylla, for she immediately launches into the following experience.

Acis, born of King Faunus and river-nymph Symaethis, was a gorgeous sixteen-year-old, a great pleasure to his parents, and a great deal more to me. He was crazy about me. And I was always after him. But this Cyclops was always after me. I hated him as much as I loved Acis. Bountiful Venus is indeed of limitless power, for look at the effect she had on that frightful, man-killing, god-despising Polyphemus. She set him afire. And he prettified himself, stopped being a cannibal, forgot to wreck ships, and stupidly turned witty. He behaved like a silly shepherd in love, sitting on a cliff and blowing his one-hundred-reed panpipe so loud that the rocks actually felt the whistling and so did the waves. I was far away under a rock, lying with Acis, but I could hear his song, and I remember every word.

Galatea then sings Polyphemus' pastoral, an uncouth love song, verbatim. She has an excellent memory, fortunately, because not many girls receive such a comic valentine. Polyphemus mixes pleasing images with homey, low, or unflattering ones, ones that do not fit, and at least one that is unintentionally sexual. The lyrics suit Polyphemus' experience, though they are not startlingly original in declaring that Galatea is sweeter than ripe grapes, smoother than sea-polished shells, and more gratifying than shade in summer. But when they compare her to a wild heifer (for obstinacy) and curded milk (for softness), the metaphors are clearly low. To say that she is more savage than a female bear because she runs from him or crueler than fire is to create inept comparison, inept because it does not fit the circumstances. And the line that, if she did not flee from him, she would be more finely formed than a well-watered garden is not only illogical but contains symbols of the female genitalia (garden) and their fertilization (watering).

After praising Galatea's physical qualities and deploring her coyness, Polyphemus lists his possessions to show that he is a good husbandman and man of property: he has real estate (a mountainside with caves), fruits, nuts, sheep, goats, curded milk and drinking milk, and unusual pets (two bear cubs). Just in passing, Polyphemus delivers himself of a sententia: " ' "He who can count his flocks is poor." ' "

The Cyclops expresses pride in his looks, recently mirrored in a pool to his gratification, and his bigness. At this point and elsewhere, one is slightly nudged to wonder about the capacity of Galatea to love a giant. Sounding hideously contemporary, he praises hair, his all-over hair, and his large single eye. (Like most of us, he naturally uses himself as the measure of everything, and thus while he is being satirized, he satirizes us. Given his physique, it is natural for him to equate bigness with goodness and beauty, but it is also amusing.) He mentions the power and dominion of his father, Neptune, and the grand alliance that Galatea will be making if she takes Polyphemus. He resents her relationship with Acis, cannot understand it, deplores it, and threatens to fragment Acis and throw him into the sea, where he can mingle with Galatea. Polyphemus also burns and despairs.

Shortly after this song, Polyphemus saw Acis and me, Galatea resumes, in what he referred to as our " ' "last venereal concord." ' " I panicked and dove into the sea. Acis called for help, but Polyphemus buried him under a section of mountain. I did the little I could. By making use of powers descended to him from his ancestors, I changed the bleeding buried boy into a stream, and he leapt forth bigger than life and blue-faced, a river-god. She ends.

And so in myth even romantic agony is metamorphosed into joyous serenity, that of the emblem.

One notes that as stream, Acis would flow into the sea, and thus ironically both he, who prayed that Galatea would take him to her abode, and Polyphemus, who hoped that the dead Acis would mingle with Galatea in the sea, get their wishes. Oddly enough, though Galatea expresses wonder at this marvel, she does not express gratification that she can possess her lover in this new form. She liked the prince.

Her story done, Galatea swims off with her sister Nereids. Scylla, not daring to follow them to mid ocean, swims back to land. The Love Story might have been useful to her, had she looked for its point. But she simply wanders naked along the shore, occasionally taking a cooling dip in a pool. Along comes Glaucus upon the sea, blowing his horn. He spies Scylla and immediately falls in love. (This is not the only time in Ovid that nakedness is Venus enough.) Glaucus tries to become acquainted with the maid, but Scylla departs in haste to a mountaintop overlooking the sea, a vantage point foreshadowing her later permanent abode. There she safely looks over Glaucus and tries to decide whether he is a freak or a deity, an interesting juxtaposition. For he has very long hair, dark green and blue arms; and from the groins he is piscine. Scylla's indecision is odd, because she is perfectly familiar with the Nereids, some of whom must have looked somewhat similar.

Glaucus continues to woo Scylla from a distance, telling her that he is neither monster nor wild animal, but sea-god, a new one with great powers. Earlier he was a Greek fisherman. In the course of his fishing from the shore, he stumbled upon a meadow untouched since the beginning of time. The details are familiar, for we have encountered them in connection with the pools of Salmacis and Narcissus, and, therefore, we know that we have come to a magic place, one where an individual's being is changed because something about it is realized. It is here that Glaucus discovers, not the feminine component in his nature nor his fascination with himself, but his immortality. Ovid's moving us back in time by means of this setting has another eerie effect: we feel that we are going back to a Golden Age—hence such a condition is possible—and that, therefore, time may be cyclical. Thus Ovid foreshadows a cyclical progress that will come upon Augustus as the bringer of a return to the Silver Age and an argent existence.

In this untouched spot the meadow grass was so powerfully beneficent that it restored Glaucus' dead fish to life (a second resurrection story), and they swam through the grass into the sea. Amazed, Glaucus cannily chewed some of the grass, felt himself shaking within because of a desire for another nature, and bidding farewell to earth, took to the sea. The sea-gods accepted him as one of them, but his mortality had to be sung away and washed away by the waters of a hundred rivers. He then went into a trance out of which he came physically and mentally changed. But, Glaucus adds, what is the point of being a sea-god if Scylla is not impressed?

Scylla is not impressed. Indeed, she does not like suitors, and she will not trust herself to the deep sea. She moves off. And so does Glaucus, in a rage, to the reception hall of the witch-goddess Circe. Love has been offered and rejected; the dramatis personae have left, and there is only the serenity of sky, cliff, and sea.

Two other matters in Book XIII need attention besides the narrative line. One is the motif of ashes: from Memnon's rise his birds, from those of Orion's daughters come the Coroni, so that one gets the distinct impression that from Troy's will arise a new Troy, as, indeed, even in western Greece Trojan Helenus, one of Priam's sons, has erected a replica of Troy. Thus the rise of Rome is foreshadowed; it will be a new Troy.

Last, Book XIII has two major sections, one dealing with heroic material and one dealing with love, so that the two are contrasted. The contrast makes the point that no matter how sad or frustrating love may be, it is infinitely preferable to war.

METAMORPHOSES XIV: The Better People

Like much of Book XIII, Book XIV is a progress, that of the events and the people leading to the founding of Rome and to her first great king, Romulus. It is given in the form of dateless itinerary and annals. These are studded with tales that are complete episodes. The emphases are curious and unsettling, for the tales are brilliants adorning a string of comparatively lackluster beads, but the worth of the beads is at least as great as that of the sparklers. This surprise is the result of shift in values. In Book XIII love and romance provided a welcome relief from the epic material, whereas in Book XIV a better kind of love appears, and it has a more important function. In Book XIII the epic adventures themselves modulated from the craftiness and brutality of the Greek heroes to the endurance and piety of the Trojans seeking self-preservation and a great destiny. In Book XIV the epic material undergoes further amelioration as a result of contrast between Greek and Trojan. After leaving Troy, the Greeks were punished by the storm sent by Minerva, and Diomedes was later punished for wounding Venus. These incidents are brief indicators that the Greeks tend to be impious. In contrast, the Trojans are led by pious Anchises and by a son whose piety is stressed, once by Caieta's epitaph and once by the Cumaean Sibyl. It is not surprising that they have a destiny, which the Greeks have not, and that they are sustained by the gods, as demonstrated by the deification of Aeneas and by Cybele's metamorphosing the Trojan ships into sea-nymphs. These new sea divinities aid mariners in distress, but refuse to help storm-tossed vessels carrying Greeks, and they rejoice in the wreck of Ulysses' ship. It is because Venus supports the Trojans that Diomedes refuses to aid the Rutulian opponents of Aeneas.

Furthermore, the Trojans and their leaders display great humanity by rescuing the abandoned Achaemenides, a Greek who fought against them at Troy. This compassion, it is implied, impresses a fellow Greek and leads to Macareus' giving the Trojans a most useful bit of advice, namely, that they shun Circe's shores. Thus goodness of heart builds constructive relationships.

The progress ends with Rome firmly established and its two peoples being given just laws by a strong military leader and able king, or political administrator. He is taken away by the gods and deified when his work is accomplished, additional proof that the gods have Rome under beneficent consideration.

Amelioration occurs in the love stories also. They form most of the brilliants in the sequence. But wherever one or more of the principal characters comes from Greek myth, an ungratified passion produces disaster. Examples include Glaucus and Scylla; Circe and Picus; the Cumaean Sibyl and Apollo; and Anaxarete and Iphis. In contrast, the love stories from Italian myth or Italo-Roman legend deal with happy, mutual loves, those of Picus and Canens, Pomona and Vertumnus, and Romulus

181

and Hersilia. This last pair is important, not only because both are deified, but also because both are joined by marital love. Their reunion in heaven is the exaltation of effective political administration and of respectable mutual love. Thus love and the heroic are bonded and raised aloft for all to admire.

To summarize this overview of Book XIV, the Italo-Romans are superior to the Greeks in love, in just government and relations to other peoples, and in humanitarianism. The gods favor them, and so does destiny. As we shall see, Ovid does not present them as perfect, but they are surely the better people.

Ovid, on the other hand, is not a Graecophobe. The myths thus far have been mostly Greek ones, perforce. But in Book XIV Ovid stresses the Greek element in the larger Italian matrix. He uses *Zanclen*, a Greek accusative form, for example, and though he has done the same in preceding books, the incidence of Greek forms of names seems heavy in this one. Unlike Homer, whose Circe, Sirens, and Aeolus seem located in some area of the imagination, Ovid places them on or near the west coast of Italy. He tells us, too, that not only is Glaucus from the Greek island of Euboea, but that the Italian community of Cumae is also Euboean. Parthenope, not very far from Cumae, is another Greek city, from its name. Aeneas saves Achaemenides, a Greek, from a life of despair and takes him to Italy; he also encounters another Greek, Macareus, who has decided to leave Ulysses and abide in Italy. Aeneas receives aid from Evander, yet another Greek, and we learn that Diomedes, an old enemy of the Trojans, has settled in southern Italy and married the daughter of a native king. Ovid even refers to Diomedes' new realm by using the name of his birthplace, calling it "the Calydonian kingdom," as though to stress the Greek element in the population of Italy. It is also surprising to find an old love of Apollo's, namely the Sibyl, firmly implanted on Italian soil. In short, Ovid is certainly willing to give the Greeks their lesser due.

Book XIV begins with images alluding to past violence, to the battle between the Olympians and the Giants, and to the murderous rage of the Cyclops that Galatea had told about. These last two and the dangerous straits of Messina are left behind by a strong swimmer going west and then up the west coast of Italy to herb-bearing hills and the reception halls of Circe and the violence done by unrequited love.

Rustic who stumbled into godhood, Glaucus rushes into his plea as soon as he has looked upon Circe and they have exchanged greetings. His first words indicate that he is in love and that only Circe can help him. Such a beginning is bound to interest any functioning female because, the love object being unnamed and the petitioner looking at her under the stress of evident passion, she is likely to speed to the conclusion that flatters her, namely, that the speaker is in love with her. Disappointingly enough, Glaucus immediately proceeds to clarify his desires: he wishes Circe to cause Scylla to fall in love with him. And he has the temerity to tell the professional the means she can use, a song or an herbal concoction.

Like Medea, also descended from the Sun, Circe is a passionate witch, but unlike Medea, who was constant in love, Circe falls in love upon the sight of any strong, handsome male, even one blue, green, and fish-tailed. Ovid offers alternative explanations for her amorousness. The first is that that is the way she is—a statement that explains nothing. The second is that Venus has punished Circe for the Sun's tattling on her and Mars—a reason containing a wild inconsistency. For Venus must consider love a good thing, but if she punishes her offender the Sun through his daughter Circe, she does so by conferring a benefit, amorousness.

To continue, Circe is unwilling to lose a possible lover. Therefore, she declares her desire for Glaucus and gives him sensible advice that works in her own interest: he should forget about Scylla, take up with Circe, and thus have his revenge. Glaucus, however, is not very acute. Knowing what his own love has led him to do and knowing Circe's powers, he yet persists in loving Scylla and saying so. His expression of devotion is unfortunate. Nature, he says in effect, would have to be metamorphosed into unnatural reversals before his love for Scylla, provided she is safe and sound, would change. "Safe and sound" provide the hint, apparently unneeded by Circe, since she wants to fix her rival. (She cannot harm another god, nor does she wish to.)

Circe fixes Scylla nicely. Using song and herbs, Circe poisons Scylla's favorite bathing spot. The area is sickle shaped and, therefore, suggests the unsexing of Uranus and moon-goddess Diana's aversion to sexual union. Thus when Scylla bathes there ordinarily, she is expressing her Diana-like attachment to virginity. We have earlier been made aware of Scylla's practice of rejecting suitors and enjoying it, so that when Circe hexes the spot, she merely makes Scylla's attitude repulsively apparent. For when Scylla bathes there, she becomes most unsound: she loses her legs and develops instead a pedestal of barking dogs. She is thus rendered completely unappealing as a sexual partner. On the other hand, Circe does not seem very inviting, either, and Glaucus flees both. Scylla, who becomes fixed in one place, gets back at Circe by destroying shipmates of Circe's former lover Ulysses. The Trojans are spared her ravages because she is turned into a rock before they come upon her.

But pass her way they do. Ovid now moves from the engaging divertissement of myth to pedestrian geography made a part of heroic legend. The Strait of Messina is now perfectly passable; no myth bogies haunt it. The Trojans avoid Scylla's rock and Charybdis' whirlpool, and their problem turns out to be a real wind that sends them scudding from their objective, Italy, off across the Mediterranean to Dido's Carthage and its queen's tragedy. For three hundred and eighty-three lines Ovid follows more of the journeyings of Aeneas, all of which had been covered earlier in detail in the *Aeneid*. Obviously Aeneas is needed to switch the narrative from the Greek to the Italian and Roman and from myth-legend to what passed for Roman history. Equally clear, the inclusion of Aeneas is a tribute to the Julian clan and to Augustus, as well as to Venus, who figures so prominently in the *Metamorphoses*. But it is also clear that Ovid's artistic problem is that of using Aeneas without repeating the *Aeneid*. The result is not to the advantage of Aeneas. He remains a shadowy figure in this book, his piety and humaneness being sketched or attested to by others. This procedure in itself is novel, but the annalistic approach to the hero's career undercuts his achievements.

Aeneas' character is not without flaw, either. In his brief encounter with Dido, Ovid labels Aeneas Dido's husband, does not justify his leaving Dido, and, indeed, says that Dido was deceived. The brevity of treatment given the passionate love of Dido and Aeneas may imply that in matters of great moment, love and women are negligible. This attitude sounds Roman enough, but it seems an unlikely explanation here. Ovid is too warmhearted, for one thing. For another, the passage displays Aeneas as one who is ungrateful and one who betrays the heart by means of deceit. There is a good deal of treachery and deceit in Book XIV. Circe deceives Glaucus, ruins the unwitting Scylla, and tricks the companions of Ulysses. The Sirens deceive by means of their song; the Cercopians engage in tricks, lies, fraud, and perjury. Ulysses' shipmates suspect that the big bag given him by Aeolus is a device for cheating them of gold. Circe deludes Picus with a phantom boar and his retinue with mists and fogs. Aeneas is superior to these deceivers, for he is pious in adhering to the quest for the homeland, but because of his lapse in accepting Dido's love and hospitality, he shares in their deceit. Shape-changer Vertumnus alone uses deceit for a praiseworthy end, that of obtaining and, in a sense, fulfilling the right bride. And so does Aeneas, one must admit. Still, as Ovid writes the tale, mortal Aeneas has deceived a wife, and his character is tarnished.

In other circumstances, Aeneas does measure up. He sails from Carthage to Eryx and there piously sacrifices to his dead father. He avoids the King of the Winds, the dangerous Phlegraean Plains, the Sirens, and the degenerate inhabitants of Pithecusae. His lack of curiosity and his prudently avoiding dangerous situations characterize him as a realist and as unlike the romantic Ulysses. He is thus in keeping with Virgil's presentation of Aeneas, that of the man dedicated to a mission. But he has forfeited knowing some of the wonders of the world, and he seems dull.

At this point Ovid plays some of his tricks upon his reader. He makes Aeneas' route geographically impossible, as Mr. Simmons notes; and his chronology is in error, for he has Aeneas come upon the tomb of his trumpeter Misenus without bothering to bury the man first. Since Ovid is accurate about other geographic matters in this very passage and since he avoids Virgil's mistake of calling a place Caieta before it was named for the old lady, Ovid is seeing whether his readers are nodding, and he is also making fun of Virgil by duplicating at least one kind of mistake made by

Virgil. Ovid played another trick on his audience earlier in connection with Dido. He might have been expected to give the loving queen and her emotions extended treatment, as he had given Byblis, Scylla, and other heroines. True, in his *Heroides*, Dido had written a letter to Aeneas, but Ovid's audience might have expected the more mature poet to surpass his earlier performance. Yet he touches only on her opened-armed reception of Aeneas and her death, saying that as she was deceived, so she deceived others. And so Ovid has deceived any reader who expected a searing account of Dido's passion.

The account of Aeneas' first landing in Italy is a similar cheat. Any poet who had done what Ovid had with the house of Fame, with Hunger, and with the Cave of Sleep, might have been expected to make the Sibyl a figure of mantic awesomeness or to make her guided tour through Hell better than Virgil's. But Ovid flats the whole passage. Indeed, his emphases are disappointing. He stresses Aeneas' politeness and has the hero praise the Sibyl for taking him into Death's house and bringing him safely out of it. (Aeneas' words are more meaningful than he can guess, for later Venus will use this trip as an argument for his being made immortal.) As for the remarkable journey through the realm of Dis, Ovid largely ignores it and concentrates instead upon the Sibyl's love story, hardly an acceptable replacement even for that of Dido and Aeneas.

The Sibyl's sad and wistful story shows that unyielding virginity has led to a wasted and wasting life. Once Apollo had offered her the opportunity to be forever, a gift she accepted, and then the chance to be endlessly young, would she but be his love. She refused. Now, seven hundred years old and fated to live three hundred more, she feels that no one, not even Apollo, will ever believe her worthy of being loved. And as she talks, she reveals that she has always been completely wrapped up in herself and isolated.

From Cumae Aeneas sails to the spot where he will bury his nurse, Caieta. Her urn will bear an epitaph praising Aeneas' piety as well as identifying her ashes. The epigraph is composed as though Caieta spoke it, but only pious Aeneas could have had the sententious inscription engraved to enhance his glory.

At this place two former comrades of Ulysses meet, Macareus and Achaemenides. Macareus had stayed in Italy because he had tired of journeying. He knows that Achaemenides had been left in the land of the Cyclops, and he is surprised that Trojans would aid a former enemy Greek. Here Ovid's emphases are those of Virgil in the *Aeneid*: the brutality of Polyphemus and the implicit relentless hatred of the Greeks are contrasted with the humaneness of the Trojans, which by descent, of course, flows down through the Romans. Achaemenides expresses a boundless gratitude that glorifies Aeneas and all his descendants.

Macareus also pays his respects to Aeneas' justness and thus contributes to the hero's fame. But he also addresses him with the

Virgilian formula " 'nate dea,' " which Ovid had Cygnus use earlier to effect a comic devaluation of the phrase, so that here it lacks its full Virgilian grandeur. Macareus also points out that, the war over, Aeneas is no longer an enemy; and he warns him against Circe. These details, as noted above, stress the possibility of friendly relations between former enemies, say, conquering Roman and conquered Greek, and present a useful political principle.

Macareus' account of his adventures includes encounters with Aeolus and the Laestrygonians. But after Achaemenides' description of a Polyphemus that longs to have human limbs quivering between his teeth, that crunches human bones whose marrow is still warm, and that vomits blood, wine, and human flesh, Macareus wisely speeds over the horrors of cannibalism. He treats the envy and rebellious greed of Ulysses' crew in summary fashion also. His sensational figure is Circe, whose trickiness and amorousness are displayed in her dealings with Ulysses and his crew. These qualities and spitefulness appear in her pursuit of Picus. It is the tale of the Italian prince that is the novel portion of Macareus' account.

In the first part of Macareus' tale, Ulysses is shown to be very unwise. His men have learned from the Cyclops and the Laestrygonians not to be too curious, but Ulysses has not. He forces his men to explore, and they are bewitched. If Eurylochus had not remained aloof and if Mercury had not brought the moly to Ulysses, Macareus and his fellows would have remained pigs. Thus Ulysses is woefully deficient as a responsible leader.

Circe emerges as something of a Mycenaean merchant princess, resembling the lords of the archaeological Pylos, but grander. Her abode is like a city; her halls are marble; her throne recess, beautiful; her veil, gold; her robe, sparkling. Her Nereids and nymphs are engaged, not in domesticities such as producing woolen goods, but in sorting, weighing, and combining flowers and herbs. In short, Circe has the largest pharmaceutical manufactory of ancient classical myth, and, since she is a witch and we know some of her performances, we doubt that she is engaged in promoting longevity. She has more testimonials than any other herbalist of myth: one thousand denatured wild beasts, once, presumably, men and women. These animals are apparently happy to receive the new group of conversions, to whom Circe appeared a hospitable lady. She had no trouble in bewitching the newcomers, for the way to a man's core, it is well known, is through a home-cooked meal. After Ulysses' men eat and drink, a touch of Circe's wand is sufficient to bring out their innate piggishness.

Ulysses' protection against enchantment is an herb, which is appropriate for conflict with Circe. However, its appearance in the text so close to Aeneas' golden bough suggests that their bearers differ markedly in fates, abilities, and seriousness. Ulysses needs protection against a female and enchantment; Aeneas has a device that allows him to pass through Hades and return and that, therefore, helps him to gain immortality.

Another implicit contrast between the Greek and the Trojan lies in their relationships with the opposite sex. Aeneas married Dido, but left her; she committed suicide. He did the proper thing in Roman eyes and is dishonored by his deceit; she is weak. The affair is a tragedy. Ulysses has a similarly brief relationship; however, his is with a supernatural being. He cannot be her eternal companion, so that the affair must be of limited duration and happiness. It is happy, and the liaison would seem to redound to his glory, for in it mortal mates with deity and controls her destructiveness. Thus far Ovid seems to elevate Ulysses above Aeneas. But Circe is fairyland compared with the founder of an actual Carthage. Furthermore, Ulysses' consorting so long with such an evil and vindictive personage is not to his credit. One may confront the evil existing in the universe and best it, without cohabiting with it for a year.

Whereas Achaemenides excelled in the techniques of the horror story, Marcareus has the talents of a Disney cartoonist. They are displayed chiefly in his story of native Italian prince Picus ("woodpecker"), for whom Circe had constructed a shrine and whom she worshiped by hanging wreaths on his statue. This snowy marble shows the young king with a woodpecker on his head. Although humor varies from nation to nation and although Romans took woodpeckers seriously in a number of ways, the image of a man with a bird on his head is likely to strike an American as funny. One of Aristophanes' birds cites similar statues to prove the importance of birds, but the vogue does not seem to have lasted in ancient Greek sculpture, and Aristophanes may be ridiculing it in his comedy. In any case, by beginning the tale of Picus with such a statue, Macareus makes Picus seem affectionately silly; later he portrays him as devotedly sweet. Both the affectionate ridicule and the sentimental purity may be found in cartoon heroes, as may the sketchy characterization that Macareus gives the prince.

Ovid does not state precisely how old Picus is, but he is young, somewhere between fifteen and twenty. Thus when Circe falls in love with him and spitefully enchants him, she is not only disrupting a happy young home, she is practically robbing the cradle. Picus is handsome; the wife of his choosing, young and beautiful. She has a marvelous voice, its powers resembling those of Orpheus', so that it is oddly humorous that her singing, moving to rocks, trees, and wild beasts, arresting to birds and rivers, is powerless to keep Picus, fond of horseflesh and hunting, at home. One day as she trills in her wonted way, Picus fares forth in his, off into his Latin kingdom with its hills full of the drug-producing plants so dear to Circe. Circe is there, naturally, to lure him off by himself, using a phantom boar. When she confronts him with her love and proposes an alliance and when he staunchly refuses to be disloyal to his wife and to his own affections, Circe turns him into a woodpecker. After a spectacular magic show for his attendants, she changes them into various wild beasts. Canens grieves herself into nothingness. And we latter-day beings have been with Titania—for so Ovid calls Circe—and her magic wand.

After piously burying Caieta and receiving proper credit for the act and after heeding Macareus' advice to avoid Circe, Aeneas, who is vague but seems more real than either Circe or Picus, fights a war to win an Italian bride. All combatants are properly hardy. Aeneas has the aid of Greek immigrant Evander. Turnus, his Rutulian opponent, sends Venulus to Diomedes for aid, a long trip from the Tiber area to Arpi. The aid does not materialize, for the real purposes of this rather lengthy digression are those of revealing that Greek fortunes are on the decline and that it is disastrous to offend Venus. Diomedes describes how the homecoming Greeks were mostly destroyed in a storm brought on by the sin of one man, Ajax, son of Oileus, who ravished Cassandra and thus offended Minerva. Venus, he adds, retaliated for the wound that Diomedes had given her during the Trojan War and caused him to be driven from his natal Argos. She also metamorphosed many of his comrades into swanlike birds for insulting her. And now Diomedes is the king of a difficult, arid land and is condemned to hard work. Diomedes is definitely reduced in heroic magnitude. On the credit side, however, he has a proper understanding of kingship: his function is to protect his people, keep his city in existence, and exert himself so that his realm is productive. Diomedes is not Aeneas' opponent, but his foil, for he shows that Greek and Trojan alike must face the realities of existence and of divine will.

The most curious narrative in Book XIV, tantalizingly odd because so seemingly out of place, is that of the wild olive, formerly a boorish Apulian shepherd. Venulus picks it up as he returns, otherwise empty-handed, from his embassy to Diomedes. It is as crude, naive, and pious as its native land and as artless. In its way, through the impiety of the shepherd punished for scaring and mocking the dancing nymphs, the sketch represents the sort of colorless religion found in indigenous Italy before the Greek myths were introduced: nothing great to write about, but conspicuous for respecting the forces dwelling in things, in short, for piety. Noteworthy, too, is the shepherd's hostility to art, here the dance, one of the most primitive forms of art. Since the nymphs perform a ring, or fertility, dance, the shepherd's antagonism to it is inverted love or admiration for what he cannot submit to, understand, or participate in. He behaves like the pre-adolescent boy who shows his attraction to girls by teasing them. However, he did not have to be abusive and obscene. He lacks refinement, or cultivation, and seems to indicate that the primitive Italians themselves had not understood or valued or even known of it. The cave, Ovid notes, was once the sacred abode of anonymous nymphs; now it is the dwelling of Pan, an import of the rural Greek imagination. Indeed, in the *Fasti* Ovid says that Arcadian Evander brought the worship of Pan to Latium. The male has replaced the female, but the reeds before the cave recall Syrinx and suggest that the new rustic deity appreciates art, music, and femininity.

Following the Diomedes episode, in which Greeks refuse to war on Trojans and to get involved with the wrong side of proto-Roman politics, this tale of the uncultivated shepherd shows where the desirable Greek impact should occur, namely, in the sphere of culture and refinement.

To the crude slapstick, miming, and buffoonery of the tale, Ovid adds the use of metamorphosis as metaphor: the Apulian clown is comparable to the wild olive and the bitterness of its fruit. The implications of the analogy are that Italian peasants have a talent for saying nasty, derogatory, vile things that leave a bad taste in one's mouth; that they have a propensity to crudely satiric imitation; and that even when they have been shut up, they have ways of getting back.

The Apulian is not one of the better people, nor is Turnus, to whom the narrative now returns. He, too, offends—the protectress of nymphs, Cybele, this time, rather than the nymphs themselves. For when he attempts to burn the Trojan ships, a reasonable military maneuver, he experiences the noisy and awesome epiphany of the mother-goddess. She tells him that his efforts are impious and vain. Then she rescues the trees that were once part of her sacred groves by providing a most unusual metamorphosis. She turns the remains of the tree-nymphs into sea-nymphs and dead matter back to nature spirits, but they are now ones appropriate to their marine function. Turnus is faulted for impiety, and a hint is given as to who will win the war. There is no mistaking who has divine support; Cybele is the mother of the gods and of all living things, and she has demonstrated in favor of regeneration and the Trojans. The opponents of the Rutulians hope that they will take the hint and cease fighting, but they do not until Turnus is killed and his city burned. From its ashes its namesake, the heron, arises to beat its wings in mourning.

But other things—indeed, all things—change. Because Aeneas' son Iulus is growing up and is properly established and because the war is over and the bride and kingdom are won, Aeneas is ready for heaven. His mission accomplished, his time is past. All the deities, even Juno, now favor Aeneas because of his merits. As a result, Venus petitions Jove that Aeneas be made a divinity, no matter how minor. After all, she reasons, he has been to the repulsive kingdom of Hades already, and once should be enough. Jove grants her request. Then, like Glaucus to a degree, but unlike Hercules, Aeneas is made immortal by water. His merits have outweighed his flaws, so that now he is unmistakably one of the better people. However, the circumstances are a bit odd. In all of this, Aeneas is not consulted. Venus orders the river Numicius to wash away the mortal element. He does. Venus anoints the remaining body and touches its lips with ambrosia, thus making a god of Aeneas, a relatively unimportant one known as *Indiges*. Thus Venus gets her wish, Aeneas rises in stature, and the later deifications of important Julians are prepared for and given the authority of precedent. But there is something ominous about the process of deification here, for in order to become a god, the candidate has to die. Aeneas' taking-off sounds like a violent one by drowning.

However, his descendants now have the benefit of a divine ancestor whose name indicates, according to Mr. Wilson, that he has been naturalized.

Aeneas' successors are named with a detail or two in a kind of epic catalog that advances the poem chronologically and gives evidence that there are outstanding figures among the better people, for example, founders like Aeneas, and those who simply provide continuing rule, such as Epytus and Capys. Not all of these successors are equal in merit or ability. Remulus is impious; Acrota resigns the throne. Finally a bare entity, Proca, is reached.

Proca is unexpectedly made illustrious by Pomona and Vertumnus. In his reign the Italian seasons wedded garden and orchard. Thus one of the minor better people is glorified by something that happened in his reign, but that he had no part in.

Ovid's telling of Pomona's wooing is another example of what the master can do with native myth. He takes a good, down-to-earth, industrious hamadryad who loves her fields, garden, and fruit trees, being especially fond of the last, pruning, grafting, and watering them. She is a modest maid, unstirred by sexual desires; and, afraid that some rural type would force her, she stays shut up in her domain. (In her avoidance of males, she is like Scylla and the Sibyl.) All desire her—satyrs, Pans, Silenus, Priapus, and especially Vertumnus, an obscure deity of the changing year and its vegetation. A shape-changer himself and, therefore, resembling all other deceivers that the reader has encountered, he disguises himself and works for Pomona as reaper, ox-driver, mower, leaf-collector, vine-pruner, or apple-picker. Or in the guise of soldier, fisherman, or other, he would come to gaze upon her beauty. Finally he becomes bolder. Entering the garden as an old woman, he praises Pomona's fruit and her beauty and kisses her as no old woman would. Thus Ovid indicates Vertumnus' eagerness and Pomona's innocence. The old dame preaches to Pomona about the garden elm and its mate, the vine: were they not joined, the vine would be worthless. She points out that all the locals desire to marry her and recommends Vertumnus, all a bride could wish for: obedient, loving, loyal, versatile, he shares her interests and is honored among gardens. The old woman adds, quite honestly, that no one knows him as well as she does. She also warns Pomona against offending Venus and Nemesis, telling the tale of Iphis ("strength") and Anaxarete ("queenly excellence"?) to prove her point.

Iphis, a young man of humble birth, fell in love with Anaxarete, descended from the Greek founder of Cyprian Salamis, just by seeing her. (The parallels to Vertumnus and Pomona flatter her: Vertumnus is the humble youth; Pomona, the princess.) He did everything he could to win her—hung around her door, pestered her nurse and other servants, sent Anaxarete love letters, garlanded her door, wept all over it, lay across its step, lamented. Indeed, he did all the things that Tarpeia's lover did in one of Propertius' sophisticated Roman elegies. But Anaxarete spurned, scorned, and ridiculed him, at a distance or through the door, for there is no indication that she met him face to face. Hopeless Iphis finally sent her a suicide note in which he wrote that he was certain that he deserved her, that his love in some way pleased her, that his love for her could end only with death, which he hoped would make him famous, that cruel she has won and may enjoy the sight of his dead body, for he has arranged for that. Then he hanged himself from her lintel, kicking the door convulsively as he strangled. The sound was ominous. The horrified servants cut him down—Anaxarete did not look on him—and rushed the corpse to his widowed mother. His funeral passed Anaxarete's house. Though hard of heart, Anaxarete was touched when she heard the mourning and went to a high window to behold the corpse. (An avenging deity, Nemesis, was operating.) When she saw the dead youth, she tried to turn away, but was turned to stone. So she was punished for rejecting love. This is a true story, for her statue witnesses it.

This tale, a combination of the simple and the sophisticated, has no effect upon Pomona. Indeed, its point has to do with seeing and loving, and the tale ought to have been more a guide to Vertumnus than to Pomona, for she has never really seen him. He has always been in disguise. Now in frustration Vertumnus strips and reveals his naked self ready to force the nymph. But nakedness is enough. The watching Pomona is stimulated to love by his beauty. All ends in reciprocal love.

This comedy depends on the unexpected reversal: it was Vertumnus who needed the instructional tale, not Pomona. All his earlier approaches had been the wrong kind. There is another reversal involved: one would expect helpfulness or the cautionary tale to win the shy, retiring maiden, but the rude, bold, and basic approach is the one that wins her. For it reveals to her the deity that she has been devoted to and serving all along.

On the purely human and realistic level of this allegory, Ovid is praising the industrious, modest, fertile rural Italian maid and also the Italian soil and its productivity and climate and basic Italian sensible sexuality. All that one needs for a sound match and marriage are two healthy persons of the opposite sex of sufficient physical attractiveness and complementary interests. Of course, Ovid is praising the hardworking, considerate, and forceful Italian farmer, too. The tale of Pomona and Vertumnus is his amorous georgics.

Pomona's tale done, Ovid marches on in time through the annals of the kings, not all of whom are praiseworthy. Amulius the despot rules; then Numitor regains his throne. Then Tatius and the Sabines war upon newly founded Rome. Tarpeia commits treason and is crushed to death by the comtemptuous Sabine enemy. Juno similarly betrays Rome to the Sabine men of Cures, but loyal Venus thwarts their takeover with scalding water. The war with the Sabines continues, but finally both parties decide that peace is preferable to war and arrange a compromise, joint rule by Sabine Tatius and Roman Romulus. This is a high point, for reason prevails, and one can see that the Sabine War is unlike the vengeance-fulfilling Trojan War. Italian common sense rises above Greek meanness, greed, and ambition. The national honor is upheld, and the idea of compromise works in practice.

Thus far the annals are uneven: some rulers are mere names; some, impious or vicious; some, outstanding. Ovid is realistic and does not exalt the whole of Rome's early history. It is noteworthy that, a Paelignian and tribally belonging to the Roman Socii, or Allies, he gives some stress to the fact that the Romans benefited from merging with other peoples.

The climax in the annals is yet to come. As Venus had for Aeneas when his service had been completed, so now Mars petitions Jove for the deification of his son Romulus, founder of Rome, when his city-state is strong enough to stand alone. With Jove's permission, Mars whisks Romulus from the administration of justice and carries him off to heaven so fast that his mortal part is purified away by air. This apotheosis is grand enough, but again it has the ominous undertone of something sinister, namely, death by violence, for Mars is metonomy for war and physical assault, and it is he who removes Romulus from the mortal scene. Associated with the deifications of Aeneas and Romulus is the smell of death.

It is masked, however, by the glorification, for Romulus becomes the secondary war-god Quirinus. In addition, without asking the permission of anyone, Juno, goddess of marriage, rewards Romulus' loving wife, Hersilia, by transporting her to heaven. Quirinus receives her lovingly, makes her immortal, and gives her a new name, Hora.

This episode is the climax of the annals. Not even Aeneas can match it, for his wife was not deified, nor was he made such an important god. The Greeks cannot match it, not with Glaucus, Ganymede, or even Hercules. The Roman virtues—public service, private sacrifice, justice, humaneness, harmony, and family love and devotion—all are awarded the highest recognition. And yet the climax is flat, subdued, lacking in panoply, and magnificence. For there is more to come: the fulfillment of the Roman dream.

But the end is in sight. The Roman tradition has been initiated and defined by Aeneas and defined and matured by Romulus. But how will Destiny, the Fates, almighty Jove, and Ovid work matters out? What more has Ovid to reveal about the better people, who surpass the Greeks and the Italians of Aeneas' time? The materials are known, but not their shaping and the artist's vision. Somehow Romulus and Hersilia must be surpassed. Climax must cap climax. This is Ovid's challenge—and his means of suspense.

METAMORPHOSES XV: Healers

And what is Rome besides piety, success in war, sensible use of victory, effective government, and respectable love? To these sterling achievements exemplified in Book XIV, Ovid adds peace, harmony, health, and world domination. The better people become the best. This new status and these additional accomplishments are Ovid's climax. Augustus is its pinnacle.

Toward this apex Ovid builds with a number of unexpected but carefully chosen figures from Roman legend, beginning with Numa, the first philosopher king and advocate of lasting peace, and his tutor, the Sage, who is the philosopher of peace. Then comes Cipus, the self-sacrificing citizen-general who represses ambition so that rule by the Senate and the people will not be overthrown. Last is the first historical emperor-*princeps*, Augustus, first in war and first in peace, arbiter of mores, divinely foreseen ruler of the world. Thus Ovid arranges his material so that this book caps the preceding one.

Because Ovid adds the tales of Aesculapius and of Hippolytus, the assortment of material at first seems definitely heterogeneous, but Ovid deftly builds it into an all-embracing theme, using his usual ability to throw the reader off balance and to surprise. All the major figures in this book in some way, directly or metaphorically, have to do with healing, that is, with bringing health, harmony, concord, or wholeness to men singly or collectively and even to their relationship with animals. Numa heals the warlike natures of his people and prevents wounds by training Romans to be peaceable. The Pythagorean sage protests against bloodshed and tries to bring peace of mind and peace between men and beasts. Hippolytus would heal the grief of Egeria, as his torn body had been healed in the Underworld by Aesculapius. Cipus refuses to harm the state. Aesculapius, of course, is the main figure of healing and wholeness in this book, its emblem and divine representative. But Augustus, who caused wounds in the name of piety, binds them up, too, and is an establisher of peace and just lawgiver. Even Caesar, most famous in war and peace, has done nothing so great as his becoming the father of Augustus.

All in all, then, Book XV is in general a serious glorification of Rome and the figures that establish and sustain her in peace. But like Book XIV, Book XV has its lighter moments. They have nothing to do with amour, which is absent, but with the heavier theme of the book. One, which will serve as representative, carries over from Book XIV. There Mars asserted that Rome was firmly established and did not have to rely upon a single guardian for its well-being. As a result, in Book XV one might expect government by a senate or assembly. Not at all. Mars seems to be all wrong, for the Romans look for yet another king. Even worse for Mars, the man picked for the throne is not warlike. He is a pacifist, a follower of the Italian Muses, a philosopher, a major in religious studies, and a social psychologist. Numa puts Mars out of business for the length of his reign—all because Mars desired the deification of his son. The lesson for readers may be that the goal of war is peace. Nevertheless, Mars seems dimwitted.

In addition, the narrative continues, Fama picks this new king. There is a bit of suspense and humor here, for Fama is a varied and spotted creature. As we know from preceding books, she is equivalent to Rumor. Thus the choice of Numa seems a questionable one.

But Numa has qualifications for kingship. First, he has extensive knowledge of the religion and religious practices of his own people, the Sabines. Second, he has great plans and a roomy mind capable of much more learning, so that he wishes to know "the nature of things." By echoing the title of Lucretius' famous philosophical poem, dedicated to Venus, this last phrase suggests the Numa is going to study philosophy, one that is materialistic, Epicurean, and not essentially religious and one that stresses change. Just what Numa's qualities and interests will produce in the way of a ruler, Ovid does not explain. The proof lies in the results, and there is no evidence that Numa's reign was anything but good, peaceful, and happy.

According to Ovid's chronology, Numa, driven by the desire for knowledge, goes to "the city of Hercules the Guest," and the first thing he learns there is a digression, an account of the founding of Crotona by the visiting Hercules. Hercules had been the guest of Croton in southern Italy as he returned from Spain with the cattle of Geryon. He promised his host that two generations later, there would be a city on the spot. And so there was. Hercules, through dreams, bullied Myscelus of Argos into leaving his native city and founding a new one in Italy, which he names after Croton. Before leaving Argos, Myscelus was charged with the capital crime of intending to leave the city and was convicted by an all black vote of the jury, but Hercules performed a miracle and changed all the ballots to white. Hence, Myscelus was able to leave.

The story is a form of knowledge, but it is probably more instructive for the reader than for Numa, for the peaceable king makes nothing of it. Neither does Ovid. Yet the story does function within its context. It presents a Greek parallel to Rome, for both cities are founded by immigrants who are driven to Italy by superior powers. Myscelus and Hercules, then, are parallels of Aeneas and Jove, or Fate. Of course, the Greek city cannot compare with Rome, for it has no destiny—the comparison reveals this difference. But curious phenomena are operating here. Once the bases for the comparison are provided by this tale, it is possible for the comparison itself to suddenly snap into focus for us, and thus we become aware of the relative greatness of Aeneas and the city his endeavors lead to. If this happens, Ovid's ingenuity and obliqueness have paid off. He has scored in his game. If the significance and importance of the story elude us and if we are puzzled by Ovid's using it, then Ovid also wins.

Aside from the implicit comparison, there are other things to be gained from the story. It stresses the importance of hospitality and gratitude. It teaches that prophecies—Hercules' promise to his host is also a prophecy—do come true, and teaching this lesson, it prepares for the prophecy made later about Rome by the Sage and may even lend a touch of credibility to it. It also demonstrates that the gods are, or can be, involved in the founding of city states. But Ovid is also back at his old game of belittling Greeks. Myscelus ("little mouse"?), touted as being most approved of by the gods during his time, is not only nominally comic, he is a nonentity. That the gods look on him with favor may mean merely that he is pious. He is described as *squalidus,* and though the term may mean only that he appeared in court looking distraught and wretched in his worst old clothes, it does not describe him as heroic. As far as Ovid informs us about him, his father is not a man of note, and Myscelus himself might have had trouble founding even a farmhouse. In short, this mousy agent of the gods is mock heroic. He is one of those mortals who have greatness thrust upon them. Ovid pads his story, taking two lines to say, in effect, "the next night" and devoting six lines out of its thirty-eight to an itinerary that fills space but lacks interest. The list has all the pretentiousness of mediocrity imitating epic. Hence, while it serves to type Myscelus, it serves as contrast with the preceding travels of Aeneas and the progress of Aesculapius, which is to come.

There is something wry about the god's using other people to pay his promissory notes and in his getting as much glory as the person he repays. And there is something amusing about promising to reward a host after he is long dead. To a rationalist, of course, the story of the founding seems to have been concocted long after Hercules' visit to Italy.

This tale, like others in the *Metamorphoses,* adds to the evidence that the Greek presence in and influence on Italy is very old, indeed, and that it is a civilizing one. In Numa's day, according to Ovid, that effect included the study of philosophy, for Numa goes to Crotona to listen to a voluntary exile from Greek Samos expound ideas. He is described as one who hated tyranny. Ovid does not name this exile, but he is often identified with Pythagoras, who was a Samian and who is known to have been active in Crotona. However, Ovid's allusion to Lucretius' *De Rerum Natura* suggests that the philosopher of Crotona may be a composite. Mr. Galinsky supports this view when he notes "several precise terminological affinities with Aristotle and Posidonius in Pythagoras' disquisition on change"—that is, the exposition presented in Book XV. In short, it may be better to think of Numa's philosopher as the Sage, or as Pythagoras somewhat modified.

What Ovid has his Pythagoras-Sage do in the longest single episode in Book XV is deliver a philosophy lecture in poetic form. Ovid thus adds another genre to his repertoire and another novelty to delight his readers. Part of the fun is the self-characterization that emerges as the Philosopher rolls majestically along. He is clearly self-important. But he is also well meaning. For example, he strives to eliminate the very human and very vexing fear of death. He is also a windbag. He belabors the obvious, the very obvious of Ovid's time, about the way the sun and moon change their appearance and day follows night. He is sensuous in his description of the seasons, but never rivals Keats on Autumn, and he brings in a number of old chestnuts like the Golden Age, aged Helen lamenting her lost beauty, and the four seasons as parallels of four human periods of development. Like a pedant, he cites too many instances in his list of marvelous changes in natural phenomena, some of which are most unnatural, some mere superstitions. He is also an analyst of some subtlety.

The Sage does furnish Numa with indoctrination about the way to peace; in fact, the Sage's whole speech is an extended piece of persuasion and thus another variety of oratory. It aims at giving man peace of mind by giving him an understanding of the nature of things and by removing the fear of death through understanding. It also strives to give men peaceful relations with animals and with other human beings. And to these it adds by example an appreciation of the goodness of bountiful Nature and of her beauty and wonders.

The Philosopher's peace program is essentially dietary. One should eat fruit, grain, vegetables, and milk products and use honey and wine. Meat is forbidden. The Sage gives reasons religious, ethical, aesthetic, and psychological. Killing animals trains one in cruelty and brutality and psychologically prepares one for killing human beings. The shedding of blood and the tearing open of animals to inspect their quivering inner organs is revolting, whereas the intact sacrificial animal is itself beautiful. It is as unethical to deceive, betray, or be ungrateful to animals as it is, by implication, to do so or be so to men. It is impious to sacrifice animals to the gods because the act implicates the gods in a human crime. It is impious to kill animals and a crime to do it because the flesh obtained is cruel and unnatural food; that is, it is essentially cannibalistic to feed, or nourish, flesh with its own kind, namely, other flesh. Killing animals is wrong unless one is protecting oneself or one's livelihood. Further, since souls shift about from human beings to beasts and back, one may, by killing an animal, be harming a former human soul, even that of a relative. Such killing is a step on the path to shedding human blood.

Ovid notes that the Philosopher's argument against eating meat convinced no one. Thus he undercuts the Sage. Appetite is stronger than reason. And it is easy to find objections to the Philosopher's theories about the soul. But many might find his refinement and gentleness appealing. Others might be attracted to his rational rejection of superstition—where that is operating. His novel epic catalog of natural wonders may seem inferior parallels to Ovid's own array of metamorphoses, as one modern critic suggests, or it may be regarded as another display of Ovidian virtuosity and an extension of Ovid's theme as stated in Book I. Actually it is all three. For human beings, the Grand Canyon is spectacular and wonder-filling, but Marilyn Monroe or Cleopatra is probably more interesting, because she is human. Hence, Ovid's catalog of deities, men, and women is superior to the Sage's list of ntural wonders because more engrossing. But the Philosopher adds to our understanding of metamorphosis. In Book I Ovid stated his subject: bodies changed into new forms. In Book XV the Philosopher reveals the reason that the changes have a consistency to them: the soul does not die, but during the change passes from one body to the other, and thus its characteristics are transferred to the new being. Lotis as nymph was unwilling to be violated; when she became a tree, she was similarly unwilling.

Taking an overview of the Philosopher's speech, we see that, just as the Sage seems to be Pythagoras plus and functions as Ovid wishes him to, so Ovid makes our reactions to the Sage varied and multivalent.

In general, Ovid uses the Philosopher to promote the Princeps' program of peace and piety. This support is indicated by the Sage's claim that he is inspired by Apollo and his describing the god's mind with a word that immediately suggests Augustus Caesar: " '*augustae.*' " Thus god and emperor are linked in a way that Augustus would applaud: the god seems to have Augustus as a dimension of his mind. Most supportive of the Princeps is the Sage's prophecy of the coming greatness of Rome, his praise of the Julian ancestor Aeneas, and the laudation of Augustus, who is not identified by name. (The Philosopher knew all this because he was once the Trojan hero Euphorbus and heard Helenus give the original prediction.)

The Philosopher prepares for Augustus in another way. His theorizing emphasizes change as the major phenomenon in the universe. This change, however, is cyclic, so that having seen Aeneas, Romulus, and Numa, one can expect to see their like again—not an exact replica. That likeness, of course, will be Augustus.

Ovid himself is, and has been, using this cyclic movement in his repeating types with variation. He has here come back to his subject, metamorphosis, by having the Sage explain it. And Ovid has returned to the four elements. In Book I, Ovid presented them as the bases for all things and each as having its proper sphere. The Sage sees the four elements themselves involved in the universal process of constant change. His system is thus more consistent and complex than Ovid's, but it is more improbable. Ovid's seems to represent more recent philosophical views. Both Ovid and the Philosopher himself describe the Philosopher as intellectual and contemplative, reaching toward the realm of the divine with his mind. He is also a collector of information and observation. But he is more speculative and opinionated in dealing with his data than practical. His opposites are not so much Plato, Zeno, or Diogenes as Vitruvius, Pliny the Elder, Celsus, and Columella.

After learning all that the Sage has to impart, Numa returns to Rome, is offered the kingship, and rules for many years. His learning is supplemented by his having nymph Egeria for his wife and the guidance of the Italian Muses, the Camenae, and so all goes well. He is not taken in by the Sage's arguments about killing animals, for he teaches the sacrificial rituals to his people and turns warlike citizens into peaceful ones anyway. Unlike Aeneas and Romulus, Numa dies of natural causes.

Like Romulus, however, Numa leaves behind his helpmate, who parallels Hersilia and suggests that a good wife is an asset. Everyone mourns him, but Egeria, like that other faithful Italian nymph Canens, is distraught and takes to the woods at Aricia. These are suitably thick to cover her moans and laments, but she is so loud that she hinders the local worship of Diana, imported by Orestes. Wood- and water-nymph warn Egeria to desist and say consoling things. Then Hippolytus takes her in hand. He attempts to cure her of grief. Repeatedly. And in the same words. With the wrong approach.

" 'Stop it,' " he says understandingly. " 'You are not the only one with something to complain about. Think of similar misfortunes that have happened to others; then yours will not be so hard to bear.' " The command and the unsympathetic reasoning do not work. Why should the grief of other people make Egeria's loss any the less? Hippolytus, who is pompous, egotistical, and painful, proceeds to relieve Egeria's mind by telling her of his earlier troubles, the if-you-think-you've-got-troubles-listen-to-mine approach. His, of course, are all in the past, done and gone.

Hippolytus first reveals his true, but hardly believable, identity and then sketches Phaedra's attempt to seduce him and his father's banishing him. The sensational consequences he relates in detail: the swelling of the sea, the enormous bull that stampeded his horses, the broken wheel, his horrible wounds. At this point he loftily produces his most devastating argument by asking Egeria, " 'Now can you, dare you, nymph, compare your loss with my disaster?' " The *nymph* is condescending, and the answer is "no." Feeling the loss of someone irreplaceable and experiencing violent death are not comparable situations. Hippolytus further nullifies his argument by pointing out that he was reassembled, healed, and restored to life, none of which will happen to Numa, who is gone forever. In short, Hippolytus' situation is no consolation for Egeria. Hippolytus himself has benefited from his painful death, because he is now a minor deity. As far as personality goes, he is a prig and know-it-all. That Diana should countenance such a follower makes one wonder about Diana.

Egeria weeps on. Finally Diana, out of pity for her piety, turns Egeria into a stream. This metamorphosis astonishes the local nymphs, and Hippolytus-Virbius is as stupefied as an Etruscan farmer was when he saw one of his clods turn into a man and this native become a prophet or as Romulus was at finding his spear transformed into a peaceful shade tree. The nymphs' ohs and staring immobility caused by surprise are normal reactions to Egeria's sudden change, but Hippolytus, who should be beyond surprise because of his experience, overreacts grossly. Moreover, there is something comic about having a clod become a seer and a warrior's spear become an unthrowable transplant. Each example of the surprising is slightly more unexpected than the preceding one. Cipus and his horns make a good climax.

Cipus is a startling arrival at this point. If one were aware of the theme of Book XV, one would expect Ovid to deal next with Aesculapius because he had healed Hippolytus and because Hippolytus had told Egeria about his healing him. Thus Cipus seems an unwarranted intrusion. If one has not discovered Ovid's theme, Cipus is equally unexpected, just as inexplicable as his horns were to him.

A conquering Roman hero on his way home from the enemy, Cipus is, of course, alarmed when his reflection in the river shows him that he has been growing horns. He had not been aware that anything was going on on his head. Naturally upset by this unnatural change in his appearance, he consults a seer, who is naturally Etruscan. The seer inspects the quivering entrails of an inoffensive sheep, the sort of thing that the Philosopher preached against, looks at Cipus' horns, puts two and two together, and explains: if Cipus enters Rome, he will become king. The Etruscan, who is reliable as a fortune-teller, but not as a political adviser to a Roman citizen-general, urges Cipus to enter the city. Cipus, however, turns out to be a good, patriotic Roman republican to whom the idea of kingship is abhorrent. He arranges a dramatic event outside the walls of Rome, a meeting with the Senate and the Roman People. There he reveals the prophecy and, lifting his laurel wreath, the ominous horns. The Senate and the Roman People groan because this meritorious man must be excluded from the city. They replace his victory wreath, and the Senate gives him as much farmland as he can plow a line around in one day. With this tale Ovid moves his narrative from outstanding kings, namely, Romulus and Numa, to the ideal Roman of the Republican era. Cipus serves the state, the common good, before himself. The state rewards him. He keeps the peace.

The symbolism of this exemplary tale is interesting. The horns growing on Cipus' head suggest those of the ambitious bull who battles for herd leadership; hence, they indicate the civil pain and degradation and even the strife and bloodshed that Cipus' becoming king might cause in Rome. The crown that Cipus puts on to cover up or cancel the dreadful horns is that of Apollo's "peaceful laurel"—the phrase is Ovid's. By a symbol and a gesture, that of covering the horns with laurel, Cipus chooses peace, and the Romans by restoring the crown, second the motion. Cipus' major victory, of course, is over himself and over ambition.

It is about time to include an invocation to the Muses, epic poets needing renewal of inspiration from time to time. Ovid did not call on them specifically when he began his poem, but he does so now and introduces another generic device and a change of pace and tone as well. The invocation allows Ovid to jettison his usual practice of contriving a clever transition and arbitrarily jump to Aesculapius, a god of healing most important to Book XV. It is a comic invocation, too, because it is unnecessary. The bringing of the god to Rome was historical fact and could be learned about from historical sources.

The sound city must have healthy citizens, free from fear, from ritual pollution, from civic disorder, and from physical disease. Aesculapius brings this last freedom, one of great concern to peoples of antiquity because they could do little to stave off epidemics. He is another deity brought to Rome from another city to contribute to the prestige, welfare, and power of the City. Cybele, the Trojan gods, and the Palladium are other examples. Ovid presents the coming of Aesculapius as historical, as the result of the epidemic and two Roman embassies, one to Delphi and one to Epidaurus; and so it was in fact, having occurred in 293 or 291 B.C., though not exactly as Ovid presents it, of course. He embroiders for the greater glory of his adopted city, just as he refers to the Romans as *Aeneadae* for the greater glory of Augustus. When Ovid gives Aesculapius' itinerary and alludes to the piety of Aeneas in burying his nurse at Caieta, Ovid sheds glory on Augustus by referring to the piety of the stock from which Augustus came. The reference to "Trojan Vesta" functions in the same way, for pious Aeneas brought this important goddess to Italy. Most of the embroidery, however, is devoted to enhancing the image of the god in serpent form. He is a splendid beast—golden, crested, huge, most beautiful. The Roman ship settles under his weight. His golden scales chink as he furrows the sand. He is dignified and gracious when he hisses to assert his presence or his favor and when he rests his head on the high stern of the ship. And his worth is recognized not only by the people, but by Apollo, who provides him hospitality.

Such details mingle realism and fantasy. But the serpent's progress is realistic in that almost all the places named in it can be identified geographically. As an itinerary it is four to five times longer than that of Myscelus and longer than that of Aeneas in number of places mentioned; but except for the stopover at the temple of Father Apollo (further validation of the serpent's divinity and identity), the journey has few embellishments, and those consist of a few descriptive phrases. In this way the god is given proper, though not excessive, attention; the Greeks are incorporated into the Italian landscape, for all the identifiable place-names, Greek or native, pertain to Italy; and Italo-Roman tastes are gratified. The end of the journey and its high point is Rome.

The beginning of the journey, amusingly enough, occurs on the eastern Adriatic coast at an important Greek trading post in Illyricum, not at the more famous shrine of Aesculapius in the Argolid Epidaurus, a fact that explains why the itinerary mentions no mainland Greek cities and why Apollo says that Epidaurus is closer to Rome than Delphi is. This western Epidaurus is not described as having the splendid facilities for the worship of Aesculapius and for the care of medical patients that the Epidaurus of eastern Greece had. And being closer to Rome, it was more likely to release its patron deity, but, as Ovid's story goes, it had no choice. The god made the decision to leave. Even so, a god might prefer to leave a relatively unimportant community for great Rome. The move would be one of self-aggrandizement.

There is, therefore, something entertaining about the put-down of this minor Epidaurus and about other details in the story. When the serpent god first appears, it takes the priest of Aesculapius to recognize him. The god expresses his approval of the Roman ambassadors by nodding and by hissing at them an appropriate number of times. Then he snakes off to the waiting ship for all the world like a pompous portly politico. Finally, when he arrives at the Tiber island, he resumes his celestial body, becoming either a constellation (Serpens, Ophiuchus, or Draco) or a statue and thus conveniently eliminating the care, feeding, and replacement of the sacred serpent.

On the whole, the humor is delicate. What reverberates throughout the tale is the praise of Rome and Augustus. Rome is described as the "head of things." Not only is Apollo helpful to the Romans, but Aesculapius decides on his own without a moment's hesitation to leave his old home in Illyricum for a new one in Latium, and he materializes. The already mentioned references to pious Aeneas and to Romans as the "sons of Aeneas" are compliments to his closest living descendant, Augustus. Ovid caps these with an astonishing transition that combines chauvinism and flattery: "Nevertheless, Aesculapius came an alien to our shrines; Caesar is a god in his native city."

Ovid continues his extravagant praise: Caesar's achievements in war and peace did not speed him faster to celestial status than did his child. (Since Caesar was assassinated, Augustus' unqualified acceleration of Caesar to stardom carries with it the unfortunate overtone of violent death, reminding one of the taking-off of Aeneas and Romulus.) Setting innuendo aside for the moment, a rapid charitable or unsuspicious reading of the passage would see it as high praise of Julius Caesar that Ovid tops with even higher praise of Augustus. After listing some of Caesar's triumphs, Ovid reasserts the opinion that Caesar's greatest feat was producing someone as great as Augustus. It was to glorify Augustus that Caesar had to be made a god. (Here again there may be covert ridicule of Augustus, for the sequence of statements suggests that Augustus deified Julius Caesar in order to be glorified himself. Thus Augustus seems nothing more than a political opportunist.)

There follows an account of the activities of Venus, who is aware of conspiracies against Caesar and protests about them to all the other gods. The gods, however, are inferior to the decrees of the Fates and cannot change them, but they do provide a host of hideous omens foretelling the heinous murder of Caesar. Venus is frantic. She resorts to the epic device of trying to conceal Caesar in a cloud, as she had Paris and Aeneas. Jove reproves her by telling her that the Fates' decrees cannot be altered. But knowing them, Jove can tell her that, through her efforts and those of Augustus, Caesar will be deified. Augustus will avenge his

201

father's death and go on to rule the world. Therefore, Jove reveals that Augustus will be a pious son. He further describes the Princeps as an able and just judge, lawgiver, and censor who will be aided by his wife's son. He will bring peace and set the moral tone by his own example. He will live as long as Nestor and finally be deified and mount to the stars. Venus is to make a star now of the slain Caesar's soul. So say the Fates.

Fostering Venus goes to the senate house, catches the soul of dying Caesar, and initiates his godhood, which continues in splendor as a star. Ovid in his own voice praises Augustus as exceeding his father in achievement and compares Augustus with Jove: each has his realm, and each is father and governor. This is a climax. Ovid touched on the comparison of the two in Book I. Now the cycle is complete. Augustus comes at the end of a long series of changes flowing from the creation and the Golden Age and initiates another era of peace that is a human triumph. Ovid's exaltation of Augustus ends with a prayer that mentions, very appropriately, Aeneas, Quirinus-Romulus, the Di Indigetes, Vesta, Caesar's penates, Apollo, and Jupiter and adds a blanket invocation to all other suitable deities. It asks for a long, long life for the Princeps before he is taken to the heavens, there to favor men's prayers.

The entire section after Aesculapius is magnificent and laudatory. There is nothing in it that might directly undermine the position of Augustus by suggesting that he be hastened off like Julius Caesar or that Augustus' task is fulfilled and that he is, therefore, ripe and ready for the next life, as Romulus and Aeneas were. However, Augustus was in his early seventies in 7 A.D., by which time the *Metamorphoses* were probably completed, and, although not as old as Nestor, he was an old man by ancient standards. Hence, by this time in his long reign, many might regard his task as done and his effectiveness over. Many might think his death imminent. And many might wish it. Thus it was not politic to suggest, as Ovid does, that Augustus was flagging under the burden of ruling or to even mention death in connection with the Princeps.

Another impolitic act may have been Ovid's presenting Jove and Venus as subordinate to the Fates, as Ovid also presented the gods in Book IX. It is odd that in both books, the passages about Fate or the Fates and the gods' position relative to them, bring up major issues in minor or unnecessary episodes. The rejuvenation of Iolaüs in Book IX could have been presented solely as a special act of wifely devotion on the part of Hebe and the maturing of Callirhoë's sons as a special dispensation obtained through the mediation of Jove, and the poet could have said simply that of all men only these three were so changed. The Fates need not have been brought in, and, as a result, the gods would have remained in control of things. Minos and the Miletus could have been introduced in Book IX simply by the poet's noting that Minos, unfortunately, was not one of those three and that in his old age he feared Miletus. In Book XV Venus need not have been made sick with anxiety and ineffective in her efforts to save Julius Caesar. The Fates could have been omitted. Jove could have prophesied and instructed Venus on his own, or Venus could have entered the scene after the conspirators had slain Caesar and simply led his soul aloft. In both Book IX and Book XV, the wrangling about rejuvenation and the helpless complaining about and anticipation of Caesar's death make the gods seem puny. Hence, their power and worth are called into question. It is true that in the passage, Augustus becomes Destiny's child, but it is also true that his ancestress would be more glorious if she and Jove had elevated Caesar on their own, an act that would also have shed splendor on Augustus.

As they stand, the two passages about the Fates are either glaringly unlike the surrounding context or unsuitable or both. They seem dragged in. And because they seem so, their common principle, the idea that the gods are inferior to Fate, is forced upon our attention, and it invites speculation. It makes us ask, how does the concept of the Fates or Fate make us see the gods? And the answer, already given, is, it makes them appear weak and ineffectual.

Presenting the gods in this way does not accord with the way Augustus presented them to the public. And the net effect is that Ovid's treatment of the gods undermines Augustus' official religious program, as well as reducing the glory of his divine patronage and descent.

There are other flaws in this laudatory passage. The praise piles up and piles up, so that it seems almost excessive, a tour de force, a display of the poet's rhetoric, ingenuity, and virtuosity, more than sincere tribute. Jove's prophecy about Augustus' greatness is bogus, too: the poet can put it in Jove's mouth because it has already happened. This ex post facto foretelling of the future had already been used by Virgil in the *Aeneid*; even there it is easy to spot and is effective only for the gullible or the cynical. Once spotted, the device reveals that destiny is not destined, but manufactured later.

And there are the little things. It is one thing to refer to the victorious fleets of Caesar going up the seven mouths of the Nile, for the numbers sound impressive. But it is ridiculous rhetoric to speak of one man's leading seven fleets up seven separate related branches of the river. Ovid's vocabulary in connection with the Caesar-Augustus relationship connotes a father-son and sire-offspring one that is literally untrue. Julius did not beget Augustus. And to say, "So then, that his son might not be born of mortal seed, Caesar must needs be made a god," is laughable, for it is so illogical. In additon, the reader is once again faced with an ex post facto act, a mortal insemination that was made divine eighteen for more years *after* it did not occur, for Caesar was not Augustus' physical father. The point is not that the compliment of divine descent could not be made, but that it cannot be made seriously in the way that Ovid does it here.

A few lines after Augustus is presented as coming from the seed of Julius Caesar, Venus complains, most contradictorily, that if Caesar is murdered, no descendant of Trojan Iülus will remain. Thus, though Ovid has claimed that Augustus is descended from Caesar, Venus does not regard him so. Jove finally gets the relationship right when he refers to Augustus as the "heir to the name," but he, too, calls Augustus Caesar's son.

The praise is further muddied when, in asserting that Augustus' deeds surpass Caesar's, Ovid brings in other examples of the father-son pattern: Atreus, who prepared the Thyestian banquet, a bit of family horror that Ovid called attention to in the Philosopher's lecture, yields to the renown of Agamemnon, who also offended the gods. Theseus, however, did achieve much more than his father, but here the comparison is flat. Not only has Ovid consistently slighted Theseus in earlier books, but Aegeus is no Caesar; that is, he is not much to surpass. The same is true of Achilles, whom Ovid has also belittled: it would not be difficult to improve upon a father who did little and who killed his half brother. Hence, though it is praise to be compared with Theseus and Achilles, it is disappointing to have one's adoptive father, Caesar, compared with Aegeus and Peleus. To be compared with Agamemnon is worse. Finally, there are Saturn and Jove. Saturn was sent off to Tartarus rather mysteriously, and his Golden Age was replaced by Jove's Silver Age; hence, it is debatable whether this son surpassed his father. He may even have overthrown him. In overview, it gives Augustus and Caesar a tarnished splendor to be compared with these exalted personages.

As a whole, then, the praise of Caesar and Augustus is not unqualified. It is imperfect, and these imperfections suggest a covert ridicule. At the end Ovid caps it with what was referred to earlier as a smashing bit of comic effrontery, his epilog. For in the epilog he asserts magnificently that no one and no thing can destroy his work, and he not only will be immortal, but will far transcend the stars and thus, we note, move above and beyond the realms inhabited by the souls of Caesar and Augustus. People, Ovid adds, will read him, and his fame will endure throughout all ages.

But the epilog, like the section praising Caesar and his heir, is a game. It is both serious and not serious. Take it as you will. It is hyperbolic and contingent. Ovid's assertion that nothing could destroy his work can hardly be taken seriously. Ovid himself must have known that the Sibylline Books had been destroyed by fire and that Rome itself had been sacked. Besides, Ovid's fame depends upon Augustus in a way, for it depends upon Rome's ruling the world so that Latin is its major language and Latin literature is something prestigious. The relationship between Prince and Poet is symbiotic. As for Ovid's spirit's transcending the wrath of Jove or of Augustus and rising aloft farther than the souls of Caesar or Augustus, that is a matter of point of view. Men of affairs tend to laugh at poets, and vice versa. A tolerant ruler might be annoyed by Ovid's belittling epilog, or he might find it a joke. After all, as Ovid says, his claim to lasting fame depends upon the validity of his own prophecy. And we know that he is biased. But with regard to gamesmanship, Ovid has verbally outwitted his prince. There is no way that the prince could beat the poet at his own game.

And so the poem remains, long ages past, a monument not to the greatness of Augustus, but to the glory of Ovid.

XVI. A Backward Glance

And now our game has ended. In sober retrospect, what can be said about the *Metamorphoses*?

Most important, perhaps, is that it is a very lively and artful poem, rich in insight, humor, variety, and breadth of human feeling. This would no doubt be the consensus of those who have studied the poem with unbiased minds. If one wishes a fuller appreciation and understanding of the poem, however, one must engage in considerations like the following, which arise from the preceding inspection.

Most obvious from the foregoing pages is the fact that the poem is a unit. Its delightful transitions provide the unity of continuity and give a sense that the episodes are linked in time. But the poem is a complicated unit because it is an aggregate and because the poet uses many other means to unify its components.

First, the poem has an overall purpose that binds its parts. One sees this only in overview. At the outset, the poem promises only a consecutive account of changes from the creation to the poet's own time. Then it takes the reader through a large number of Greek tales and a vast amount of clutter, varied activities, and elegant entertainment that seem to be going nowhere in particular but finally do bring him to Italy and to Rome and to its leader, Augustus, the climax of civilization. The Greeks, Lycians, Lydians, Phrygians, Aethiopians, Cretans, Babylonians, Persians, Thracians, and Phoenicians of the Greek myths and legends and of other tales may be interesting, instructive, and amusing as the subjects of tales, but Rome and Augustus dominate the world because, not only are they better than other peoples and their leaders, they are the best. They are the best because they are the most humane and the most effective and responsible in the use of force and in peaceful government, as Aeneas, Romulus, Cipus and Numa foretell. They also are given to the best kinds of love: devotion to family and to nation (seen in Aeneas); compassion (shown by the Trojans to Achaemenides); the most sober, fruitful, and productive kind of love (exemplified by Vertumnus and Pomona), and respectable and supportive love in high places (represented by Canens and Picus, Hersilia and Romulus, Egeria and Numa). Finally, Rome, in the form of her two greatest leaders, is given divine status and the poet confers it upon himself. Thus in overview the theme of the poem is the glorification of Rome.

The above survey, however, gives only one-half of the overall theme. The other half is change. This theme is announced initially in the restricted form of metamorphosis and finally expanded to change in general, including metempsychosis, by the Samian sage of Book XV. The relationship between the two themes is that of means (change) to effect (the resulting new forms and their chronological sequence). Though Ovid focuses on the more sensational theme of metamorphosis, the Sage sees metamorphosis as merely a part of the larger phenomenon of change, to which time, the very elements, and all natural phenomena are subject. Even the gods must be thought of as superior forms of natural phenomena and in that sense supernatural, for Ovid made it clear in Book I that the various known deities came into being after some unknown god or better nature caused the universe to be created. Hence, it is not surprising that the gods also change, coming to include demigods like Hercules and Aesculapius, remoter descendants of gods like Caesar and Augustus, and talented mortals like Ovid. Although metamorphosis and change function in a number of meaningful ways, to be discussed later, the pertinent one at the moment is that they give Ovid's poem a pervasive but unobtrusive coherence, that of focus upon like phenomena. This coherence is so obvious, however, that one is likely not to notice it.

A second kind of unity binds together each book so that it has its own focus, one that does not conflict with the glorification of Rome, for the Greeks and others have the problems, whereas the Romans are blessed with success. Little needs to be said about the matter. Each book has its own core theme, which has been indicated by the title of the pertinent chapter; for example, Book I deals with the theme of concord and discord, and Book V with two different kinds of artist. This practice not only enhances the cohesiveness of the poem, but it enriches it a great deal.

Third, within the all-embracing double theme there are numerous recurrent motifs that appear in various books, for example, the hero (Cadmus in Book III; Perseus in IV and V; Jason in VII; Meleager in VIII; Hercules in IX; Nestor and Achiles in XII; etc.) or the maid who rejects men (Daphne, Syrinx, Arethusa, Lotis, Dryope, Scylla, and Anaxarete, etc.). Such recurrent motifs provide another sort of unity, a sense of the continuity and coherence of experience because human types and situations keep reappearing.

Fourth, within the overall thematic pattern of change-cum-progress, major secondary themes, or subjects, work with the recurrent motifs and like them bind the poem together in a fugal fashion, for Ovid presents many variations on each major secondary theme, as he does on love, or such a theme may dominate an entire book, as piety does Book VIII, as well as appearing in portions of other books.

The first of the secondary themes is love, or Venus, appropriately, because the goddess is the progenitrix of Augustus' mother and also of his adoptive father; and in the *Metamorphoses* Venus will lead to Julius Caesar and to his even greater heir. Love is not present in every tale— one thinks of those of Pyreneus, the Pierides, Pentheus, Niobe, Cipus, Battus, Atlas, Arachne, and the bloody fights that result from love—but it is one of the clearest and most pervasive of the secondary themes.

Also appearing with great frequency and closely related to the theme of love are those of concord and piety and their opposites. The parts of each pair are inseparable, and the negative component is important because it shows how things can go wrong and because it makes one understand the value of the other partner.

/Just as important are the facts that the themes of piety, concord, and love are closely related and reinforce each other. If concord is not a nascent form of love, it is surely a ground for and a concomitant of love. Love qua lust may require nothing more than an object to gratify it at the moment and the ability to overcome resistance, but a fuller heterosexual relationship of any duration is likely to entail or require harmony, or concord—that companionship, agreeing with, and getting along with another person that meets daily emotional needs./ The tale of Cephalus and Procris demonstrates the need for harmony in love and also the fact that this more complete relationship probably includes affection and periods of more intense love.

Likely to accompany concord is piety, which is, minimally, a respect for and sense of obligation to those with whom one ought to be on close terms. One may observe piety in a dutiful way, but it is certainly made more viable if accompanied by concord and love, both of which are likely to produce piety. Hence, the three conditions are not the same, but they go together and support and augment each other. Indeed, piety is a particular form of concord, for it consists of observing one's duties towards one's parents, relatives and other members of one's extended family, one's comrades, one's native land, and its deities. If one is pious, one will show respect to all of these, and if one is thoroughly pious, one will want to do so. By showing respect and doing one's duty, one is in harmony with the customs and religion of his country or community, and one is not upsetting one's parents or relatives. Such behavior need not entail love, but it is likely that one will feel affection for the members of one's family and one's land, especially since piety involves the obligations of parents to children, as well as of children to parents, and if parents take care of children as they should, mutual love will probably develop if it does not exist in the parents to begin with. In sum, piety is likely to promote family concord and love.

The result of having these prominent related themes running throughout the *Metamorphoses* is more extensive coherence. By this means Ovid has solved the problem of providing a high degree of unity and continuity to the material that fills in the time between creation and the arrival of Augustus.

More striking to a historian of literary form, perhaps, is Ovid's ability to sense that themes were built into the tales he used, that there is such a phenomenon as subsurface unity, and that as a result he can juxtapose stories with related themes and have significance emerge from their being placed next to one another and in sequences. These realizations and their utilization make Ovid appear very modern. It is the same sense that enabled Ezra Pound to perceive the unity underlying much of the early version of Eliot's *The Waste Land* and to assist in turning it into an episodic poem having unity because of subsurface theme and thematic development. A similar idea of overall form is implicit in Pound's *Cantos*. That Ovid should have conducted a major experiment in the use of such form is much to his credit as an artist. It is even more remarkable that he should have used the same principle in a more subtle and somewhat different way in each book.

His use of so many related myths results in variations on his basic themes, as well as surveys of the subjects, and these variations have significance because, for one thing, they are evaluatory. The theme of love, or Venus, serves as an example. The *Metamorphoses* is, indeed, a veritable catalog of the varieties of love. There are at least five marital kinds: the young married love of Deucalion and Pyrrha and of Canens and Picus; middle-aged love—anxiety-ridden for Ceyx and Alcyone, stable and calm for Romulus and Hersilia, Numa and Egeria; the placid devotion of aging Baucis and Philemon; the rash lust of newlyweds Atalanta and Hippomenes; and the tempestuous, somewhat racy love of Cephalus and Procris. For almost all of these true married lovers, the relationship is enduring, and that of Ceyx and Alcyone almost amounts to identification with one another. For some of them, love lasts beyond death. But there is also a negative side to married love. For Tereus and Procne, Orpheus and Eurydice have marriages that fail to bond the couples in mutual love. Tereus becomes an adulterer, but he is not alone. Adulterous love is amply represented by Jove and his inamoratas, by Venus and Mars, and by Venus and Adonis.

Outside of marriage, love is found in the courtships of Iphis and Anaxarete and of Pyramus and Thisbe, which turn out badly. The occasional bachelor chase is engaged in by Apollo, Pan, and Mercury. This type of love is varied by having the lady proposition the male, as Salmacis, Scylla of Megara, and Circe do in their various fashions. Such loves and the adulterous ones are short-lived, and many are more or less frustrated. Indeed, there is a fair amount of frustrated love—e.g., Orpheus' for Eurydice and that of Pyramus and Thisbe—partly because this category includes the unrequited love of Pan for Syrinx, Apollo for Daphne, Iphis for Anaxarete, and Echo for Narcissus and the unfaithful love of Coronis, as well as the frustration caused by cruel fathers such as Perimele's and Leucothoë's. Arising out of frustration because there are no suitable love objects is Pygmalion's idealized love for his statue, which represents for him the ultimate in love. In contrast, there is the relationship between Jove and Semele in which the lady seeks the ultimate in sexual experience. Tiresias represents a variety of this sort, for he experiences sexual intercourse as both sexes do. The antithesis of Semele's sexual encounter is the debased love of the Propoetides, intercourse without feeling. And beyond this type lies the rejection of heterosexual love by Daphne, Syrinx, Lotis, Caenis, and, by implication, Hippolytus, the divine form of which is Diana.

Then there is rape, attack of the female by the male (Hades, Boreas, Jove, Tereus, the centaurs), by the female upon the male (Salmacis, Aurora), even by male upon male (Jove, disguised as his eagle, upon

Ganymede). There is also the near rape of Deianira by Nessus and, somewhat different, that of Thetis by Peleus. Beyond these is the vengeful love of predatory Circe, experienced by Scylla and Picus. And exceeding all of these is criminal love: the impious loves of Megarian Scylla and Medea; the incestuous desires of Byblis and Myrrha; the bestial love of Pasiphaë.

Ovid includes even the infantile love of a boy for a pet stag and homosexual love of males for males (Orpheus for Thracian boys, Jove for Ganymede, Apollo for Hyacinthus and Cyparissus) and of female for female (Iphis, initially, for Ianthe and possibly Diana for Callisto), and of this last, there is a further sort, the momentary pseudo-homosexual erotic approach of Jove, disguised as Diana, to Callisto. There are also the self-love of Narcissus and Dryope's love of a certain stage of life.

Running over this list, one sees that it is sensational enough, and if one remembers the stories themselves, one is aware that Ovid handles the sensational with a certain delicacy, avoiding pornographic detail. The list also shows that Ovid's variations on the theme constitute an extensive, though not complete, survey of love and that his variations are sometimes relatively subtle ones. It does not reveal what the fuller study of the poem has, for example, a tolerant attitude toward most of the various kinds of love, if not approval; a sense of the all-pervasiveness of love; and an acceptance of the anti-Eros type of personality, which is given recognition and status by Diana; and it does not everywhere stress the fact that, as the varieties are presented, they are ranked, or evaluated. Nor does one get from the list what one gets from reading episode after episode, namely, a sense of the importance of variations in a basic story. Pan's pursuit of Syrinx can never be as elegant or entertaining or complicated as Apollo's of Daphne. Pan is a rustic often thought of as part goat; his nymph becomes a clump of marsh reeds; his head is wreathed in pine needles. Apollo is an urbane Olympian of many powers, articulate and suave, burning with love; his miss becomes a beautiful tree and the garland of victorious generals and of emperors; he is all brightness and manliness, though a bit out of condition. Neither's pursuit has the tone of Jove's. Mature and expert at the hunt, more powerful than the others, he obtains his desire, aided by an effortless bit of weather magic. In comparison, Pan and Apollo are amateurs. Aside from the newness that such changes contribute to the same story line, even these three variations on one basic love plot demonstrate that love qua the chase affects males of various ranks, ages, cultural background, and power, and, in view of what Jove does for Io later, ability to reward a lady who has obliged. One learns from the differences in the stories that not all nymphs will yield, nor need they. But despite the differences between stories, all insist that love obligates the pursuer, especially the successful one.

The entire list of the varieties of love indicates that gods have few restrictions on their loving where they will. Nymphs and mortals are fair game, even princesses and queens, though a maid may refuse a god (the Cumaean Sibyl), and a nymph may thwart him (Daphne, Syrinx). Gods have fewer opportunities among the goddesses. Juno is out because she is Jove's wife and a mother figure. Vesta, Minerva, and Diana are committed to virginity, and their views are respected. Only Venus is bedded by Mars, who has children by her. Among the Titanesses, Jove has marked success with Dione, Latona, Maia, and Mnemosyne. And he has a child by his sister Ceres. Incest is allowed the gods: Jove with Juno and Ceres; Hades with his niece, Proserpina, and here even rape is excused (Hades' of Proserpina). A number of nymphs (Io, Callisto) and women (Dryope, Caenis, Erysichthon's daughter, Orithyia, Europa) are raped by gods, and the gods do not suffer.

When amorous relationships occur between gods and mortal women, status and power carry with them privilege and immunity, but the mortal women sometimes suffer. Perimele and Leucothoë, who succumb to gods, are punished by their parents. Women who are forced may resent the experience, like Caenis, or be the objects of a certain amount of shame, like Dryope. Or they may be punished, as Semele and Io are by Juno. In addition, women who reject sexual congress with male deities may fare badly, as Scylla and the Cumaean Sibyl demonstrate. They are not alone, for their male counterparts Picus and Cephalus also suffer. Indeed, the rejection of Venus qua physical love is a punishable offense, as Anaxarete and Narcissus find out.

But the gods are in a class by themselves and are above criticism. Different rules apply to mortals. For them, rape and incest are crimes, as is love that leads to impiety. This last includes religious impiety, such as Atalanta and Hippomenes' copulating before the images of the gods; familial impiety, such as Perimele and Leucothoë's offending their fathers by having affairs with gods; and treasonable love, engaged in by Scylla of Megara and Medea. There are only two instances in which one mortal engages in adultery with another—Tereus with Philomela and Paris with Helen, and there the woman is forced, and the act is clearly wrong. There are two attempted rapes by centaurs (Nessus' of Deianira and the centaurs' of the Lapith women), and these are presented as criminal assaults. Mortals who have amorous affairs with mortals are few (the budding romance of Pyramus and Thisbe and the torrid liaison of Coronis with the young Thessalian), and these amours, though not condemned outright, are unfortunate. All in all, as far as love between mortals is concerned, respectable love in marriage and ideal love are the preferred kinds.

It is obvious, then, that Ovid's survey of love turns out to be evaluatory. Some kinds of love are better than others; some kinds are wrong. But, as indicated, double standards operate in these evaluations. There is one set of rules for mortals and one for deities; there is another for males and yet another for females. The double standard for deities is indicated in the debate about sexual pleasure that occurs between Jove and Juno and in the infidelity of Venus with Mars. Goddesses are not punished either for unfaithfulness or for experiencing sexual pleasure, but both are regarded as bringing a degree of disgrace. Gods, in contrast, revel in their sexual powers and have no inhibitions. Juno can do little about Jove's escapades except make his mistresses or their families suffer. Incest is not a crime for gods or goddesses. But mortals pay when they commit it. And mortals do not attack the gods for having affairs with women. The passionately erotic women who might be regarded as mortal equivalents of Venus have sorry careers: Megarian Scylla, Medea, Byblis, Myrrha—even Procris). Their male counterparts are not so unfortunate. True, Tereus is punished, and Cephalus is badly treated for his marital fidelity, but tender and devoted Pygmalion is rewarded by Venus. As for love between men and women, men are allowed more freedom in extramarital affairs. Ulysses marries the nymph or goddess Circe and is not blamed for it; Cephalus is abducted by a goddess. Hercules is only rumored to have supplanted Deianira with Iole. The married males who have affairs with women are almost nil. The women who have, or try to have, affairs with men are Coronis, Phaedra, Scylla of Megara, Byblis, and Myrrha. None of the affairs is happy. None is a mere affair, for all are tainted with two-timing, impiety, or incest. Apparently, no decent woman or no woman in her right mind would have an affair. In number, Ovid's tales about mortal heterosexual love favors, if only slightly, marital relations of a stable, durable, companionate nature. The irregular human relationships may be more erotically stimulating, but they are brief and disastrous. Thus Ovid seems, because of his selection and weighting of tales, to approve solidly of enduring conventional love and marriage.

On the other hand, if one recalls Arachne's tapestry and the loves of the gods displayed there and other tales about their amours in the *Metamorphoses*, one might agree with Arachne that the Greek gods are less than edifying. He might conclude, too, that the Greeks, not the Romans, have sullied Venus with incest, adultery, and worse, because, whatever her own behavior, they have not demonstrated that she is not responsible for those kinds of love in mortals.

So much for the theme of love in the *Metamorphoses*. More might be said about it, but the above survey and commentary indicate the kind of thoroughness needed in order to make satisfactory generalizations or properly qualified and supported conclusions.

As for the theme of concord and discord, there is conflict, or discord, in chaos and in most of the episodes thereafter, so that it is not difficult to find examples of it. Concord is rarer, though even in chaos the particles of each element have the harmony of identity. The mention of the phenomenon of change in the opening lines of the poem and the title itself suggests that stability of being exists with its opposite and is in conflict with the law of change. No matter how much change there is or how drastic it is, matter and recognizable forms persist of necessity. Concord, however, rises above change and conflict, and there is no doubt that it is more valuable than its opposite. This fact is established at the outset of the *Metamorphoses* in the description of chaos: nothing can come of such discord but more discord; no forms, no life can exist under its conditions. Thus Ovid indirectly condemns the primal conflict and through it all later kinds, from harassment to murder and war. Nevertheless, men are such mixed creatures that they are more interested in the excitement, sensationalism, and novelty of discord and more inclined to it. Ovid instructs them about conflict, its kinds, its results, and its causes, so that if they wish to learn, they can avoid it.

As with love, discord, and concord, Ovid is evaluatory about piety and impiety. There is no indication that he is unconventional on this topic or that he disagrees with the Greeks about the worth of piety, but he does not hesitate to use material demonstrating that the Greeks left the subject in some confusion. Just as Venus emerges from Greek myth sullied and reprehensible, so piety there is not always unmistakably just or beneficient. As Althaea learned, there may be conflicting pieties with equally valid claims: her brothers require pious vengeance; but if Althaea takes it, she will commit the heinous impiety of causing her son's death. Inequity may appear in the results of piety: Acheloüs punishes nymphs who slight him by turning them into islands, but he rewards Perimele, who has gratified him, by having her turned into one. It seems unfair that the results of piety and impiety should be the same.

Piety is an ideal and a reality. In principle, it consists of a series of obligations or duties that keep the family unit intact and flourishing, that define reciprocal relationships with the gods qua natural and humanizing forces, and that allow some stabilizing relationships with those outside these groups, namely, one's community and strangers. As a reality, it does not operate uniformly, nor do its infractions bring inevitable or uniform retribution. Human nature often prevents pious behavior. King Oeneus forgets or neglects to honor Diana. Nymphs slight river-god Acheloüs. Romantic love confounds familial piety, as Scylla, Ariadne, Medea, and Meleager show; bestial love subverts it—Pasiphaë is evidence. Indeed, love of one's family or one's country, which should sustain piety, seems as nothing before Venus and Cupid. As far as punishment for impiety goes, Scylla and Meleager receive it; Ariadne is abandoned after committing it, but is later gratefully rewarded by a god for her favors; Medea escapes punishment imposed from without. Hercules and Peleus wrestle with minor deities and win. Pirithoüs scoffs at the gods and goes unpunished. Niobe and Arachne offend deities and are punished at once. In short, though the *Metamorphoses* insists that there is such a thing as piety and the words *piety, impiety, pious,* and *impious* appear frequently in it, the Greek myths there are neither clear nor consistent on the subject.

Perhaps two important things to learn from Greek confusion about love and piety are that even these important values can on occasion change into their opposites and that the safest thing a human being can do is to adhere to the conventional and to avoid the irregular, the extreme or overly intense, and the sensational.

Metamorphosis needs some attention because it is the declared theme of the poem. First, as noted earlier, the idea expands to that of change in general, which includes geological and biological change and, in the process, the movement of the soul from one body to another, or metempsychosis. This expansion of meaning is accomplished by the Sage in his lecture and is one of his functions in the poem. The expansion is useful to Ovid because it gives him the prestige of a philosophic basis for his subject. His poem thus celebrates a great principle, that of change, to which all things are subject. As the Sage develops the principle, he stresses the newness of each moment and its phenomena, the cycles characterizing existence—and by implication the idea that motifs recur and are new with each recurrence—and the reassurance that nothing is ever lost. Combining these principles with that of metempsychosis, one has the persistence of the soul, which changes but is never lost, and its entering into the new forms that nature is constantly generating. This combination is also useful to Ovid for it explains or provides a basis for Callisto's becoming a bear and then a constellation and for the soul-stars of Augustus and Ovid.

Furthermore, the Sage's principles, or unalterable givens, are the philosophic equivalents of the Fate of folklore and myth. One of these givens is the principle that change is cyclic. And this cycle takes the form of creation, decay, and renewal or favorable condition, decline, and return to a favorable state. The result is that when the Sage speaks of day and night's following one another and of the moon's waxing and waning, he is speaking on a small scale of the creation and of the Four Ages of Man and also of the progress that brings Augustus and peace, for all are parts of cycles. As the *Metamorphoses* presents cyclic movement, it reaches the nadir only once in chaos and the zenith once in creation and the Golden Age. Thereafter, the highs and lows are relative: Phaethon's scorching the earth is not as bad as the Flood, and neither is as bad as the original chaos; the Trojan War is not as degenerate as the behavior of the time of Lycaon; the re-creation after the Flood, accomplished by the action of heat upon slime and by Deucalion and Pyrrha's throwing stones, is neither so grand nor so beautiful as the original creation. Thus the continuity produced by change has a peculiar cyclic nature in which there are highs and lows that finally lead to a marked change of the human condition. Metamorphosis by itself is not the whole show, and without such ups and downs and the flow of time, it would not be possible to have a paragon such as Augustus. But the arrival of Augustus upon the mortal scene, as well as other evidence in the poem, suggests that there is some god, better nature, or fate that operates in a long-range beneficent fashion. This is one of the things that the age-long cycle of change teaches.

The Sage, in addition, focuses in part on a particular variety of metamorphosis, metempsychosis, and uses it to promote kindliness and peace and to condemn the practice of eating meat. In this way he and metamorphosis lend practical support to Augustus' political program: peace is the desirable condition. His claims that all things change—hence, change is fated—and that change is cyclic, support Augustus, too, for what happens is destiny, and Augustus crowns the cycles produced by destiny.

Second, Ovid has indicated five possible causes, very broad ones, for the various changes. In the opening lines of the poem, he says that the gods have brought them about. Toward the end of it, another cause of change is flow, or movement in a given direction. Flow is modified by a cyclic twist that is given it, so that although flow moves on, it also moves up and down. Sometimes a particular pattern of change is decreed; hence, fate is the cause. Next, personality is at times responsible for change. And last, sometimes chance is.

The first cause, not always clearly operative, is significant because it makes the gods important. The second cause of change, its inherent cyclic nature, is not always apparent, because it may operate over long periods. It allows for an obvious dimension in human affairs, the improvement, deterioration, and improvement of circumstances. Of course, cycles, or parts of them, may appear in an individual's life; then they are like the reversals of Greek tragedy and epic. One sweeping cycle is the downswing from the Golden Age and the varying ups and downs through the Greeks and their myths to the Romans and finally Augustus. The third cause, fate, of which the gods are sometimes presented as agents, seems to operate, too. Ovid does not always state which cause effected a metamorphosis or what the reason for it was, but the information is often implied or indicated. When Ocyrhoë is changed into a horse, she implies that the Fates have wrought the transformation and that they have done so because she engaged in prophecy without their permission. It is implied further that men should be permitted to know the future only when the Fates see fit to permit their authorized agents, such as Jove, to speak. The fourth cause, character, operates much of the time, except when a god rewards a person for pleasing behavior, as Jove does by making Callisto a constellation or Bacchus does by making one of Ariadne's crown. Dryope's personality causes her to pluck flowers from the lotus and thus brings about her change. The last cause is chance. Someone stumbles upon a magical or sacred place; once he is there, the metamorphosis follows almost automatically. Glaucus and Actaeon are prime examples.

None of the causes is operative all of the time, but if both gods and mortals are given their individual characteristics, powers, and goals, then their natures are fated and so are the changes that their natures bring about. Much of change, then, may be regarded as the result of some variety of fate; even chance may. However, fate receives but fitful treatment, operating conspicuously only three times: once when Ocyrhoë speaks of it as preventing her soothsaying and twice when Jove refers to it (in connection with age change and with Caesar's future). It receives passing mention in a few more places. In other passages, gods and mortals appear to behave independently. Hence, it is not clear whether all acts and events are determined by the Fates. Perhaps they come into play only in connection with the most important matters or at the poet's whim. Ovid leaves the matter unresolved. The net result is that both fate and freedom from fate are operative.

Perhaps the important thing to note is that metamorphosis does have some underlying causes that are inherent in the nature of things, and, as speculated in Chapter I, what is inherent may result from the predominance of one or more of the elements in an individual's makeup. Thus Ovid provides a rough and fairly satisfying explanation of change for an unscientific era.

Third, as noted in divers places earlier, metamorphosis functions in various ways in the poem. Morpheus assumes the form of Ceyx so that he can deliver Juno's message to Alcyone: Ceyx is dead. A god may change shape in order to warn a mortal, as Minerva does to urge Arachne to repent, or to free a mortal, as Mercury does so that Io may be released from captivity. A god may change shape in order to lure a mortal to destruction, as Juno does with Semele. Jove may metamorphose himself in order to win a Callisto or a Europa. A deity may also transform himself in order to test someone, as Mercury does with Battus; to fend off unwanted advances, as Thetis does; or to travel about, as Jove and Mercury do. Thus the evidence indicates that the gods change themselves in order to obtain some end: to realize desire, to test, to punish, or to be incognito. Whatever their reasons, the gods' metamorphoses have purpose and are not permanent. Nor are they serious matters for them, for the gods may change their shapes at will. The motive for a change may reveal how tricky, lustful, powerful, vengeful, just, grateful, or beneficent a particular deity is, but his own metamorphosis does not bare his personality problems the way Echo's and Dryope's do. Nor is it a punishment for a god in the *Metamorphoses*. Minor deities, however, do not have the power that the celestials have. Thetis' metamorphoses are finally futile against Peleus because he is backed by Jove. Acheloüs is subdued by Hercules for a somewhat similar reason, despite Acheloüs' godhood and shape-changing. In addition, changing things is one of a god's powers, for example, Arachne into a spider, Battus to touchstone, chaos to an orderly universe. In addition, a great function of the gods in the poem is to cause major changes: Jove brings about the end of Iron Age degeneracy and causes new constellations to appear; Minerva brings olive culture; Ceres causes Triptolemus to spread the knowledge of grain cultivation; and Venus brings love to the realm of Hades. The gods, of course, do not completely control all change, for human beings can decide to be uppity, like Arachne, or vile, like Lycaon, and thus invite punitive alteration. Whatever the case and the magnitude of the change, the gods do direct change significantly; that is, the miraculous metamorphoses are mostly purposeful and always meaningful change. And beyond the gods lies fate.

The picture is different when metamorphosis affects nymphs, satyrs, or human beings. For them change is permanent. Aglauros and Anaxarete turn into lifeless statues, and there is no indication that the process will be reversed or that it can be. Dryope and Daphne will remain trees;

217

Byblis, a fountain. The change may be a punishment, as it is when Niobe is turned into a weeping stone figure. If the change is a punishment, then it is likely to fit the crime, as it does when hardhearted Anaxarete is turned to stone or when fraudulent Battus is made a stone that detects fraud. The change may be more or less excruciating: Marsyas becomes an overall wound; Niobe, even though stone, does not cease to express grief; Midas' pride will always be vexed by his ass's ears. Cybele, indeed, regards the change of Atalanta and Hippomenes into lions as a punishment worse than death. However, some changes are the equivalent of mere death, for example, those effected by the head of Medusa. At other times the punitive change is a life sentence, as it is for Atalanta and Hippomenes or Dryope.

But metamorphosis is sometimes aid. Daphne prays that her river-god father take her away her beautiful appearance; he does: she is changed into a tree. Something similar happens to Syrinx. However, since the change diminishes being, it seems as much punishment as assistance, especially since a similar change was punishment for Dryope. Anius is not overly happy that Dionysus, to save Anius' daughters from Agamemnon, changed them into doves. Sometimes the alteration is an act of lifesaving, as it is with Daedalus' nephew, who loses his talents in the process. And sometimes the lifesaving mutation is a frustration, witness Aesacus. Or it is the best thing available at the time, for example, Galatea's changing Acis into a river-god. These metamorphoses are help, but there is something wry about them. On the other hand, the metamorphosis of a mortal or nymph may be a true reward: Io becomes a goddess; Hercules, an Olympian; Callisto, a constellation; Caesar, a star-god. Baucis and Philemon truly have their wishes fulfilled when they become trees growing from a double trunk. And the change of Ceyx and Alcyone into halcyons is both a resurrection for Ceyx and a way of perpetuating their love, as well as an endorsement of it.

But metamorphosis does other things besides rewarding or punishing. Sometimes it reveals a latent or unconscious desire, as well as the chancy nature of life, as it does with Dryope. At other times it exposes the psychological horror inherent in one's pursuits: the hunter may become the hunted, as Actaeon did. Or it may not grow out of personality at all, for chance and a magic herb make Glaucus a sea-god. It may even occur at the instigation of a goddess, not because of the intent of the mortal involved, for Pallas orders Cadmus to plant the magic teeth that become warriors.

Yet metamorphosis is often closely related to character. It may reveal its essence, but more often metamorphosis sums up character or emphasizes something about it or evaluates it. Daphne wanted to remain virgin before Apollo saw her, and her turning into a living log is merely an analog that stresses her already apparent frigidity. But the change is also an evaluation of her rejection of men and her desire to be stripped of her beauty. For these attitudes caused her to lose much that goes with being human: mobility, grace, the ability to draw others to her, sociability, communication, and the ability to have chldren. Circe's nastiness, however, is revealed by her deceiving illusions and by her transforming human beings into beasts. Dryope wished to retain her nymph-like freedom and attractiveness and, therefore, worshiped the nymphs, but in doing so, she incurred the wrath of a nymph and, as a result, found that she had lost much that she loved, such as her child. Thus her desire is condemned. Yet the metamorphosis does help one realize what her personality is like and shows that it is a psychologically disturbed one. In contrast, the reader is aware of Narcissus' aloofness and lack of warmth and the evaluation of them long before Narcissus finds the fatal pool. His change involves a psychological process that reveals how his personality malfunctions, and his flower form emphasizes only the fragility both of his psyche and his beauty. Thus there are two changes, and the psychological deterioration is more marvelous than the miraculous bloom.

The tale of Narcissus, the Sage's lecture, and Medea's biography indicate that metamorphosis, as Ovid deals with the phenomenon, must be defined broadly, as *The American Heritage Dictionary* (1976) does, namely, as any "marked change in appearance, character, condition, or function." Medea does not undergo physical metamorphosis, but her character certainly changes for the worse with each evil act that she performs. From a young woman with many admirable qualities, she turns into the epitome of the wicked witch. Megarian Scylla undergoes a similar change of character. At first a lonely romantic child, she becomes a loathsome traitor, and then, when refused the reward she hopes for, she turns on the man she loves and slings mud. Her change to a bird exposes nothing about her character; it is an evaluation of it, for it demonstrates that she is an animal who should be denied land and sea. Hence, metamorphosis includes progressive deterioration of character or personality, as with Narcissus, Scylla, and Medea.

Whether metamorphosis involves physical change or not, its evaluations are sometimes complicated. Having Ceyx and Alcyone turn into halcyons manifests divine condemnation of their being anxiety ridden and divine approval of their peace-loving natures and of their devoted love. Arachne's becoming a spider shows how good and how industrious a weaver she was, how her behavior reduced her to the status of bug, and how ugly a person she was inside. Acheloüs' changing both the offensive nymphs and affectionate Perimele brings up another complication, for the same transfiguration may be either a punishment or a reward.

All in all, metamorphosis is not a single, simple, uniform thing. For it functions in many ways other than those already mentioned. The magical transformations and the changes resulting normally from the effect of behavior on personality both provide warnings to the reader, telling him to beware of doing this or that. Frequently the metamorphoses explain the origins of something, such as the windflower, the red of the mulberry, or the name of the Icarian Sea. But in doing this they also soften the force of catastrophe or bereavement; they divert the mind from agony to beauty or marvel; or they memorialize past events and link them and their emotions with the present. Like all myths, they perform another bonding, for the metamorphoses orient man with regard to the phenomenal world by giving it human characteristics and sometimes human origins or human affiliations. Sun, moon, lightning, rivers, trees, and so forth, are given emotional, ethical, psychological, artistic, and aesthetic dimensions. They love, hate, have palaces, are just or unjust, appreciate beauty, have it, or create it. Other phenomena weave, make things grow, have children, want to be left alone, like telling stories. Because the myth view of the world personifies its aspects, making nature like man, man can feel comfortable in his surroundings. He is akin to phenomena. He knows what to expect from them and how to behave toward them. They are with him, built into him sometimes, and he and his past are part of them. Metamorphosis also implies that the world is marvelous, comprehensible, and orderly. It is orderly because it operates on a cause-and-effect basis, because like produces like, and because characteristics are passed on from one form to its successor. And it is disorderly. Nothing is cut-and-dried in myth, Ovid's poem, or in life.

Since Ovid's poem makes metamorphosis include change in general, it is multifaceted, indeed. Even metamorphosis metamorphoses. In book after book the myths maintain that once there were nymphs in the trees, pools, rivers, and seas and that once the gods did visit them and mortals. But by the time of the Sage, things have changed. Ovid leads into the Sage's lecture by saying that the gods are far off in the heavens in the Sage's day and that the Sage communicates with them by means of his mind. Thus Ovid indicates that in his own day they are no longer on earth with men. Hence, the changers of things have changed, too. And when a man of Ovid's time and temperament looks back at earlier men's visions of the gods, he cannot take the gods or the myths about them as seriously or as literally as could the men who first made and believed in them. For the Sage and for Ovid, the rational soul dominates the scene. The Sage tries to determine the causes of things by the use of it. He is, as a result, concerned with natural, not mythic, metamorphoses for a long passage that includes mention of the development of frogs from tadpoles. Ovid uses the rational mind to adapt the myths to game-playing.

In addition, according to the Sage, not to Ovid, who comes later, even the elements change, one into the other. And the Sage introduces a new kind of metamorphosis, metempsychosis. This idea leads to a new moral stance, the desire to preserve all creatures of the flesh. Being philosophic, the Sage adds a new ingredient to the poem, a realistic or balanced optimism, for he believes in the durability of souls, and his cyclic view of change is as much optimistic as pessimistic.

But Ovid is not the Sage. As Ovid presents the course of events, they lead beyond change to the deified Augustus and to the deified Ovid, prince of poets. According to the end of the *Metamorphoses*, both princes will dwell in immutability with or beyond the stars. Both will have everlasting fame on earth. Both will be beyond time and change and metempsychosis. Thus changelessness becomes a transcendent variation on the theme of change.

Moreover, in a world in which all things flow, Ovid's metamorphoses likewise present values that, if not beyond change, are close to being so. Piety in its various forms is one. So is human beauty. Sensuous and aesthetic appreciation of trees, flowers, streams, pools, groves, vales, and seas is another. Respect for all these and kindliness toward men are others. So are fruitfulness; artistry; inventiveness; love within proper limits; loyalty and honesty; grace; civilized elegance; wisdom; peace; harmonious marital existence; healing; the founding of cities; the gift of prophecy; strength; power and beneficent use of it. Rape and cruelty are wrong. Incest, greed, insensitivity, trouble-making, plundering, bestiality, deceit, hardheartedness, breach of hospitality, war, murder, and hubris are wrong. Also faulted to varying degrees are the following behavior patterns: being overly attached to pets, homosexuality, rashness, refusal to accept release from tension, the desire for the extreme in sexual experience, self-absorption, being other-directed, trying to be what one is not, aggressiveness on the part of the female, refusal to grow up, groundless suspicion of infidelity, excessive grieving, excessive feelings of guilt.

The amazing thing about these lists is that there is nothing unusual about them. Except for our not recognizing many forms of piety because the label is out of fashion and for a current tendency to accept aggressiveness in women and perhaps to be more tolerant of homosexuality, there is almost nothing in the lists that most twentieth-century persons in western civilization would not find familiar and agree with. This fact suggests that many of our human values have remained constant for a long time, though much else has changed. In the end, it is the human types and situations and values that endure.

And to this the *Metamorphoses* adds by means of illustration, there are so many variables in life that one must pick one's way carefully as one moves amid love, piety, discord, and change. Change, piety, love, and discord and their permutations and combinations make life bewildering, as well as exciting and agonizing. Being changed to bovine form is a punishment of the Cerastes; a protection for Io, though it offends her feelings; and a lark for Jove.

As for the miraculous transfigurations themselves, they are as numerous as Greek myth will allow and as sensational and as varied as the Greeks and Ovid could make them: blood to snakes, seaweed to coral, ships to sea-nymphs, ashes to birds, tears to amber; persons or personages to rock, fountain, river, flower, plant, tree, spider, bat, fish, snake, bird, bear, bovine, stag, or lion. Stone comes to life. Dragon's teeth and ants change into men; men become women; women, men; a male and a female become a new creature, a hermaphrodite; a male changes sex twice. Deities become human beings, bulls, tigers. Persons become gods of the river, sea, or Olympus. Or they become star-gods, heavenly bodies. All these mutations are as novel, as gratifying, and as amazing as one could wish. But the greatest surprise is the fact that they rank themselves in a comparative system, in a hierarchy of values.

And so the idea that the *Metamorphoses* is immoral or amoral, that it is without values, can be put to rest. And some of the reasons for the durability of the poem have been indicated.

There can be little doubt that Ovid enjoyed the Greek myths and knew what could be done to make them new and to revitalize them. He admired Greek culture, and in this respect he was like many upper-class Roman citizens. But, like his fellows, he also felt superior to the Greeks. As Ovid presents Achilles in combat and in his tent, the Greek is an excellent fighter; he is courteous, but socially not very astute. Ovid treats other Greek heroes in a belittling or derogatory fashion. The only exception is Hercules, a Roman favorite who had visited the city's site and destroyed the monster Cacus in a cave on the Palatine. Using their own myths, Ovid displays the Greeks as they revealed themselves: frequently cruel, unjust, impious, undiginified, unruly, and foolish. They reach their nadir in the contention of Ajax and Ulysses for the armor of Achilles and the psychological dismemberment of Hecuba, where they expose their selfishness and baseness. Ovid's Romans and Italians are paragons by comparison. Even the Samian philosopher of Book XV is an extremist—and in that respect foolish—needed to rectify the Greek propensity to shed blood and to be cruel. Often, however, Ovid uses the Greeks in their myths and legends as though they were figures in light opera or tragi-comedy. This approach in another way transmits Ovid's sense of superiority. Indeed, in the *Metamorphoseon*—Ovid's use of a Greek title calls attention to the fact that a Latin poet has mastered Greek—Ovid is putting down the Greeks by doing them one better at their own game of telling myths and at Callimachus' efforts in the *Aetia*, a book-length series of myths about origins.

Furthermore, as Ovid tells the myths generated by the Greeks, he exposes some of the muddle that they incorporate. For example, as mentioned above, Acheloüs punishes some impious nymphs by changing them into islands; he preserves the swimming Perimele, a nymph he loved, by having her changed into an island also. Acheloüs is neither admirable nor discriminating if he gives his love a reward used to punish the offending nymphs. Byblis points out that it is very confusing for mortals to have incestuous deities. Anyone may note that Venus and Amor represent lust and love and then reasonably ask, how can one clear them of causing traitorous, incestuous, or bestial love? If Venus and Amor clearly operate on some occasions, how does one explain love's happening without them? These failures in consistency or thoroughness undercut the value of Greek myth and at times make it comic. Here again the Greeks are quietly made fun of.

Ovid also spoofs the gods. His treatment of them is too urbane and carefree to be serious and completely honorific. He stresses their imperfections, their weaknesses, their errors and strayings, not their aloof grandeur, their unerring rightness, or the monumental nature of their benefactions. Ancient Greeks had done the same in a Homeric hymn to Hermes (Number IV in the Loeb edition), for example, but Ovid does it rather consistently. Most of his technique for doing so is his making the gods very human, though very powerful, so that their frailties seem natural and inevitable. As he does this, Ovid seems to be writing of the human counterparts of the gods, the high and mighty of the earth. Thus the process equally reduces them in stature. Something of this sort happens in Book I where Ovid compares Augustus to Jove and the Palatine to the Milky Way and where Apollo becomes the city slicker chasing the country girl. At the very end of Book XV Ovid has to appear to abandon this gentle ridicule, though it remains undercover—as his epilog bears witness. When all is said and done, Ovid tells us little about the gods, but a great deal about mortals and does so mostly with urbane lightness.

There can be little doubt, either, that Ovid enjoyed writing the *Metamorphoses*. It allowed him to employ his talents to the fullest, to gambol, frolic, frisk, and sport with them in a bewildering, splendid, and dazzling way. His powers must have been at their height. And as far as adhering to rules of any sort, he must have said, "The rules be damned!"

Deserving recognition because of their playfulness and ingenuity are his artificial transitions, produced with all the flourish and skill of a magician's paper flowers; the richness of his stories; and his ability to turn even a dull tale into a brilliantly functioning part of a context. Equally brilliant are his use of the sententia and his creation (as far as I know) of the emblem—the arresting story, incident, or image that is suspended in the context, unexplained, like a bee in amber. The extent of Ovid's virtuosity is indicated by his ability to move with great speed and ease from one tone or mood to another, to insert a grace note of novelty, and, more impressively, perhaps, to exploit a number of genres or generic bits. He has built into the *Metamorphoses* numerous epyllia, such as those of Pygmalion and Daedalus. But there are also a Homeric hymn dealing with Ceres' search for Proserpina, a parthenion, a comic idyll (Polyphemus' love song), a lover's complaint (Iphis' to Anaxarete), an anti-pastoral (Latona and the Lycian boors), deliberative oratory (the speeches of Ajax and Ulysses), a philosophical poem (the Sage's lecture), philosophical aetiology (the account of chaos and creation), a marine idyll (Galatea's seaside conversation with Scylla), high comedy (Nestor's handling of Achilles at the banquet), an epic invocation, epic catalogues, standing epithets, and interior monologues (Medea's). In this profusion of genres contained in one work, Ovid surpasses the Greeks, as far as we can tell; and in using their forms in new and original ways, he goes beyond them.

His poem is rich in literary allusion, neologisms, and rhetorical devices, but these are all matters for specialized studies. It abounds in wit and humor, as the preceding chapters testify, and it goes a long way toward classifying the various types of human personality. And there is much wisdom in it, part of it consisting of a wealth of psychological insight.

Of variety of personalities in the poem, little needs to be said here beyond pointing to the teasing, verbally abusive Apulian shepherd, the sadistic Lycian rustics, the inhospitable neighbors of Philemon, the kindly Baucis and Philemon, greedy horse-tender Battus, the rude boy who taunts thirsty Ceres, and Peleus' long-winded herdsman—all rustics. Of psychological insight, Ovid provides numerous examples, e.g., the personality inflation of Apollo after his killing Python, Phaëthon's insecurity and desire to establish his identity, Echo's other-directedness, Dryope's attachment to the nymph stage of human life, and the progressive deterioration of the personalities of Medea and Hecuba, one because of her abuse of power, the other under the accumulation of anguish caused by the loss of her husband, home, city, and one child after another. Ovid provides numerous less arresting analyses of character, as any author would: that of Apollo as a parent dealing with a daring darling son or that of Aglauros as a greedy and pruriently envious sister, for examples.

Perhaps the most novel thing about the *Metamorphoses* because the most amazing is the fact that it is a set of games. Not only does Ovid pit himself against the Greeks—and if not outdo them, put them down—but against Augustus and the common reader. Part of the game with Augustus amounts to undercutting Augustus' program and prestige without ostensibly doing so. Ovid carries out this process by playing a double game. On the one hand, he glorifies Rome and extols Augustus. On the other, he contrives a poem that would never encourage the youth of Italy to fill the gaps in Augustus' legions, the military force upon which the emporer and the empire depended. Nor would it support sober veneration of the gods, the public religion that Augustus also relied on and took such pains to revitalize.

What the poem chiefly promotes is an interest in love, often love in forms that Augustus could not publicly countenance because of his attempts at moral reform. It also gently and indirectly urges a tolerant attitude toward amour.

This indirect pleading is the second part of Ovid's game with Augustus, and it, too, is a double one. For the poem deals sympathetically with many kinds of love. Only incest, traitorous love, and love without feeling are condemned outright, and of these Ovid fails to give sympathetic understanding only to the Propoetides. Ovid's detailing the ways lovers' minds work either implies or is accompanied by a warm identification with the lovers, though he may deplore their kind of love. Often he handles the amorous situation with a light touch. By such means he projects an amiable tolerance, half excusing the lax behavior and sexual immorality of many of his lovers by being so understanding. Because of the moral reforms and legislation that Augustus had espoused and was serious about, he could not publicly approve of such latitudinarianism. Nor could he condone it in his own family because such laxity undermined his dynastic endeavors, exposed him to public ridicule, and could even lead to conspiracy against him.

The second part of this double game is that, though Ovid's poem works for tolerance of love and against Augustus' interests, the poet could still argue that he, too, takes love seriously and is a man of probity. On the basis of comparison of his love stories from Greek myth and legend with his Roman ones, as shown above, he could reasonably assert that the Greek Aphrodite produces some noteworthy honorable loves, namely those of Deucalion and Pyrrha, Baucis and Philemon, Ceyx and Alcyone, among a host of disreputable amours, whereas the Roman Venus is outstanding in the production of honorable ones, displaying for models the loves of Romulus and Hersilia, Pomona and Vertumnus, Picus and Canens, and Numa and Egeria and, most important, in causing no lurid loves in the Roman past. Not in Ovid's poem. It is love as practiced by the non-Romans that is marred by discord, crime, and the reprehensible. And if one reads the *Metamorphoses* carefully and thoughtfully, one may conclude that Ovid is more moral in his love tales than one first suspects, for the Roman is soberly superior to the Greek in love, and even the Greeks condemned certain kinds of passion.

But who reads so carefully? The preceding argument available to Ovid is half the picture, for it fails to consider the selectivity with which human beings read. Most of the non-Roman love in the *Metamorphoses* is unconventional and thus, from Augustus' view, damned; but it is damned engrossing because damned exciting, and it is to love as excitement, adventure, conquest, and thrill that many persons are drawn. The Greek stories gratify the desire for novelty and, while doing so, fan the desire for erotic thrill. Hence, they encourage throwing off caution, prudence, morality, convention, and piety in order to gratify oneself sensationally, for example, as Medea did for a grand passion. In short, the wanton tales of the *Metamorphoses* could cause the susceptible among Ovid's readers to follow their lead. Thus the poem undermines Augustus' moral position.

In addition to such oblique opposition to Augustus on the matter of sexual behavior, Ovid's comparing the Imperator with an unjust and unwise Jove (Book I), who wenches, parades his marital infidelity, and twits his jealous spouse, does not build the image of an august or even respectable ruler, either of gods or of men. The comparison certainly undercuts Augustus' attempt to produce marital fidelity among Romans and his own image of a sagacious and sober ruler. Ovid's concluding assertion that not even Jove's wrath can destroy Ovid's poem is a slap at the earthly Jove who banned Ovid's works from public libraries. The epilog also deifies Ovid and puts him on a higher level than Augustus. However, Ovid has constructed his poem in such a way that he can explain away all such charges, even though the evidence for them exists. After all, his poem is sportive, and he has extolled Caesar and, even more, Augustus.

In the elaborate game with the reader, Ovid is matching wits in a different way. He sets himself an impossible task and, like a poetic Hercules, does it, bringing his continuous poem from the creation to the time of Augustus. No audience could conceive how anyone could accomplish such a task unless he were writing a history of the world, a sober undertaking. This Ovid does not do, but using myth-legend instead of history, he faces the equally difficult problem of unifying disparate tales from widely separated locales. To write a continuous poem, he must overcome the staggering difficulty of linking the episodes so that they all cohere. This is minimal. He does it. No reader approaching the poem for the first time in an edition without subheadings could guess which tale would follow which or how the author could get from one to the next. No reader could be sure how successive books would begin or how Ovid would treat the well-known stories. And no reader would be likely to anticipate the various thematic devices that Ovid would further use to unify his material. In solving the problems confronting him, problems that the reader cannot even conjecture about, Ovid dominates the reader and keeps him in suspense. And to further complicate matters and confuse him, Ovid clutters up his narrative with verbosity and apparently unnecessary detail. Often he leaves his reader to infer what is going on, as he does with the tale of Ceyx and Alcyone or with the emblem of the uncatchable beast and the dog that can catch anything. Often the reader has to think matters through or remain bewildered. Nor is it easy for him to see that the *Metamorphoses* as a whole is a meaningful statement, for there are too many threads running through its tapestry and too many scenes to mull over.

In this game Ovid wins. If the reader's wit and will are keen enough, he will pursue the fox over the pastureland and through the thickets and woods. At a certain point, if his experience is like mine, he will divide and stand with the fox at the side of the scene and watch the hunt go on until at the very end the fox metamorphoses into the poet's person and ascends.

INDEX

(This index is limited almost exclusively to the names of significant personages.)

Cybele, 48, 134, 145, 162, 181, 189, 200, 218.

Cycnus, Cygnus, of Liguria, 20, 22; son of Neptune, 160-63, 165-67, 186.

Cyparissus, 131, 134 f., 211.

Daedalion, 147-49, 154-56.

Daedalus, 103-05, 127, 218, 223.

Danaë, 44 f.

Daphne, xiii, 8-14, 19-22, 30, 38, 41, 78, 81, 134, 144, 208, 210 f., 218.

Deianira, 115-18, 127 f., 211-13.

Deucalion, 7 f., 52, 127, 210, 215, 225.

Diana, 11, 20, 31-33, 36, 40, 45, 50, 52, 54, 64-66, 74, 98, 106-09, 113.

Dido, 183-85, 187.

Diomedes, 169, 172 f., 181 f., 188.

Dionysus, 218 (see Bacchus).

Dryope, 120-23, 126-28, 141, 208, 211 f., 216-19, 224.

Echo, 30, 35-37, 41, 210, 217, 224.

Egeria, 193, 197-99, 207, 210, 225.

Eliot, T. S., 209.

Envy, 25 f.

Erysichthon, 112, 115, 127, 212.

Europa, xiii, 25 f., 29, 33, 41, 43, 81, 99, 212, 217.

Eurydice, 63, 131-33, 137 f., 142, 144, 147-51, 158, 210.

Eurystheus, 119.

Evander, 182, 188.

Fama, 160 f., 164, 185, 194 (also called Fame and Rumor).

Famine, 112 f.

Fate(s), 23, 65, 67, 82, 123 f., 127, 133, 155, 192, 194, 202 f., 216.

Faunus, xiv.

Fury, Furies, 77 f., 133, 140 142.

Galanthis, 120, 127.

Galatea, xvii, 169, 176-78, 182, 218, 223.

Games, xiii-xviii, 224-26.

Ganymede, 132, 136, 192, 211.

Glaucus, 161, 169, 178 f., 181-84, 198, 192, 216, 218.

Hades, 57, 63 f., 66-68, 80, 131-33, 137, 151, 171, 185, 189, 210, 212, 217.

Harmonia, 31, 46, 52, 55.

Hector, 149, 160 f., 170 f., 173 f.

Hecuba, 174 f., 222, 224.

Helen, 159, 196, 212.

Helenus, 176, 179.

Hercules, xiv, 93, 115-20, 123, 127-29, 149, 153, 165 f., 171, 174, 189, 192, 194 f., 208, 213 f., 217 f., 222, 225.

229

Hermaphroditus, 44, 47, 50 f.

Hermes, 44, 154 (see Mercury).

Herse, 25, 29, 41.

Hersilia, 182, 192, 198, 207, 210, 225.

Hippolytus, 193, 198 f., 210.

Hippomenes, 45, 142-45, 210, 212, 218.

Homer, xiii, 160, 182.

Hyacinthus, 132, 136 f., 174, 211.

Hymen, 77, 139.

Ianthe, 126-29, 211.

Icarus, 103-05.

Ino, 42-46, 51.

Io, xvii, 12-14, 17, 21, 23, 51, 77, 81, 211 f., 217, 221.

Iolaüs, 119, 123, 127 f., 202.

Iole, 120-23, 127, 213.

Iphis, of Crete, 125-29, 211 (see Ianthe); of Cyprus, 181, 190 f., 210, 223 (see Anaxarete).

Isis, 126.

Iulus, 203.

Ixion, 166.

Jason, 83-92, 94, 103, 106, 208.

Jove, 4-8, 10, 12-14, 17, 20 f., 23, 25 f., 29, 33 f., 36, 41, 43-46, 50, 52-54, 60, 64 f., 68, 73, 75, 81, 83, 95, 116, 119, f., 123 f., 127, 134, 136 f., 144, 153 f.,
170-172, 174, 189, 192, 194, 201-204, 210-213, 216 f., 221, 223, 225.

Juno, 12-14, 21, 33 f., 36, 40 f., 44-46, 51 f., 75, 77, 95, 115, 120, 126 f., 144, 157, 189, 191 f., 212 f., 217.

Laomedon, 147, 149, 152 f.

Latona, 74-76, 212, 223.

Lelex, 110-112.

Leuconoë, 49.

Leucothoë, 44, 49 f., 55, 210, 212.

Lotis, xiv, 122, 128, 134, 208, 210.

Lucina, 120.

Lycaon, 4-6, 14, 21, 41, 75, 138, 215, 217.

Lyncus, 64, 66.

Macareus, 181 f., 185-188.

Mars, xiv, 29-31, 36, 43, 45 f., 52, 55, 183, 192 f., 210, 212.

Marsyas, 76, 80, 82, 218.

Medea, xiii f., 83-94, 100 f., 144, 183, 211-214, 219, 223-225.

Medusa, 52-57, 58-60, 218.

Meleager, 106-109, 113, 127, 208, 214.

Memnon, 169, 174.

Mercury, xvii, 13 f., 24 f., 54, 154, 172, 186, 210, 217.

Merops, 18, 26.

230

Midas, 147 f., 152, 159, 162, 175, 218.

Minerva, 22-25, 29, 54, 59-63, 65, 69, 71-73, 82, 163, 173, 181, 188, 212, 217.

Minos, 26, 94, 102-104.

Minyeïdes, 43 f., 46 f., 49-51, 55, 71, 81, 131, 158.

Morpheus, 217.

Muse(s), 60-63, 67-69, 71, 81 f., 123, 158, 199.

Myrmidons, 95.

Myrrha, xiv, 125, 132, 136, 138-142, 144 f., 211, 213.

Myscelus, 194 f.

Narcissus, 30, 35-38, 41, 46, 74, 81, 131, 179, 210-212, 219.

Neptune, 12, 73, 112, 153, 161, f., 164, 167, 178.

Nessus, 117 f., 127 f., 211 f.

Nestor, 106, 159, 163-167, 171, 202, 208, 223.

Niobe, 74-76, 79, 82, 100, 160, 208, 214, 218.

Numa, 193-198, 207, 210, 225.

Ocyrhoë, 23 f., 26, 41, 216.

Odysseus, see Ulysses.

Oeneus, 45, 106, 109, 113, 214.

Orchamus, 50.

Orion (Orion's daughters), 169, 175, 179.

Orithyia, 80, 97, 212.

Orpheus, 63, 131-145, 147-152, 155, 157 f., 160, 210 f.

Palamedes, 171, 173.

Pan, 13, 24, 62, 81, 144, 148 f., 152, 188, 190, 210 f.

Pandion, 77 f., 80.

Paris, 167, 174, 212.

Pasiphaë, 113, 127, 211, 214.

Pegasus, 60.

Peleus, 147-149, 153-155, 164 f., 204, 211, 214, 217, 224.

Pelias, 91-93.

Pelops, xiii, 76, 79, 82, 150.

Pentheus, 30, 35, 38 f., 51, 74, 208.

Perdix, Daedalus' nephew, 104 f.

Perimele, 109, 114, 116, 127, 210, 212, 214, 219, 222.

Persephone, see Proserpina.

Perseus, 43, 45 f., 52-55, 57-62, 65, 67-69, 71, 93, 208.

Phaedra, 213.

Phaëthon, xiii, 14, 17-19, 21 f., 26, 29, 34, 41, 43, 52, 158, 224.

Philemon, 110 f., 127, 210, 218, 224 f.

Philoctetes, 119, 171, 173 f.

Philomela, 78-80, 212.

DATE DUE

OCT 18 '87			
MAR 8 '88			
DEC 6 '88			
JUN 6 '89			
DEC 3			
JAN 8 '90			
MAR 5 1991			
SEP 29 1993			
261-2500			Printed in USA